ON THIS ROCK

Heresies

Arianism The teaching that Christ was not divine.

Donatism The teaching that sacraments celebrated by a priest who had once lapsed or was in a state of sin were invalid.

Gallicanism The nationalist doctrine which stated that the authority of national Churches (particularly in France) should increase at the expense of papal influence.

Gnosticism A religious and philosophical movement whose members were selective about which parts of Christ's teachings they chose to apply to their own lives and beliefs. They claimed Christ had imparted special teachings to a select few, that the world and the flesh were inherently bad, and that no God worth the name would have sent his son to the earth to be crucified.

Jansenism The teaching, based on the notion of a harsh, punishing God, that human freedom does not exist and that Christ did not die for the salvation of all.

Manichaeism A Persian heresy, comprising a mixture of Gnosticism, Buddhism and Zoroastrianism.

Monophysitism The teaching that Christ's nature was solely divine, rather than human and divine.

Monothelitism The teaching that Christ's will was solely divine, rather than human and divine.

Montanism The teachings of Montanus, who took a pessimistic view of the sinfulness of humanity and preached extreme asceticism. His followers considered themselves a Christian elite.

Nestorianism The teaching that there were two separate persons, one human, one divine, in the incarnate Christ.

Pelagianism The teachings of the British monk Pelagius, that humans can save themselves and therefore do not need divine grace.

Quietism The teaching that, to achieve salvation, people must abandon themselves completely to God to such an extent that they cease to care about heaven, hell and even their own salvation.

Waldenshianism A reformist movement which in the sixteenth century embraced predestination, renounced the Catholic Church and accepted the marriage of clergy.

On This Rock

The Popes
and their times:
St Peter to John Paul II

Tony Castle
and
Peter McGrath

ST PAULS

The potographs of the popes are taken from
the mosaics in the Basilica of St Paul, Rome

ST PAULS Publishing
187 Battersea Bridge Road, London SW11 3AS, UK
www.stpauls.ie

ISBN 085439 602 0

Set by Tukan DTP, Fareham, Hampshire, UK
Printed by Interprint Limited, Marsa, Malta

ST PAULS is an activity of the priests and brothers
of the Society of St Paul who proclaim the Gospel
through the media of social communication

Contents

General Introduction   6

0–330   From the Upper Room to Rome   7
             The Popes: 0–335   20

330–700   The spread of Christianity and the birth of Islam   33
             The Popes: 336–701   47

700–1050   A Christian Europe under siege from Viking
             and Islamic invaders   67
             The Popes: 701–1054   81

1050–1400   Dark Ages for Europe and the Church   105
             The Popes: 1055–1404   121

1400–1600   Reformation; Counter Reformation
             and exploration   143
             The Popes: 1404–1605   161

1600–1700   Europe at War and the growth of colonialism   175
             The Popes: 1605–1700   192

1700–1800   A century of revolutions   197
             The Popes: 1700–1799   213

1800–1900   Marxism, empires and missionary Christianity   219
             The Popes: 1800–1903   236

1900–present A century of warfare and the present growth
             of the secular society   241
             The Popes: 1903 to the present   265

General Introduction

Almost 2,000 years ago a former fisherman was given a remarkable new job description: 'You are Peter, and on this rock I will build my Church.' With those few words Jesus Christ founded the earthly government of the Roman Catholic Church.

The papacy is, arguably, the longest-established government in history. It has survived the Roman Empire, which tried to eliminate the upstart Christians; a split with the Eastern Church in Constantinople; barbarian invasions of Europe, the corrupt Middle Ages and Renaissance popes; the Reformation; revolutions, invasions; and Communism. These are just a few of the historical events that have impinged directly on the papacy, an institution that in 2002 still claims spiritual authority over an estimated 850 million Roman Catholics.

The papacy is remarkable not only in its longevity, but also in its authority. The reigning Pope claims the authority of Christ's Vicar on earth, and embodies the so-called magisterium of the Church – the right to interpret Christian teaching into a code of conduct for Roman Catholics. The Pope's authority to act in this manner is one of the fundamental divides between Catholic and Protestant Christianity.

All history needs a context and when considering an institution as powerful as the papacy that context is huge. In the Middle Ages popes could and did force kings to their knees, begging forgiveness. Popes both created history and were affected by historical events. For example, it is arguable that modern relations between Islam and the western world would have been different had the popes not rallied Christian warriors to the Crusades.

Such a massive historical context can only be skimmed in a book of this size and inevitably there are areas that do not receive the treatment they deserve or are omitted completely. We hope that this book helps to explain the durability of the papacy and, given the constraints, provides as accurate as possible a portrait of each pope and the world in which he occupied the Throne of Peter. If it excites an interest in the popes and in the wider historical events they defined and were defined by, then it will have succeeded.

0–330
From the Upper Room
to Rome

Timeline 0–330

30   Jesus is crucified. Peter assumes leadership of the disciples.

44-49   Paul becomes the first missionary.

60   The evangelist Mark writes his Gospel.

64   The Roman Emperor Nero persecutes Roman Christians. Peter is martyred.

67   Paul is martyred in Rome.

84   Christians are excommunicated from the Jewish synagogues.

112   A Roman governor writes to the Emperor Trajan, calling Christians 'harmless'.

144   The first recorded schism: Marcion rejects the Old Testament and is excommunicated.

180   Christianity gains a foothold in northern Europe: Irenaeus becomes bishop of Lyons in France.

250   Roman Emperor Decius persecutes Roman Christians. Fabian, the Bishop of Rome is killed.

303   Emperor Diocletian oppresses Christians.

306   Constantine is proclaimed Emperor of Rome.

312   Constantine wins the battle of Milvan Bridge using Christian battle standards.

313   The Edict of Milan allows Christians freedom of worship in the Roman Empire.

325   The Council of Nicaea proclaims that Christ and God the Father are one.

330   Emperor Constantine renames Byzantium Constantinople, and declares it 'the new Rome'.

Introduction

The early Christians lived in first-century Palestine, a place where cultures, languages and religions were strangely mixed.

Alexander the Great conquered Palestine around 330 BC, introducing Greek culture, gods and language to the area. By 200 BC, however, the rapidly expanding Roman Empire had come to regard the unstable political situation in the eastern Mediterranean as a problem, and initially became involved in Palestine through a series of alliances aimed at stabilising the region. However, the political instability persisted and threatened trading routes – trade that was crucial to the survival of the large, resource-hungry Roman Empire. By 64 BC the problem of piracy at sea was making life difficult for Roman merchants, so the Roman general, Pompey, led his forces in a successful campaign against the Mediterranean pirates, and went on to conquer Palestine, which became a Roman province.

So the early followers of Christ lived in a region with a strong Greek heritage, a well-organised Roman administration and a pervasive, ancient Jewish religion.

History shows that both the Roman authorities and the local placemen they imposed as rulers could be utterly ruthless: Herod, the king of Judea at the time of Christ's birth, dealt with a Jewish riot by crucifying 2,000 people. Yet the Romans allowed the Jews of Palestine to practise their religion unmolested: the Romans by now had a great deal of experience of being an occupying army, and knew that trying to suppress a deep-seated faith would only provoke hostility from an already resentful conquered nation. The followers of Christ lived in this minor Roman province, controlled by a military and a religious administration, but significantly, part of the massive Roman Empire.

The early Christian Church underwent a remarkable transformation following the Resurrection. With the death of Jesus his followers went into hiding – their leader had suffered the most degrading, painful, prolonged death that the Roman authorities in occupied Palestine could impose. The same fate could easily be in store for his followers.

However, instead of withering away through lack of leadership and low morale, the earliest Christians found the strength and courage not only to found a Church in Palestine, but to engage in early missionary activity around the Mediterranean basin. Although there is some debate about the exact time of the crucifixion, the time was around what we now call 30 AD.

The civilised world around Europe, the Mediterranean and North Africa was occupied by the forces of Imperial Rome. Pompey's intervention had reduced piracy to the levels where sea travel, if not safe (the Mediterranean is a notoriously stormy sea), was safer than when pirates roamed the shipping lanes. The Romans were also great road builders, so the Empire soon also benefited from the world's first paved highway network. The followers of Christ had the means to take their new message to all parts of the Roman Empire.

Travellers on foot (or by donkey if they could afford such a luxury) could rely on roads kept moderately safe by Roman army patrols, with inns providing food and shelter at regular intervals along the way. Even so, travel in first-century Palestine could not have been rapid or pleasant.

The early missionaries – notably Peter and Paul – could therefore take their teaching beyond the confines of Judæa. Peter travelled initially to Jerusalem and Antioch, and then to the heart of the Roman Empire, Rome itself, although it has to be said that independent records of Peter's time in Rome are scarce.

Paul's travels are well documented. From Palestine he travelled hundreds of kilometres into what we now know as Turkey, Greece, Cyprus and ultimately Italy. The work of the early missionaries would often start in the synagogue, preaching Christ's message (Christ was a Jew, so were the apostles) and forming house churches, then using personal contacts to bring new members into the churches.

The early Christian message was a new, powerful one for people used to Roman occupation and the rigid observances of first-century Jewish practice: Christians held property in common, and did not distinguish between nationalities, social status or gender.

Many authorities agree that early Christianity was a religion of the towns and cities – this is where missionaries could spread their word to best effect because of population density and because of the synagogue as the starting point for missionary contact. The Syrian city of Antioch had a great Greek heritage and was a centre of commerce and learning – after Pompey's occupation in 64 AD, the Romans granted the city freedom within the Empire. It was here, according to the Acts of the Apostles, that the term 'Christians' was first applied to Christ's followers. Peter, Paul and the Apostle James (leader of the Church in Jerusalem) visited Antioch on their missionary travels, and it is believed that Matthew's Gospel was written in the city. It was a rich city with great patronage and influence in the Roman Empire, positioned on key trade routes, and was a tremendous springboard for early Christians wanting to move from Syria into 'Asia Minor' – the lands around what is now Turkey.

Another important centre for early Christianity was Ephesus, yet another Roman conquest and again a powerful city. Paul visited it several times, and was reported to have not only preached, but healed the sick. His teachings caused a riot, since they offended followers of the goddess Artemis, whose cult was massive in Ephesus. The towns and cities evangelised by Paul were under Roman rule, there was an Empire-wide language (Greek) and the means for a missionary to travel in safety: thus the Romans, while occasionally trying to persecute Christians out of existence actually enhanced the spread of Christ's message by their well-ordered Empire.

By the time Peter and Paul had arrived in Rome, the seeds of Christianity had begun to shoot throughout the eastern and northern Mediterranean. A further significant centre of Christianity developed in Alexandria, on the Nile Delta. Founded by Alexander the Great, Alexandria became a seat of great learning, a very cosmopolitan city occupied by Greeks and native Egyptians and with a vigorous Jewish population. It was one of the most prosperous trading ports in the region, with shipping links to the rest of the Mediterranean and overland routes deep into Egypt, Iran and Iraq. Alexandria became Christianity's bridgehead into North Africa, as Christian missionaries thrived in the city's cosmopolitan environment and spread the new religion. Tradition holds that St Mark visited Alexandria to teach, then settled and wrote his Gospel while in residence.

But it was Rome, the heart of the Empire, that attracted Peter and Paul and became a focus for the struggle for Christianity first to survive, then to flourish. The Romans could be tolerant of what they regarded as alternative cults, or could suddenly develop an antipathy to a certain cult – the followers of Bacchus and of both Greek and Egyptian gods all suffered persecution at some time in the first centuries AD, so Christianity was by no means alone in occasionally falling foul of Roman ill-will. Christians enjoyed periods of toleration as well as bouts of persecution. Nero's barbaric persecution of Christians in 64 AD was reported to have elicited pro-Christian sympathy among some parts of the Roman population. Despite fluctuating fortunes, Christianity survived in Rome, weathering bouts of persecution in

250 and 303 AD, until to be a Christian was beginning to be fashionable for Roman upper classes. The Emperor Constantine was said to have been influenced by his mother, who had sympathy with the Christians.

The Roman Empire was incredibly significant in forming the early Christian Church: it provided the roads and shipping routes for the early missionaries to travel, and imposed a common language so that the message could be understood throughout the Empire. It gave the Church the solidarity that goes with being an oppressed minority, and provided the Church with its early icons by martyring Church leaders such as Peter and Paul, and many thousands of faithful thereafter. With the death of martyrs, the living members of the Church began to venerate their remains, and when Constantine allowed Christians to own property, churches became centres where the relics of martyrs could be venerated, and the Christian tradition of pilgrimage to visit churches housing significant relics began. Constantine himself commissioned St Peter's Basilica to be built on the site of St Peter's tomb on Vatican Hill.

'When it was evening on that day, the first day of the week, and the doors of the house where the disciples had met were locked for fear of the Jews...' (Jn 20:19). One can imagine the demoralised state of the disciples – Jesus taken and crucified, betrayed by Judas, one of their own number. Peter had denied he knew Jesus, and now they were behind barred doors, in fear of their own lives. Yet these terrified men and women, in about 30 AD found the courage to go out into the Roman Empire and preach a new religion. Three hundred years later Constantine the Great, Emperor of Rome, was christened on his deathbed and was buried surrounded by gold statues of the twelve apostles, the implication being that he really deserved to be thirteenth. In three hundred years, Christianity had captured the Roman Empire.

Early Christian worship

Early Christianity developed among the pervasive Jewish religious culture that dominated first-century Palestine. The early Christians developed a form of worship that soon became distinct from the Jewish religious ceremonies which would have dominated their pre-Christian spiritual lives. Sunday replaced Saturday as the day of worship, and the focus of the Christian ceremony became the commemoration of Christ's Resurrection.

St Paul

St Paul, known as Saul of Tarsus, was a Jewish Roman citizen. He was believed to have played a part in suppressing the early Church – guarding cloaks while a mob stoned St Stephen to death, and dragging known Christians from their homes and taking them to prison. On the road to Damascus, Saul was confronted by the risen Christ and temporarily struck blind. Converted, inspired, his eyesight restored and his name changed to Paul, he became one of the leading figures in taking Christ's message to the Gentile (non-Jewish) world. In a time without fast mass transportation, his travels were astounding: through Palestine and Syria into modern-day Greece, Albania, Cyprus and Turkey.

During his travels, he was not only a missionary: he became a travelling leader of the Church, arbitrating in disputes, settling matters of theological debate and instructing the new and growing Church how to behave and what God, as revealed in Jesus Christ, wanted for his Church. Paul's many letters – his epistles – became so central to the early Church that they were included in the Canon of the New Testament – the list of Gospels and writings that the leaders of the early Church agreed should become the New Testament.

Paul's missionary activity ultimately so enraged the Jewish authorities in Roman occupied Palestine that he was arrested in the temple in Jerusalem. The authorities in Jerusalem were not allowed to sit in judgement on Paul, since he was a Roman citizen, and he insisted on his right to be examined in Rome, so in the year 59 AD he set sail from Sidon in the eastern Mediterranean to Rome, where he continued preaching the Gospel and the Word of Christ even in custody.

Paul, having been an uncompromising Jewish Pharisee, became an uncompromising Christian missionary, and continued his missionary work in Rome until his execution by beheading, which is thought to have taken place around the year 67. Although the Christian Church did not gain freedom of worship until 330, by the year 165 AD the Church in Rome had raised a memorial to Paul on the road to Ostia, the supposed site of his burial.

The format of early Christian worship would be familiar to a Catholic attending Mass today. There was what we now call the liturgy of the Word, involving Gospel readings, reciting the psalms, and a sermon. Then followed what we would now call the liturgy of the Eucharist, where bread and wine were consecrated and distributed to the faithful. The Eucharist, drawing its authority from Christ's words at the Last Supper, was used to affirm the congregation's membership of the Church.

Christians stopped the Jewish practice of male circumcision, and instead instituted baptism, echoing Christ's immersion in the River Jordan by John the Baptist. Baptism was followed by confirmation, where the new communicant would be received into full membership of the Church by the deacon laying hands on the candidate. Confirmation allowed the new Christian to receive the Eucharist, and brought with it an obligation to behave according to the rules of the Church. If a communicant was found to have sinned, they would be required to leave worship after the readings, thus being denied communion. A sinner could expect severe and long-lasting penance, and a penitent could be restored to being a full member of the congregation after a further laying-on of hands – essentially a reconfirmation.

The early Church was a community of faith rather than a specified, consecrated place of worship: acts of worship were carried out in private houses, although archaeological evidence shows that early Christians soon came to regard their rooms of worship as special spaces – an excavation of a house dating from the early third century in modern-day Syria shows a room clearly used as a church. The room had a niche for the altar and wall paintings of scenes from the New Testament.

Bishops and the rise of the papacy in the early Church

In the years following the death of Jesus, the apostles acted as peripatetic Church leaders, but as the Church grew and these eyewitnesses to Christ's life died, it became necessary to develop some form of clerical and administrative structure.

The spiritual director of a local church was the deacon or presbyter, and before long one member of the clergy would become the region's principal cleric, a role that became known as a bishop.

Early bishops were, as they are now, senior priests in a given province, with the sacramental duties of baptism and confirmation of new church members, and the consecration of bread and wine at the Eucharist. The bishop also acquired administrative duties – representing his province in dealings with neighbouring provinces, and assisting in consecrating other bishops.

Since Rome was the capital of the Roman Empire, and both Peter and Paul had ended their missionary work in Rome with 'gaining the crown' of martyrdom, it is hardly surprising that the Bishop of Rome became regarded as the principal bishop of the early Christian world. Although the records are scant, there is evidence that the Bishop of Rome had begun to claim supreme authority over the Christian Church by the end of the first century AD.

Peter was regarded as the leader of the apostles and therefore of the early Church through the Petrine sections of the Gospels, most notably Matthew 16:18 'And I tell you, you are Peter, and on this rock I will build my church' and 'first, Simon, also known as Peter' (Mt 10:2). Therefore, when he arrived in Rome, he assumed leadership over the Church and is regarded as the first Bishop of Rome. Despite the universal assumption that Peter lived and was martyred in Rome, actual historical records placing him there are scant.

The cultural power of Rome and the apparent authority granted to Peter in the Petrine Gospels secured the position of the Bishop of Rome as the head of the Church. Early Christians used the Latin or Greek for 'father' as a term of respect for their bishops: the Greek is *pappas*, the Latin *papa*. The local use of these terms must have fallen out of favour as local languages became more commonplace, supplanting the ancient Greek and Latin. In Rome, Greek was the common language of early Christians until the third century, when it was replaced by Latin. Latin remains the official language of the Vatican even in the twenty-first century, so the linguistic tradition of the *pappas* or *papa* referring to the Bishops of Rome is unbroken – the election of a new pope is hailed by '*Habemus papam*'.

The Canon of the Gospels

A remarkable achievement of the early Church was codifying the teachings of Jesus and the apostles into the New Testament, changing forever the nature of Christianity.

In the immediate aftermath of Christ's crucifixion, the apostles were the source of authority on Christ's life and teachings. Their teaching was by word of mouth, a means of transmitting information which is prone to errors, variation and embellishment.

With the Church growing, its emerging leadership was concerned that Christ's message should be transmitted as accurately as possible. The Church leadership's concern for the integrity of the Gospels was twofold – first, so that Christians should have an authentic account of Christ's life and teaching, and second, to counter the dangerous Gnostic heresies that were already starting to circulate, even in the first century.

Historical records mention the existence of written Gospels by Mark and Matthew between 120 and 140, but opinion holds that these Gospels were probably written from the year 60 onwards. A fragment of the Gospel according to John originating in Egypt has been found, dating between 125 and 150 AD.

It is thought that the early Church debate about which books to include in the Canon of the New Testament centred around two points: did the Gospel represent an authentic witness to the life and teachings of Christ and the apostles, and was the text acceptable to the beliefs of the Church at the time?

Forming a definitive Old and New Testament had important implications for the Church in the first, second and third centuries, because the time was rife with Gnostic heresies. Gnostics claimed to be Christians, but were selective in which parts of Christ's teachings they chose to apply to their own lives and beliefs. Gnostics claimed that Christ had imparted special teachings to his disciples, and that only a select few were worthy to share this knowledge. They also held that things of the world and the flesh were inherently bad, and that no God worth the name would send his son to this sinful earth to be crucified. To support their views they quoted selectively from the early Gospels and put their own secret gospels into circulation. Their views did gain some support, which made it all the more important that the fledgling Christian Church confirm the book that would become the foundation for its teaching and practice until the end of time when, according to the writings they chose, God would judge us all.

The debate about which books should formally become the New Testament started and continued throughout the infant stages of Christianity, but the issue was not finally settled until a Council held by Pope Damasus (reigned 366–384) in 382.

Roman persecution of early Christians

In Christians, the Roman authorities were dealing with a new brand of rebel. The Romans had conquered much of Europe, the eastern Mediterranean and North Africa. Their efficient armies were followed by an equally efficient civil administration in their conquered lands, and many settled down under the *Pax Romana* – the Roman Peace.

The early Christians, however, were undaunted by the mighty Romans, and their opposition to the Jewish authorities in Palestine occasionally caused riots, leading to Roman retaliation. In addition, the Christians' message must have sounded unpleasantly revolutionary to the Roman conquerors, and the Christian refusal to acknowledge or sacrifice to the Roman gods was downright insulting.

The Christian view of Christ as model for living and route to eternal salvation differed from the Roman view of their many pagan gods. For the Romans, the gods had to be kept content with sacrifices, since the wellbeing of the Empire depended on their favour. When catastrophes struck the Roman Empire, emperors anxious to find a scapegoat would blame Christians, who, they claimed, had brought down luck by snubbing the gods of Rome.

Whether or not Christians were persecuted often depended on the state of mind of the local Roman rulers. Some were minded to ignore the new religion, while other Roman rulers were zealous in their persecution of Christians. The Emperor Nero was famous for having 'fiddled' (done nothing) 'while Rome burned'. Nero was either mentally ill or evil. The Greek legend of Troy describes its destruction by fire and says Nero was curious to see what this would have looked like. So Nero ordered Rome – his capital city – to be set ablaze. After his curiosity had been satisfied, he publicly blamed the arson on the Christian community, and set about a massive persecution of Christians. One of his victims was Peter, crucified head-down and entombed on Vatican Hill.

Throughout the first 200 years of Roman Christianity, Christians were subject to sporadic persecution – occasionally due to a local catastrophe, occasionally because they had provoked a governor, but more seriously when an emperor turned against them. Concerted periods of persecution occurred in 248–250 when Germanic tribes rampaged around the Roman Empire. The Emperor Decius forced all citizens to sacrifice to the Roman gods for the good of the Empire, and Christians who resisted were persecuted. In 303 the joint Emperors

Diocletian and Galerius instigated a further period of oppression, which ended with the arrival of Constantine as emperor in 306.

When the Christians did fall foul of the Roman authorities, the Romans excelled themselves in brutality. Nero had Christians coated in pitch, then set them on fire as human torches to illuminate his gardens. Some were fed to wild animals during public games in Rome's Colosseum and in other amphitheatres throughout Europe, others were tortured to extract information about their fellow Christian brethren, and yet more followed Jesus in crucifixion. Roman citizens, such as St Paul, were granted the relatively humane death of beheading.

Those not killed could be sentenced to the hardest work in penal colonies. This fate befell one future Pope, Callistus, who was pope from 217 to 222. He was reported to have provoked fights with Roman Jews, wrecking their Sacred Scriptures and was sentenced to slavery in the silver mines of Sardinia – a fate he escaped. Instead of becoming a slave he became the Bishop of Rome.

The Roman persecution of the early Christians was intended to kill off many of them and dissuade the more faint-hearted. The persecution rose and fell according to just how badly disposed the emperor of the day was to Christians, and Christians of this time did enjoy long periods of relative peace. The Roman attempts to suppress Christianity by killing its followers and hoping to terrify the rest away from their faith hit one problem: Christians were not only unafraid of dying as a witness to their faith, there is evidence they welcomed it.

Christians who were killed for the faith were called martyrs, and being martyred was hailed by Christians as 'gaining the crown'. Christians would greet each other with the phrase 'May you gain your crown', meaning 'May you die for your faith'.

To an early Christian an horrific martyr's death was an opportunity to show loyalty to the crucified Christ and to join him in paradise following death.

As a result, Roman persecution failed to break the spirit of the early Christians. Not only did the surviving Christians gain strength from their brethren 'gaining their crown' of martyrdom, these martyrs became the first generation of saints, and established the Christian practice of venerating the relics of martyrs and making pilgrimages to churches housing relics. The Roman persecution of early Christians gave them the strength and unity that comes when facing adversity, and ultimately ensured Christians had the coherence to survive.

The Roman Emperor Constantine

Christianity's breakthrough came with the election of Constantine as Roman emperor in 306. Rome had recently been through economic recession, civil war and a barbarian invasion. The new Emperor Constantine, possibly influenced by a Christian mother and appalled that the old Roman pagan gods had let the Empire down so badly, developed Christian sympathies. These grew when, outnumbered in battle, he called on the support of the Christian God, put the name of Christ on his battle flags, and gave his opponents a beating. The Romans were great believers in omens, and Christ's assistance in this unexpected victory was probably seen as a powerful omen.

In 313 Constantine (with the agreement of his pagan co-emperor in the East, Licinius) issued the Edict of Milan, which established toleration of all cults, including Christianity. This allowed the Church to own property, and this, coupled with the freedom from oppression, provided the catalyst for the expansion of the early Christian Church both in Rome and ultimately throughout Europe. Constantine's predecessors had intermittently tried to eradicate Christianity. Constantine not only officially allowed Christians to practise their faith openly, but he commissioned the building of some of early Christianity's great churches – St John Lateran and St Peter's Basilica in Rome, and the Churches of the Nativity and of the Resurrection in the Holy Land.

Constantine controlled a massive Empire, which was divided into two distinct geographical areas – the Western Empire centred around Rome, and the Eastern Empire centred around what is now Yugoslavia, Turkey and Greece. In May 330, Constantine shifted the political centre of power of the Roman Empire from Rome to Byzantium. He renamed the city Constantinople. In doing so, he weakened Rome as a political and administrative centre, creating a power vacuum that the burgeoning Christian Church, with their Bishop of Rome now firmly established as the 'successor to Peter', moved to fill.

On his deathbed Constantine received baptism and died a Christian. Nero, his predecessor, had crucified Peter, the first Bishop of Rome, and less than 300 years later, Constantine delivered Rome to the Christians and died one of their number.

THE POPES
0–335

Simon Peter

On 26 June 1968 Pope Paul VI announced that the remains of the Apostle Peter had been discovered and identified in a tomb under the high altar of St Peter's Basilica, which had been built over the traditional resting place of the Apostle. The bones were of a powerfully-built first-century man in his mid to late sixties, wrapped in a cloth of imperial purple. The Vatican has been cautious, as the evidence is not conclusive; however, many people share Pope Paul's enthusiastic belief. If reliable this discovery confirms the ancient and well-established tradition that Peter and Paul had died and were buried in the imperial city.

Symeon, or Simon, was from Bethsaida, a small town on the northern shores of Lake Tiberias, or the Sea of Galilee. The Gospels tell us that he was the son of Jonas, with a brother, Andrew. The family worked the Sea of Galilee as fishermen in partnership with the sons of Zebedee, James and John. Having called them to follow him Jesus declared that he would make them 'fishers of men'. Our knowledge of his subsequent life is derived from the Gospels, the Acts of the Apostles, St Paul's Letter to the Galatians and tradition. Jesus gave him the name Cephas, the Aramaic equivalent of the Greek *petra* meaning 'rock', from which, of course, comes Peter. Some time later he is called to be one of the Twelve Apostles, and in all the lists of these he is named first. Peter is present at all the events when Christ only admits an 'inner group'; e.g. the transfiguration. Jesus adopts Simon Peter's home at Capernaum as his headquarters while preaching in the Galilee area. (The Franciscan guardians of the excavated town claim to have discovered Peter's house.) Peter usually takes the lead and is the mouthpiece of the disciples, e.g. John 6:66–69. After his profession of faith in Jesus as the Messiah, at Caesarea Philippi (Mt 16:13–20) he receives the promise, 'You are Peter, and on this rock I will build my Church.' There follow from Christ the words on which the authority of the papacy is founded; 'I will give you the keys of the kingdom of heaven and whatever you bind on earth will be bound in heaven, and whatever you loose on earth will be loosed in heaven.'

Three times Peter denies knowing Jesus, in the courtyard of the High Priest (Mt 26:69–75); but three times the risen Christ asks for a profession of his love, on the shores of the Lake of Tiberias (where the story had begun). In return Peter hears the commission to 'feed my sheep' (Jn 21:15–19).

After the Ascension Peter immediately assumes leadership (Acts 1:15–22) and delivers the first Christian sermon, after the Pentecost experience. Throughout the first half of Acts he appears as the head and leader of the Community. Of the later years of his apostolate outside of the Holy Land very little is known. The tradition linking the Apostle Peter with Rome is early and unrivalled. St Clement of Rome (the third Bishop of Rome, ruled c.88–97) conjoins Peter and Paul as the great heroes of the Roman Church. According to the historian Eusebius (c.260–c.340) Peter was executed during the reign of the Emperor Nero (54–68), probably during the persecution of 64, following the fire of Rome.

Linus, St

Tuscany; c.67 to c.78

Traditionally it is believed that Linus, the Bishop of Rome to follow Peter, was appointed by St Peter and St Paul acting together. He may be the Linus mentioned in Paul's second letter to Timothy (4:21). Little is known of his episcopate, but during it the Romans destroyed the city of Jerusalem (70) and he may have seen the Jewish slaves brought to Rome to work on the Colosseum.

Anacletus, St (Cletus)

Rome; c.78 to 88

An obscure figure, his name suggests that he was a Greek. Eusebius of Caesarea records that he died during the reign of the Emperor Domitian. According to tradition he is honoured as a martyr.

Clement, St

Rome; 88 to 97

Tertullian and St Jerome list Clement as the immediate follower of St Peter but he is officially considered the third successor. Tradition may solve the problem, suggesting that Peter ordained Clement and that he acted as a type of assistant bishop to Linus and Anacletus. Origen identifies him as the Clement mentioned by St Paul in his letter to the Philippians (4:3). Many myths and legends are associated with Clement, including a spectacular martyrdom (being cast into the sea, in the Crimea, with an anchor round his neck!). Various writings are attributed to him but the only reliable one is his Letter to Corinthians ('First Epistle of Clement'). After the New Testament and the Didache this is considered the most important Church document of the first century.

Evaristus, St

Greece; 97 to c.109

Apart from a few obscure traditions, for example that he was a Jew from Bethlehem and that he died a martyr's death and was buried next to St Peter on Vatican Hill, there is no reliable information available.

Alexander I, St

Rome; c.109 to c.116

No reliable information about Alexander has come down to us. Even his dates are uncertain. There is a tradition that he was a Roman by birth and he was martyred during the reign of the Emperor Trajan, but the latter is considered doubtful as there is no early testimony to his martyrdom.

Sixtus I, St

Rome; c.116 to c.125

Virtually nothing is known about Sixtus. It has been suggested that he was called 'Sixth' because he was the sixth pope since St Peter. Early sources call him Yystus and declare that he was a Roman; little else is known about him.

Telesphorus, St

Greece; c.125 to c.136

His name, meaning 'fulfilling one's purpose', suggests that he was Greek. Little else is known, but it is believed that he died a martyr.

Hyginus, St

Greece; c.138 to c.142

There appears to be a two-year gap between Telesphorus and Hyginus, but this may not actually be the case as dates at this early period are very unreliable. Another Greek name, this time meaning 'healthy' or 'sound'. (It is thought by some authors that there was a custom, at this time, of taking a Greek name on becoming Bishop of Rome.) During Hyginus's episcopate a noted Gnostic leader, Valentius, came to Rome. His presence in Rome and his beliefs were to cause future problems for the popes.

Pius I, St

Aquileia, Italy; c.142 to c.155

Of Pius (Latin for 'dutiful') little is known, although tradition suggests that he was born in slavery at Aquileia. He had much to contend with in his episcopacy. Valentius, the Gnostic, was causing problems in Rome; so were a certain Cerdo, who was teaching that there were two equal gods, one good and one evil, and Marcion, who disputed the need to use and refer to the Old Testament.

Anicetus, St

Syria; c.155 to c.166

Little is known of Anicetus although tradition suggests that he was Syrian. The Christian community was plagued by various heresies (see Pius I) which Anicetus struggled with; he is reputed to have discussed the date of Easter, another live issue at the time, with St Polycarp of Smyrna.

Soter, St

Campania; c.166 to c.174

Except for a mention in the writings of Eusebius of Caesarea, who praises Soter's charity and support given to Christians in trouble, there is little information available about him. Tradition says that Soter came from Campania.

Eleutherius, St

Nicopolis, Greece; c.174 to c.189

Eleutherius is believed to have come from Greece and had been a deacon in the service of the two previous popes. During his pontificate he had to deal with the problems raised by Montanism which had not been energetically tackled earlier. (Montanus, who took a pessimistic view of the sinfulness of humanity, encouraged his followers at hysterical mass assemblies. They considered themselves a Christian elite.) Due to the more moderate approach of the Emperor Marcus Aurelius, Rome enjoyed a respite from persecution during Eleutherius' reign.

Victor I, St

Africa; c.189 to c.199

Although an African by birth, Victor was a great upholder of the Western as opposed to the Eastern ecclesiastical tradition. He advanced Latin culture in the Church and from his time can be dated the official use of Latin as the language of the Church. He insisted that the Roman date for Easter (on a Sunday) should be followed universally, rather than the Eastern practice which led to Easter falling on any day of the week. He held synods in all the chief Christian centres and he used his papal authority to excommunicate some churches of Asia Minor who would not comply.

Zephyrinus, St

Rome; c.199 to 217

Zephyrinus appears to have returned to the earlier practice of adopting a Greek papal name. He is reported to have been a weak man who failed to take the firm action needed at the time over the heresies that arose. His critics even describe him as 'ignorant and greedy' (Hippolytus in *The Refutation of all Heresies*). He used as his principal assistant, Archdeacon Callistus, who became pope himself. At this time (202) Emperor Septimus Severus launched his persecution of the Church.

Callistus, St

Rome; 217 to 222

Also known as Callixtus. The writings of the anti-pope Hippolytus (the first of thirty-nine in papal history) who was elected at the same time as Callistus, by a

rival faction, are the only source of information about Callistus. He started life as a slave and embezzled a large sum of money entrusted to him by his master, Carpophorus. He tried to escape capture but was arrested and sentenced to death. In Rome he was released after the local Christian community interceded for him; there followed an incident where he was accused of insulting the local Jewish community in their synagogue. He was condemned to the notorious mines of Sardinia but released through the kind intervention of Marcia, mistress of the Emperor Commodus. Pope Victor showed him kindness and he was ordained a deacon (216) by Pope Zephyrinus. Having won the confidence of the Roman community he was elected pope. He was firm in dealing with heretical teaching and had to deal with the presence of the anti-pope Hippolytus. Tradition records that he died heroically as a martyr.

Urban I, St

Rome; 222 to 230

Little reliable information is available about Urban. The tradition that he died a martyr's death is unreliable. However it is certain that he had a difficult reign with the presence and activity of the anti-pope Hippolytus dividing the community in Rome.

Pontian, St

Rome; 21 July 230 to 28 September 235

The first pope to abdicate, Pontian, who is believed to have been a Roman, had a very difficult pontificate. He still had to handle the schism in Rome, caused by the anti-pope Hippolytus, and the heretical teachings of Origen. The Emperor Maximinus Thrax directed a persecution at the leaders of the Roman Church so that Pontian and Hippolytus were arrested and sent to the dreadful mines of Sardinia. Pontian judged that he would never return and resigned. He and Hippolytus endured terrible conditions and both died in prison.

Anterus, St

Greece; 21 November 235 to 3 January 236

Anterus replaced Pontian for a few months after Pontian had resigned. His name is Greek and the deduction is made that he originated from Greece; little other reliable information is available. One early record states that he was martyred, but this is contradicted by another source.

Fabian, St

Rome; 10 January 236 to 20 January 250

A legend told by the historian Eusebius has it that Fabian was not expected to be elected but a dove came into the gathering and sat on his head! The crowd took this to be a sure sign of the approval of the Holy Spirit. Fabian proved to be a good leader of the Church; he ordered the improvement of the catacombs and divided the diocese of Rome into seven districts each with the leadership of a deacon. He brought back to Rome for burial the bodies of Pope Pontian and Hippolytus (See Pontian). It is believed that he died a martyr's death under the Emperor Decius.

Cornelius, St

Rome; March 251 to June 253

The persecution of the Emperor Decius was so violent that no successor to Fabian was elected for over a year. A committee governed the Church. Novatian, a well-known scholar who expected to be elected, was passed over, the electors choosing Cornelius. Novatian's supporters consecrated him and Cornelius had a difficult time holding his own. He was approved and supported by the famous St Cyprian, Bishop of Carthage and by synods of bishops at Rome and Carthage. In 252 a new persecution began and Cornelius was arrested and sent into exile; the details of his death are unknown but he is believed to have died a martyr.

Lucius I, St

Rome; 25 June 253 to 5 March 254

Soon after his election Lucius was driven from his native city of Rome by the persecuting Emperor Trebonianus Gallus, who died later the same year. Lucius was able to return when the new emperor, Valerian, relaxed the persecution of Christians. He is believed to have continued the policies of Cornelius. Two sources contradict one another over the manner of his death. The *Liber Pontificalis* states that he was martyred, but another ancient source declares that he died naturally.

Stephen I, St

Rome; 12 May 254 to 2 August 257

A Roman by birth and education, the only facts about Stephen's life come from his correspondence with Bishop St Cyprian of Cathage over several doctrinal matters, including the validity of baptism when administered by a heretic. He upheld the teaching authority of the Bishop of Rome against Cyprian and three African Councils. He is hence known for being the first pope to make formal claim for the primacy of the See of Rome. He is honoured as a martyr, but there is no evidence to support this tradition.

Sixtus II, St

Greece; 30 August 257 to 6 August 258

Also known as Xystus II. Contemporaries called this pope, Sixtus Junior. It was only when there was a further pope of the same name that he was numerically listed. More conciliatory than Stephen, the previous pope, he repaired relationships with St Cyprian and the African bishops over the issue of the re-baptism of heretics who had repented. The Emperor Valerian launched a sudden and violent persecution on the Roman community and Sixtus was caught and beheaded as he preached, on 6 August 258, at the cemetery of Praetextatus, close to the Appian Way.

Dionysius, St

possibly Greece; 22 July 260 to 26 December 268

There was no occupant of the Roman See for over a year, due to the violence of the Emperor Valerian's persecution, which had virtually annihilated all ecclesiastical leadership. Dionysius was elected as soon as news of Valerian's death in the East was received in Rome. The new emperor, Gallienus, returned the Church's property taken by Valerian and Dionysius had the task of restoring and rebuilding the shattered community. He won a reputation for his care for Christians in any kind of distress throughout the Empire.

Felix I, St

Rome; 5 January 269 to 30 December 274

Everything about this Bishop of Rome is obscure; even his dates are open to question and sources cannot agree on his manner of death. Nothing of any note is recorded of his pontificate.

Eutychian, St

possibly Tuscany; 4 January 275 to 7 December 283

No records exist that give us any reliable information about this occupant of the Holy See. The reason for this is believed to be the severe persecution of the Emperor Diocletian some twenty years later, when all records were, by imperial order, destroyed. It is known, however, that Eutychian's community did not suffer persecution.

Gaius, St

Dalmatia; 17 December 283 to 22 April 296

Sometimes known as Caius. No trustworthy records have survived of this pope. It is known that the Roman community did not suffer persecution during his period of office.

Marcellinus, St

Rome; 30 June 296 to 25 October 304

It is remarkable that later generations honoured Marcellinus as a saint in view of the contemporary sources that speak of his apostasy. It seems that after a few quiet years his pontificate, and the Church, was hit by the persecution of the Emperor Diocletian in 303. Marcellinus is reported to have handed over copies of the Scriptures to the authorities and even burnt incense to the gods. The scandal given must have been immense and it is believed that Marcellinus would not have survived as pope and must have abdicated or resigned before his death, of which nothing is known for sure. The result of the persecution and scandal was that there was no Bishop of Rome for over three years.

Marcellus I, St

Rome; 27 May 308 (or 26 June, 308) to 26 January 309

After a long interregnum, occasioned by persecution, Marcellus was elected when a new emperor, Maxentius, took the throne. Marcellus tried to reorganise the Church after the disorder of the preceding years and introduced severe penances on those Christians who had fallen away under persecution. This measure was so unpopular that there was rioting in Rome and the emperor, blaming Marcellus, banished him from the city. He died soon afterwards.

Eusebius, St

Greece; 18 April 309 to 17 August 309 (or 310)

After his election Eusebius attempted to proceed with Pope Marcellus' policy regarding the *lapsi*, that is, those who had abandoned their faith during times of persecution but looked for forgiveness and acceptance back into the community when all was quiet. However the emperor, Maxentius, struck again and Eusebius was dispatched into exile on Sicily, where he died. His body was later brought back to Rome and was buried in the Catacomb of Callistus.

Miltiades, St

from Rome? 11 July 311 to 11 January 314

The imperial Edict of Toleration, 311, brought peace at last to the Church; Emperor Maxentius, in a gesture to win the approval of Christians, restored church property. So Miltiades became Bishop of Rome at a propitious time. Constantine's victory over Maxentius at the Battle of Milvian Bridge heralded in a new age for the papacy and the Church. The new emperor gave the pope the palace of the Empress Fausta; this became the Lateran Palace, used by the popes until the fifteenth century. The reign was only seriously troubled by the Donatists, who taught that sacraments celebrated by a priest who had once lapsed, or was in a state of sin, were invalid. This was condemned by Miltiades in 313; however the controversy continued after his death.

Sylvester I, St (Silvester)

Rome; 31 January 314 to 31 December 335

In spite of a long pontificate Sylvester remains obscure, overshadowed by the dominant figure of the Emperor Constantine who took a personal interest in Church affairs. The emperor summoned the Council of Nicaea, and Sylvester sent two priests to represent him (hence establishing a practice that became traditional). As a result of Constantine's generosity Sylvester was able to construct churches, the first St Peter's, St Paul's and the Basilica, later known as St John Lateran, which Sylvester made the cathedral church of the diocese of Rome, which it still is.

330–700
The spread of Christianity
and the birth of Islam

Timeline 330–700

337   Roman Emperor Constantine baptised a Christian before his death.

381   Constantinople (now Istanbul in Turkey) is made Christianity's second city.

382   Pope Damasus defines the Bible as we know it today, listing the 'canonical' books.

395   Augustine, Bishop of Hippo writes *City of God*, one of the dominant theological texts of early Christianity.

410   Rome invaded by Goths.

431   The Council of Ephesus – the Virgin Mary is affirmed as mother of Christ, 'Godbearer'.

451   The decision by the council of Chalcedon that Christ and God the Father are one God in two forms causes dissenting Christians to split into the Orthodox Churches

455   Vandals invade Rome. The city is saved only by Pope Leo's intercession with invaders.

496   Clovis, King of the Franks is converted.

540   Benedict writes his monastic rule.

597   St Augustine arrives in England to begin the conversion of Britain.

622   First year of the Muslim calendar.

632   Prophet Mohammed dies.

638   Jerusalem overrun by Muslim (Saracen) armies.

656   Conquest of Syria, Egypt and Persia by the Arabs.

664   Synod of Whitby.

681   Third Council of Constantinople confirms the dual nature of God.

Introduction

The Germanic period between 330 and 700 AD was a time when Christianity changed profoundly. Prior to this, Christians had been a persecuted minority sect in pagan Rome, but when the Roman emperor Constantine announced toleration of Christians in 313, Christianity's fortunes immediately changed for the better. Constantine had tolerated the Christians, but following his deathbed baptism in 337 it became socially advantageous to be a Christian.

For a while, Christian and pagan ceremonies co-existed in Roman society, and to some extent borrowed from each other's practices – some Romans thought it was perfectly acceptable to worship in both early Christian rites and pagan festivals, until some Church leaders demanded with some exasperation that Romans should decide whether they wanted to worship as Christians or pagans. Once Christianity took hold, it did so with vigour, and the persecutors became the persecuted: in many towns there were riots that destroyed pagan temples. Pagan worshippers were stoned and many fled.

The period 330-700 is popularly called the Germanic period because it saw the collapse of the Roman Empire and the rise in power of the Germanic tribes from the north of Europe. Having been conquered by the Romans, they had little love for the Roman empire, and Rome was subject to invasions by the Goths, Huns and Vandals. Christian Rome not only survived these invasions, it recovered to send Christian missionaries to the Germanic states and succeeded in converting many previously hostile tribes. The Germanic period also marks the start of the Middle Ages in European history, where the upheavals of the collapse of Rome and repeated invasions caused European civilisation to stagnate – education, art and culture were limited, and with that the economy and population declined.

But while Europe languished, Christianity had stopped simply struggling to survive and was undergoing a period of growth and maturation as a religion. The Bible was defined for the first time in 382 when Pope Damasus convened a Council to list the books that now make up the Old and New Testaments. Significantly, St Jerome had translated much of the Bible into Latin in the 380s – Latin was replacing Greek as the common language of Rome, and it became the language that was understood by educated people throughout much of Europe. All of this served to reinforce Rome as the spiritual centre of early Christianity.

The period 330-700 saw some significant historical and religious developments that affect Christianity and world affairs to this day. One was the split between mainstream and Orthodox Christianity. This occurred as a result of the Council of Chalcedon, where Christian leaders decided that Christ and God the Father were two forms of the one God. Egyptian and Syrian Christians disagreed with this teaching so deeply that they split from the Church, no longer recognising the authority of the pope. A further hugely significant development that has affected the history not only of the Catholic Church but also of the world occurred with the founding of the Islamic Calendar in 622 and the death of the prophet Mohammed in 632.

But in Europe, a continent liberated from the military rule of the Roman Empire, a new power from Rome started to take control of the Germanic, Frankish and Goth states that made up post-Roman Europe. Regional rulers found power and money leaving their grasp and finding their way into the hands of bishops. From a persecuted minority in first-century Rome, Christianity had taken over much of Europe in little more than 500 years. Ignoring occasional anti-pagan riots, it was a remarkably consensual conversion in many places. Life in Middle Ages Europe must have been hard – subsistence living with the threat of capricious feudal lords or invasion from a belligerent tribe of Goths or Vandals. The appeal of a religion promising salvation and an afterlife basking in the approval of a merciful God must have been an appealing prospect.

This period of the Church's history saw two significant developments that echo in today's Christianity – the cult of the martyr developed, as did the Christian distaste for sex, an activity that was seen to be distinctly inferior to virginity and chastity, and only to be undertaken following marriage. Sexual reproduction was seen as an unfortunate consequence of Adam and Eve eating fruit from the tree of knowledge ('the fall') thereby committing the first sin. This led to some entertaining theological debates. If Adam was made by God rather than born of woman, did he have a navel? Many pictures of Adam skirt the subject, showing him with a leaf or wandering vine covering the site of his disputed navel and so avoiding the issue.

Christianity still had painful memories of some of its early followers being martyred by the Roman authorities for their determination to follow the teachings of Christ. The cult of worshipping martyrs led to growth in revering their relics. Bones, skeletons and fragments of clothing (some, it has to be said, of very dubious origins) all became items to be venerated – they represented the courage and Christian virtue of the martyrs, and the cult of venerating relics became regarded as a line to God, via the saints.

Relics were precious, and many churches were built to allow increasing numbers of the faithful to venerate them. The cult of venerating martyrs spread and became one of the central practices of Christianity. The growing ranks of the Christian faithful made pilgrimages to worship at these new shrines, so the cult of martyrs not only changed the physical shape of Europe through the number of churches it caused to be built, it also caused huge population shifts in pilgrimages.

One of the most significant popes of this period was Gregory I. Gregory's rule (590–604) came towards the end of the period under examination, and his past as a Roman urban administrator confirmed the Church's role as a cultural ambassador for Roman values in the early Christian world. He allowed monasteries and orders of monks to flourish, which had profound implications for much of western civilisation, not only in the spread of Christianity but also in the role of monasteries as places of learning.

Gregory's reforms and his inspirational spreading of Christianity to England with Augustine's mission in 597 are still being felt today. The Synod of Whitby in 664 confirmed the dominance of Roman over Celtic Christianity, and set the formula that is used to this day to determine the variable date of Easter throughout the Catholic and Protestant Christian world.

Some see Pope Gregory's rule as a turning point in Christianity. Before Gregory, the Church was struggling with pagan Roman influences and repeated invasions, fighting for survival and forging its own identity. With Pope Gregory giving the Church a missionary role to convert the Germanic states, the Church began to consolidate its religious, educational and cultural dominance over Europe.

The Byzantine Empire and Orthodox Christianity

Following his conversion to Christianity in 326, the Roman emperor Constantine proclaimed the Greek colony of Byzantium the 'new Rome'. He renamed the city Constantinople after himself and declared it the capital of the Eastern Roman Empire.

Ironically, this attempt to strengthen the Empire actually

weakened Rome, the Empire's founding city, and while the original Western Empire withered under repeated invasions by Goths, Vandals, Huns, and other barbarian tribes, the city of Constantinople and its surrounding land thrived, and became the Byzantine Empire. Byzantium's was a Greek based culture, valuing education and philosophy, and it had a flourishing economy.

Christianity was the state religion, and it permeated the life of the Empire. In its outward expression, Byzantine Christianity was rich and ostentatious – the Hagia Sophia in Constantinople (now Istanbul) was the largest church building in the world, and all visitors to Constantinople marvelled at its wealth and splendour.

Wealth and power attract trouble, and the Byzantine Empire had its share of internal and external strife – rulers were murdered, imprisoned and exiled. One deposed emperor had his nose cut off as a mark of disgrace before being sent into exile. An archbishop was excommunicated as he celebrated mass, with a messenger creeping on to the altar and pinning the notice of excommunication to the back of his vestments.

Externally, Byzantium suffered wars with Germanic, Persian and Saracen invaders in the east, and Slavic tribes in the west, and its religious relations with Roman Christianity deteriorated until in 1054 the Roman and Byzantine branches of Christianity formally split, with a cardinal acting on behalf of Rome and a patriarch from Constantinople exchanging anathemas. An anathema is a Church declaration that a person, or their religious doctrine, is 'damnable'. That move split Christianity into Roman Catholicism and Orthodox Christianity, a division that remains to this day, although the two factions are no longer as absolute in their rejection of one another's beliefs.

Byzantine Christians were as successful as their Roman cousins in missionary work: Eastern monks Cyril and Methodius created the Cyrillic alphabet and translated the Bible into Cyrillic, allowing eastern Christian missions to Russia and the Slavic countries. To this day Russia's alphabet is Cyrillic and its principal religion is Orthodox Christianity.

By the second millennium, the power of the Byzantine Empire had begun to fade, and not long after the schism with Rome, it suffered a series of military and economic setbacks: invading Seljuk Turks inflicted a grievous defeat on the armies of Byzantium at the Battle of Manzikert in 1071 and in 1204 the Fourth Crusade visited Constantinople, defeated the incumbent emperor and sacked the city, replacing the Byzantine emperor with a Latin ruler.

This new Latin dynasty lasted until 1261, when Constantinople once again fell into Byzantine hands, but the state was now severely weakened, and with much of the Empire now captured by the Ottoman Turks, Constantinople was besieged in 1395. The siege lasted an incredible fifty-eight years, since Constantinople was in a commanding, easily defended position. In 1453 the Turks breached the walls and the emperor (also called Constantine) was killed defending the city, which then fell.

The rise of Islam

Mohammed was born in Mecca in the year 570. It was as significant a birth in world history as was the birth of Jesus in Bethlehem. Like Jesus, Mohammed's ministry did not start until well into his adult years, when at the age of forty Mohammed experienced visions. They were remarkable visions, in which the Archangel Gabriel told Mohammed that he was to be the prophet of Allah (God).

Mohammed took this call seriously, and over the following years became the religious leader of Arab world, founding the religion of Islam. Islam means 'surrender', indicating not a lack of courage but a willingness to surrender completely to Allah's will. The followers of the prophet Mohammed were known as *Muslimin* – the surrendered ones. In the last years of his life, Mohammed wrote down the revelations he received from Allah, and after Mohammed's death in 632 these writings were gathered by Abu Bekr (Mohammed's chosen successor) into the Koran, which became the sacred book of the Islamic faith.

At this time, Christianity was growing into not only a widespread religion but also a powerful political system. Christianity's influence stretched from the west of Ireland to Syria at the eastern end of the Mediterranean, and into the countries of North Africa. With Islam as a focal point and Mohammed as a charismatic, able leader, the Arab countries soon began to grow in strength, and it became almost inevitable that the spread of Christianity would come into conflict with the new and vigorous religion of Islam.

The first Christian–Muslim conflict was provoked by the Orthodox Christians of the Byzantine Empire – this massive Eastern European empire stretched as far east as Syria, and here the Byzantine authorities started to persecute the local Arab population. The Arabs appealed to Abu Bekr for help, and he obliged, dispatching an army under his general,

Khaled, to aid the beleaguered Syrians. The Muslim army swept up the eastern Mediterranean coast, taking much of the Eastern Byzantine Empire and eventually reaching and besieging Constantinople, the Empire's capital. The Muslim warrior invaders became known – and feared – across Europe as Saracens, and with this first successful clash with European Christianity, the Muslims began a campaign of conquest against the Christian sites around the Mediterranean.

Jerusalem fell to a Saracen army led by Caliph Omar in 638. Jerusalem was already considered a holy city by Jews and Christians; in 622 Mohammed had visited the city and received further visions, so it also became a holy city for the Muslim world. When Jerusalem fell to the Muslim armies, Caliph Omar commissioned a mosque to be built to mark the city's holiness to Islam. The Caliph assured the Christians that their rights to worship and their property would be respected, and guaranteed these rights in a legal agreement – the Saracens might be conquerors, but they were not barbarians.

By 640, Persia – which we now know as Iran – and Egypt had fallen to the Saracens, and in 642 the famous library at Alexandria was burned by the Muslim invaders. By 650 the Saracens had conquered as far as Afghanistan in the east and to the Black Sea (in modern Russia) to the north. In 675 Christian Spain suffered a Saracen invasion, and in 697 the city of Carthage (a significant city in the history of Christianity) was conquered.

Europe rallied and ultimately defended its lands against the Saracen invaders. The siege of the Byzantine capital Constantinople was lifted in 677, but Spain and Portugal had fallen to the Saracens by 716. The Saracens pressed on into France, where they were defeated in a battle near Poitiers in 732.

The Christians had no reason to love, or indeed tolerate the Muslim invaders. Their occupation of Jerusalem was insult enough and invasions of the Byzantine Empire and western Europe were worse. The fact that Mohammed also revered Jesus as a fellow prophet of Allah made no difference to Christian or Muslim sentiments. Both believed God was on their side, and that conquest was a matter of territorial expansion and bringing the Word of God to non-believers. The antagonism between Christianity and Islam ultimately caused both great religions to develop the idea of a war in God's name. In the case of Islam this was the *jihad*, and in Christianity became the papally inspired Crusades, a series of military excursions aimed at recapturing the Holy Lands from the Muslim invaders.

The growth of Monasticism

The period 330-700 was remarkable in Christian history for the growth of monasticism. Today, we know monasteries as the religious communities of monks such as Benedictines or Dominicans, or friars such as Franciscans, but the earliest forms of monasticism were loose groups of religious hermits who lived in the desert fringes of the Holy Land and North Africa. The early monks withdrew to the wilder edges of society to practise ascetic lifestyles, aiming for a life of Christian perfection through self-denial, prayer and withdrawal from the temptations of society, possessions and relationships. These original loose groups inevitably gelled into more formal, organised communities.

The first record of a monastic community was that founded at Tabennisi in Egypt by Pachomus, (a former soldier) around 320. From Egypt, monasticism developed in the eastern Church under the guidance of Basil the Great (330–379), whose vision for monasticism was more closely involved with the wider community than the earliest ascetics. Basil also started the trend for monastic 'rules' – the written guidance that governs the way of life of each monastic order.

Monasticism entered western Christianity through St Martin of Tours, a natural hermit who, having been reluctantly persuaded to become Bishop of Tours in France, found that the life of a bishop did not sit well with his ascetic temperament; he withdrew to the countryside, setting up a monastery, from which he started the work of spreading Christianity through France.

Monasteries as centres of learning began with the Roman Cassiodorus, who was born in 490 and lived to the (for that time) incredible age of ninety-three. Having been a civil Roman administrator, he founded a monastery in southern Italy and retreated from Roman society. His community became a centre for learning, setting a trend that persisted long into the Middle Ages. Monasteries throughout Europe held large libraries, and monks came to specialise in copying and illustrating manuscripts.

But perhaps the most notable early western monk was Benedict, who was born in Nursia, in central Italy. He founded the order now known as the Benedictines, establishing its monastery at Monte Cassino, where he wrote what we call the Rule of St Benedict. Benedict's rule was centred around the twin activities of prayer and work, citing the Bible as the basis for praying seven times a day, and stating that idleness is the enemy of the soul. His rule stated that monasteries should, if possible, be self-sufficient so that monks would not need to venture outside its walls and be tempted.

By the time Gregory the Great became Pope in 590, monasticism was firmly established in Roman Christianity, and Gregory wisely encouraged the development of monasteries. Monasteries tended to be stable communities; monks laid great stress on prayer, meditation and learning, and as such made ideal missionaries. Gregory accordingly dispatched the monk Augustine to Britain, where Christianity took root. Britain, spiritually strengthened by monks from Ireland led by Columba, became a stronghold of monasticism, and monks from Britain were crucial in the subsequent evangelisation of northern Europe.

Although monasticism was principally the province of men, monastic communities of women were established. Although records of the period are sketchy, Pachomus is thought to have founded a monastic community of women in Egypt, and at the height of the monastic influence in Britain, Whitby Abbey – site of the Synod of Whitby in 664 – was a mixed community led by Abbess (later Saint) Hilda.

St Augustine and the conversion of England

Perhaps one of the most significant missions in this period was that of St Augustine and his forty fellow monks. Pope Gregory the Great was anxious to establish Roman Christianity in the British Isles, and to take the Saxon kingdom into the growing community of Christian lands – Gregory had by this time invented the idea of a Christian commonwealth, and he wanted Britain to be a part of it.

Augustine landed in Kent at Easter in the year 597, and within the year Augustine's work had secured the conversion of Ethelbert, the Anglo Saxon king of East Anglia. Ethelbert was probably a relatively easy first conversion, since his wife was already a Christian. Later in 597 Augustine was ordained Archbishop of England, and the newly converted king allowed Augustine to build a palace at Canterbury. (The head of the Church of England, which split from the Catholic papacy in the rule of King Henry VIII, still has Archbishop of Canterbury as his title.)

It would, however, be wrong to say that Augustine was the first Christianising influence on British soil – Celtic Christian missionaries, originally from Ireland, had been at work in Britain since the fourth century, encouraged by figures such as St Columba and St Patrick. Christianity had established a stronghold in the fourth and fifth centuries, but had been suppressed by repeated invasions of Angles, Saxons and Jutes from northern Europe.

St Augustine arrived into a more stable, Anglo Saxon Britain, bringing with him a very Roman, authoritarian brand of Christianity. Celtic Christianity differed from the Roman version in both tone and details – it was a more imaginative, creative version of Christianity, and at first the Celtic Christians and Augustine disagreed.

The Celtic Church had its own way of working out the date of Easter, and disagreed with Augustine's Roman practice of baptising converts. When Celtic bishops met Augustine, he was reported to have remained sitting rather than standing out of respect when he greeted them. They initially refused to join him in his papally ordered mission of evangelising Britain.

Before long, however, the two Christian factions came to terms. Northern Celtic-influenced churchmen became involved in the evangelisation, and at the Synod of Whitby in 664, the dispute between Celtic and Roman Christianity was settled in favour of the Romans.

It was not, however, a complete take-over of Celtic Christianity by the Roman tradition. The creative, spiritual nature of the Celts had permeated British Christianity, especially in the north where the monastic tradition was developing, and this fusion gave British Christianity a unique reserve of spirituality and inspired manpower that subsequently went on to provide vigorous, effective missionaries in the conversion of northern Europe.

The collapse of Rome and the conversion of Europe

The period 330–700 was a turbulent one – the Roman Empire was in decline, with legions of Roman soldiers abandoning outposts around Europe, the Mediterranean and North Africa as successive waves of invasions rocked the overstretched Empire. Tribes of Goths, Huns, Avars and Vandals filled the vacuum left by the Roman collapse, and in successive waves they rampaged through Europe. Not even the mighty city of Rome was immune. In 410 Rome fell to a Visigoth siege and once again to a Vandal invasion in 455. Christianity, by now closely identified with Rome, with the Bishop of Rome now firmly established

Asceticism

Many religious people have felt called to live lives of rigorous self denial. This lifestyle was called ascetic, and the people who followed it ascetics. Ascetics would often lead isolated lives, fasting and existing with an absolute minimum of worldly possessions.

Some ascetics became founders of the early monasteries – St Pachomus, widely credited with starting the first known monastery, started his spiritual life as an ascetic – and the role of ascetic living is echoed in many religious groups who see a simple life as more conducive to spiritual fulfilment. By the seventh century, asceticism was being compared to martyrdom as an expression of Christianity.

Some ascetics took this expression of their faith to extremes, with unpredictable consequences. The psychiatrist Anthony Storr suggests that many of the ecstatic visions described by Christian saints were in reality hallucinations brought on by malnutrition – a consequence of too ascetic a lifestyle. Early Christian authorities also recognised the danger of extreme asceticism, since ascetic Christians tended to claim that their lifestyle was a more perfect expression of Christianity than those who ate normally, engaged with the world and married.

One of the most extreme examples of asceticism was that of St Simon Stylites, a Syrian ascetic who spent the latter years of his life living on top of a pillar. St Francis of Assisi warned his Friars Minor against living too ascetic a life. Although he himself fasted, he warned that his brethren could not do God's work if they were weak with hunger.

as leader of the Christian Church, could have suffered too, but it showed a remarkable flexibility and resilience. In 452 Pope Leo persuaded Attila the Hun not to invade the city, and in 455, when Gaiseric the Vandal did invade Rome, Leo minimised the damage and effectively ransomed the city.

As the Roman Empire crumbled away from Britain and France, local rulers filled the void left by the retreating Romans. The tribes of Franks and Burgundians established large kingdoms in France, and in Britain the scattered tribes vied for land and power, while Jutes, Angles and Saxons invaded from the countries across the North Sea. Roman

Christianity took advantage of the new Europe, and in this period became a missionary church, repeating the startling success it showed in its spiritual conquest of the pagan Roman Empire. In 432 the Welshman Patrick was ordained a bishop in France and travelled to Ireland, where his missionary work founded the distinctive Celtic Christianity. By around 500 AD most of France had been converted; then in 597 Pope Gregory the Great sent the monk Augustine and forty of his brethren to England. Before long, England too was a Christian country and with Ireland became a great centre of Christian learning; was a great monastic tradition founded at centres such as Iona, Lindisfarne and Jarrow. The English and Celtic monks became powerful agents for the spread of Christianity, sending missionaries to play a significant role in Christianising the Germanic tribes of northern Europe. In this period most of Europe's kings bowed to the new Church: Clovis, King of the Franks, was baptised in 493, and the Spanish king, Recared, in 589.

The development of churches

In the Roman period, churches were a place to meet and worship, but the building itself had no innate holiness – it was the presence of the people of God that brought the sanctity to the structure. In the period 330–700, there was a growing trend of churches now being home to relics of martyrs and saints. The relics were usually placed beneath the altar, and churches became holy places in their own right, with their size, architecture and decoration starting to reflect their role as a place where people would meet in communion with God. Christians began to travel great distances to venerate particular relics (especially those with a reputation for miraculously healing the sick), and the age of pilgrimage began. The development of churches as sacred spaces in their own right began in Rome with the Emperor Constantine's toleration of Christianity – he commissioned the basilicas of St Peter (built over the tomb of the first pope) and St John Lateran. Rome led the way in churches becoming a sacred space and becoming buildings to the glory of God – pagan temples such as the Pantheon were converted for Christian worship, and with Constantine's proclamation of Constantinople as the 'new Rome', with Christianity as the state religion, massive, ostentatious churches and basilicas were built.

This trend of holiness being attached to churches was

strengthened by the start of the monastic movement, where communities of holy men or women would live in an abbey with much of their spiritual life revolving around prayer in the abbey's church. As Christianity spread throughout Europe and the Mediterranean basin, churches became a visible, impressive symbol of the power of Christianity and a focus for the Christian developing community.

Christians capture time

Julius Caesar introduced the Julian Calendar in 46 BC, and it was under this calendar that Christianity began to develop.

But as Christianity began to flourish and the Roman Empire went into decline, Christianity began to define its own religious calendar. Just as Christianity took over Roman dress, converted Roman temples and took on Roman manners, it also absorbed significant Roman festivals and renamed them as Christian feasts.

Christianity then imposed its own special days, feast days commemorating saints or martyrs, and while still using Julius Caesar's original calendar it usurped it into a new Christian annual routine. Christmas was fixed on 25 December, replacing (it is thought) the Roman feast in honour of Saturn – the earliest mention of Christmas on this date is in 336 AD. Easter became a movable feast linked to the lunar cycle.

In 527 the monk Dionysius Exiguus (Dennis the Short) first developed the term 'Anno Domini', meaning 'In the year of Our Lord'. This marked the true Christianisation of time, since time was then dated from the presumed year of Christ's birth, with BC referring to the years supposed to be before Christ's birth. In 1582 this system became formalised into a revised and corrected Gregorian Calendar by Pope Gregory XIII, replacing the Julian Calendar which by this time had lost ten days.

THE POPES
336–701

Mark, St

Rome; 18 January 336 to 7 October 336

The pontificate of Mark was overshadowed by the last few years of the Emperor Constantine, and little is known. He is remembered for founding two churches in Rome and introducing the custom of having the Bishop of Ostia consecrate the Bishop of Rome.

Julius I, St

Rome; 6 February 337 to 12 April 352

Much of Julius' pontificate was spent combating Arianism (the teaching that Christ was not divine). He gave sanctuary to St Athanasius (339) after the Arians had expelled him from his diocese of Alexandria. Julius called the Council of Sardica, 342, to condemn Arian teachings. He thereby reinforced Rome's claims of primacy over the bishops of the East.

Liberius

Rome; 17 May 352 to 24 September 366

Liberius has the distinction of being the first pope not to be honoured as a saint. This was almost certainly due to the perceived notion that he had compromised with Arianism. At first Liberius firmly refused to bow to the pressure of the pro-Arian Emperor Constantius II, but bullied by the emperor he was sent into exile (355). In Rome Felix II, an anti-pope, was chosen to replace Liberius. After two years Liberius returned, apparently after accepting a compromise settlement under duress. Faced with an anti-pope and the hostility of the Romans, Liberius' last years were marked by orthodox teaching but little regard from anyone.

Damasus I, St

Spain; 1 October 366 to 11 December 384

Of a Spanish family, Damasus grew up and was educated in Rome. Violence swept the streets of Rome when Damasus was consecrated because supporters of the previous pope preferred Ursinus, a Roman deacon. Armed gangs of Damasus' supporters routed the Ursinians; according to one historian the casualties included 137 dead. Driven out of Rome, the Ursinians continued for several years to try to overthrow Damasus. Not only did he have to work hard to restore his reputation but he had to suppress several heresies plaguing the Church at that time, notably Arianism and Donatism. Damasus resolutely advanced the claims of the Roman primacy, referring for the first time to the 'Apostolic See'. He appointed St Jerome to be his secretary and requested him to translate the Septuagint (Greek version of the Old Testament) and the New Testament into Latin, providing the Church with the authoritative translation known as the Vulgate.

Siricius, St

Rome; 15 December 384 to 26 November 399

The anti-pope Ursinus (see Pope Damasus) challenged the election of Siricius, but he was elected by unanimous vote. He continued the emphasis of the previous pope upon Roman papal supremacy and was the first Bishop of Rome to use the title 'Pope' in the sense in which we use it today. He decreed that the permission of the Holy See was necessary before any bishop could be consecrated.

Anastasius I, St

Rome; 27 November 399 to 19 December 401

A Roman by birth, Anastasius is only notable for his involvement with a bitter controversy over the writings of the Alexandrian theologian, Origen. St Jerome, whose advice he took in the conflict, admired him as 'of very rich poverty and Apostolic solicitude'.

Innocent I, St

Albano; 22 December 401 to 12 March 417

Innocent, who was believed to be the son of Pope Anastasius, was elected at one of the most terrible times in the history of Rome. The Western empire was falling apart with the invasions of Alaric I, the king of the Visigoths. Innocent went to Ravenna, Alaric's capital, to negotiate a truce. His attempt failed, and while he was away Rome was sacked (410) by Alaric. Innocent returned when the Visigoths left and devoted himself to relieving famine and the sufferings of the Roman population. The bishops of North Africa, including St Augustine, appealed to Innocent to repudiate Pelagianism (a British heresy by origin) which was disturbing the Church in Africa.

Zosimus, St

Greece; 18 March 417 to 26 December 418

Little is known about Zosimus' early life. He was believed to be heavy-handed in the use of his papal authority and lacking in tact and diplomacy in dealing with the African churches over Pelagianism, and with the bishops of Gaul. He was unpopular in Rome and his death was not mourned.

Boniface I, St

Rome; 28 December 418 to 22 September 422

Boniface's election was contested by a small group of Roman deacons who chose Eulalius as their candidate. Boniface was forced to leave the city but his appeal to the emperor, Honorius, was upheld and Eulalius was ordered to leave Rome. Settled eventually into his pontificate, Boniface sorted out the mess left by Pope Zosimus. He proved to be an able and efficient administrator. He gained the support of St Augustine for the resolute way in which he condemned Pelagianism.

Celestine I, St

Campania; 10 September 422 to 27 July 432

Celestine appears to have been a friend of St Augustine and St Ambrose of Milan before his election, and they remained friends. The greatest challenge to Celestine, apart from an on-going struggle with Pelagianism and Manichaeism, was from the East. Celestine approved the appointment of Nestorius as Patriarch of Constantinople (428–451) but from him came a new heresy, Nestorianism (the teaching that there were two separate Persons, one divine and one human, in the Incarnate Christ). This was condemned at the Council of Ephesus in 431. Celestine sent St Palladius (431) on a mission to Ireland; this was however, short-lived. The next year, in one of his last acts, Celestine sent St Patrick instead.

Sixtus III, St

Rome; 31 July 432 to 19 August 440

Elected by a unanimous vote, Sixtus continued the policies of Pope Celestine, being equally firm in confronting Nestorianism and Pelagianism. He confirmed the decrees of the Council of Ephesus (431) and built the magnificent Basilica of Santa Maria Maggiore (St Mary Major).

Leo I, the Great, St

Tuscany; 29 September 440 to 10 November 461

The first pope to be buried in St Peter's. Little is known of his early life, save that Leo had worked for the two previous popes and was already experienced in handling theological controversy before his election. His long reign was set against the background of the disintegration of the Roman Empire. His papacy is noteworthy for the safeguarding of orthodox teaching and the advancement of papal supremacy. In 449 his Tome was used to reject Eutychianism, an extreme form of the Monophysite heresy; his teaching was hailed as 'the voice of Peter' at the Council of Chalcedon

(451). Leo's many letters and ninety-six extant sermons expound on papal primacy and reveal the liturgical practices of the time and his concern for the poor. He was politically courageous in personally confronting Attila the Hun (452) and Gaiseric the Vandal (455), helping to mitigate the sack of Rome that followed. He was declared a Doctor of the Church in 1754.

Hilarus, St

Sardinia; 19 November 461 to 29 February 468

Also known as Hilary. Hilarus worked for and with Leo the Great, representing him as his legate at the Council of Ephesus (449). When elected to succeed Leo, Hilarus faithfully continued his policies; he was particularly active in advancing the rights and privileges of the Holy See in his letters to the bishops of the East. He consolidated Rome's authority over the churches of Spain and Gaul.

Simplicius, St

Tivoli; 3 March 468 to 10 March 483

Major political events reshaping the map of Europe took place during Simplicius' reign, and little is known of his life and work. The Roman Empire finally came to an end when the emperor, Romulus Augustulus, was deposed by a German chieftain, Odoacer, who was a heretic. The Western Empire disintegrated, and there followed a Germanic domination of Italy. Simplicius continued the struggle against the Monophysite heresy which was rampant in the East, receiving no help or support from the emperor. One attempt at a solution resulted in the birth of the Acacian Schism (see Felix III).

Felix III (II), St

Rome; 13 March 483 to 1 March 492

(Some lists of popes number or name him Felix II, regarding the original Felix II (355–365) an anti-pope; other lists consider the opposite!) A Roman, and believed to be an ancestor of Pope Gregory the Great, Felix raised a family before entering religious life on the death of his wife. He was mostly occupied by events in the East, particularly the activities of Acacius, the patriarch of Constantinople. Believing that the Patriarch was supporting the heresy of Monophysitism, Felix excommunicated him. The excommunication caused the Acacian Schism, which divided the Western and Eastern Churches from 484 to 519. Felix resolutely resisted overtures from the emperor, showing how confident he was, as pontiff, of his authority.

Gelasius I, St

Rome; 1 March 492 to 21 November 496

Of African descent, Gelasius was probably born in Rome. Apart from exerting his authority in ongoing difficulties with the Eastern Church over the Acacian Schism, he also spelt out to Emperor Anastasius the authority of the Church over the State. While assertive in defending the rights of the papacy, Gelasius was revered by his contemporaries for his humility and love of poverty. He was a writer of many letters and treatises, though not the famous Gelasian Sacramentary which has been wrongly attributed to him.

Anastasius II

Rome; 24 November 496 to 19 November 498

The Acacian Schism and relationship with the Eastern Church dominated Anastasius' reign. He tried to bring about a reconciliation, sending two bishops to Constantinople with the offer to negotiate a settlement. This action led to controversy and Anastasius was accused of being led into error. Rome was divided and

Anastasius' efforts were at the best inept. When he died suddenly his enemies attributed it to the wrath of God.

Symmachus, St

Sardinia; 22 November 498 to 19 July 514

The divisions in Rome over Pope Anastasius' policies led to an anti-pope, Lawrence, being elected by a small influential group shortly after Symmachus was elected. The open conflict between the two sides led to violent clashes in the streets of Rome and the murder of some priests. The enemies of Symmachus laid false charges against him, but he was vindicated. It was not until the politically powerful, King Theodoric of the Ostrogoths gave Symmachus recognition in 506, and Lawrence was banished, that he was able to achieve anything. He expelled the Manichaean sect from Rome and issued a decree tightening up electoral procedures for the Holy See.

Hormisdas, St

Frosinone; 20 July 514 to 6 August 523

From the Roman aristocracy, Hormisdas had been married before his ordination to the priesthood. More of a peacemaker than his predecessors, Hormisdas brought together the various factions in Rome and despite early overtures being rebuffed, resolved the conflict with the East. The Acacian Schism came to an end in 519, and relations with the Eastern Church were renewed, if only for a short time.

John I, St (Martyr)

Tuscany; 13 August 523 to 18 May 526

John was in the papal service as a senior deacon when he was elected to succeed Hormisdas. The Eastern emperor, Justin I, had just begun to persecute the Church in 523 and the local king, Theodoric of the

Ostrogoths, an Arian himself, ordered John to go to Constantinople to negotiate a settlement. John, the first pope to visit Constantinople, was well received but his mission was a failure. On his return Theodoric seized John at Ravenna and imprisoned him. Before Theodoric could decide what to do with him, John died; it is believed that he died of starvation (the title 'martyr' refers to this).

Felix IV (III), St

Samnium; 12 July 526 to 22 September 530

Theodoric, king of the Ostrogoths, firmly 'suggested' the election of Felix. He proved to be a competent pope, enjoying the favour of the court. He summoned the Council of Orange (529) to sort out the controversy over grace and original sin. He indicated that he wanted his archdeacon, Boniface, to succeed him, causing a later schism – the very thing Felix had feared and had sought to avoid.

Boniface II

Rome; 22 September 530 to 17 October 532

Boniface had been Felix IV's unconstitutional nomination but he was rejected by many of the Roman clergy because he was a German; they chose Dioscorus. The two were consecrated on the same day, but the anti-pope, Dioscorus, died after three weeks and Boniface worked for a reconciliation with his Roman supporters. Boniface summoned a synod and proposed that it issue a decree giving him the right to name his successor. There was much opposition to this and a third synod rescinded it. Boniface opposed the heresy of Semi-Pelagianism. His death was followed by a scandalous election campaign where bribery and intrigue were employed to influence the choice of a successor. It was only stopped by the king, Athalaric, passing a law prohibiting such behaviour.

John II

Rome; 2 January 533 to 8 May 535

Out of the appalling mess surrounding the election of a new pope came John, the first pope to change his name on election. (His original name was that of the pagan god, Mercury.) He was a compromise candidate, an elderly priest of the church of St Clemente, acceptable to the king, Athalaric, and the new Eastern emperor, Justinian I. John's principal doctrinal decision was to excommunicate, at the request of the emperor, a group of heretical Nestorian monks. (The custom of changing the name of the pope did not become the tradition until 1009.)

Agapitus I, St

Rome; 13 May 535 to 22 April 536

Agapitus, from an aristocratic background, was opposed to the Emperor Justinian I's declared intention of invading Italy to bring it back under Byzantine control. In order to travel to Constantinople to try and persuade the emperor to change his mind, Agapitus had to pawn sacred vessels to pay for the journey. He failed in his mission but did persuade the emperor that Anthimus, the Patriarch of Constantinople, was a Monophysite heretic, and had him deposed. Agapitus died in Constantinople. The empress, Theodora, a Monophysite who had supported the deposed patriarch, promised the papacy to Vigilius, a Roman deacon, if he would re-instate Anthimus. Before she could act Silverius was elected in Rome

Silverius, St (martyr)

1 (or 8) June 536 (under pressure) to 11 November 537 freely abdicated (see Agapitus I for the background to this pontificate)

Silverius was the son of Pope Homisdas, from his marriage before entering the priesthood. After his consecration, Belisarius, the Byzantine general captured

Rome and, encouraged by the empress, tried to persuade Silverius to step down in favour of Constantinople's ambitious candidate, Vigilius. When Silverius refused he was arrested on false charges of conspiring with the Goths and sent into exile. The Emperor Justinian ordered a fair trial, but Vigilius, now pope, conspired to keep him at Palmaria. Under threat of torture, Silverius was forced to abdicate. He was sent once more into exile where he died from cruel treatment and starvation.

Vigilius

Rome; 29 March 537 to probably 7 June 555, exact date unknown (see Silverius for the background to this pontificate)

Vigilius first appeared on the scene when he was nominated by Pope Boniface II to succeed him; this was quashed, but Vigilius was left with the ambition of being pope. As representative of Pope Agapitus at the imperial court Vigilius received the support of Theodora, the empress, who conspired to have him elected. When this was unsuccessful and Silverius was chosen, Theodora worked to have him removed and Vigilius was promptly elected. The new pontiff took part in the brutal treatment handed out to the exiled Silverius. Vigilius failed to keep his bargain with Theodora to have the Monophysite Patriarch of Constantinople re-instated and found himself caught between the expectations of Justinian, the emperor, and Theodora, both of whom had different theological beliefs. Finally Vigilius fell foul of the emperor. Justinian had him taken off to Constantinople and then thrown into exile for the last seven years of his life.

Pelagius I

Rome; 16 April 556 to 4 March 561

After a long and distinguished career in papal service Pelagius was sent by Pope Agapitus as papal legate to the imperial court at Constantinople. In 546 he was

Vicar of Rome while Vigilius was away in Constantinople. He courageously defended Rome against the Ostrogoths. When Vigilius gave in to the emperor over the Three Chapters controversy, Pelagius at first opposed the emperor; but he too eventually gave in. When Vigilius died, in 555, Justinian sent Pelagius back to Rome as his candidate for the papacy. He was not consecrated until 556 because of the opposition of many Western bishops. Pelagius did his best to correct the damage done to papal prestige by the previous reign and bring stability to Rome.

John III

Rome; 17 July 561 to 13 July 574

John's reign is a little obscure as it was dominated by the invasion of Italy by the Lombards. John fled to Naples to plead with Narses, a retired Byzantine general, to organise the defence of Rome. Narses was unpopular there and John was forced to retire from the city and conduct Church affairs from a church on the Via Appia outside Rome.

Benedict I

Rome; 2 June 575 to 30 July 579

An obscure figure, Benedict reigned at a time of extreme crisis in Italy. There were severe economic, social and political problems exacerbated by widespread famine. He died during the siege of Rome by the Lombards.

Pelagius II

Rome; 26 November 579 to 7 February 590

Pelagius was elected at a most desperate time; the Lombards were at the gate of Rome. After his consecration, unapproved by the emperor because of the crisis, he negotiated a truce with the Lombards, then appealed to the emperor, who was politically too weak to help. He successfully promoted the conversion of the Visigoths in Spain, insisted upon clerical celibacy and opposed the adoption by the Patriarch of Constantinople of the title 'Ecumenical Patriarch', which Pelagius interpreted as a challenge to his own authority. He died of the plague which swept Italy following vast devastating flooding.

Gregory I the Great, St

Rome; 3 September 590 to 12 May 604

Of a Roman noble family (born c.540), after a secular career in urban administration, Gregory sold his vast estates and became a monk (c.574), using his family fortune to found a monastery. Later, while abbot, he saw British slaves in Rome and passed his much quoted remark, 'Non Angli, sed angeli' ('Not Angles but angels'). In about 579 he was sent to Constantinople, as Pope Pelagius II's representative at the court of the Eastern emperor. On his return, c.585, he became the pope's advisor and was horrified at his unanimous election in 590, the first monk to occupy the papal throne.

As pope he centralised administration, reformed the Church and established its political independence in turbulent times. He sent Augustine, with forty monks from his monastery, to convert England, and began to call himself, 'the Servant of the servants of God', still a recognised papal title. His enthusiasm for the reform of the liturgy resulted in his name being given to Church music, called Plainsong or Gregorian chant. As an author his practical pastoral guide for bishops Liber Regulae Pastoralis (c.591) became the manual for the mediæval episcopate. His sermons and letters have proved of lasting importance and value. Gregory's immense influence on the papacy and the Church was acknowledged in the eighth century when he was given the title 'Doctor of the Church'.

Sabinian

Volterra in Tuscany; 13 September 604 to
22 February 606

Entrusted by Gregory the Great to represent him in 593 at the court of the Byzantine emperor, Sabinian disappointed Gregory by not resisting the claims of the Patriarch of Constantinople, which were supported by the emperor, Maurice. Brought back to Rome (595) he regained Gregory's favour and was chosen to succeed him as pope. There was a five-month delay before the emperor's approval to the election (required at that time) was granted. The following brief pontificate was remembered for – stopping Gregory's practice of advancing monks in papal service, and for selling grain to the poor at a time of great famine, when Gregory had been accustomed to giving it away. (The latter may have been invented by Gregory's biographers, who wanted to enhance Gregory's memory.) Sabinian was so unpopular that at his death, the populace of Rome blockaded the streets to prevent the passage of his funeral procession.

Boniface III

Rome; 19 February 607 to 12 November 607

A Greek by descent, Boniface served Gregory the Great, being sent by him as a legate to the court of the Emperor Phocas (603). His excellent relationship with Phocas did not speed up the approval of his election by the emperor (it took a year) but it did result in the recognition by Phocas that the Roman See was head of all the churches.

Boniface IV, St

L'Aquila, Italy; 25 August 608 to 8 May 615

Famine, plagues and earthquakes were striking Italy at the time of Boniface's election. He had been a great admirer of Gregory the Great and he was totally committed to monasticism, turning his residence into a monastery. It was during his reign that the Pantheon was converted into a church and dedicated to Santa Maria ad Martyres. Boniface died in monastic retirement.

Deusdedit, St (Adeodatus)

Rome; 19 October 615 to 8 November 618

Also known as Adeodatus I. Believed to be a Roman by birth, Deusdedit was quite elderly when he was elected pope. He is an obscure figure whose pontificate was marked by continuing natural disasters, which plagued Italy at that time, and the military campaigns of a Byzantine force against the Lombards, who were threatening Rome. During his reign the practice of sealing papal documents with leaden seals, known as bullae, was introduced.

Boniface V

Naples; 23 December 619 to 25 October 625

Boniface had to wait over a year for his election to be confirmed by the Byzantine emperor, (the city of Rome was under threat at the time by a rebel force led by a certain Eleutherius). Little is known of Boniface, but he is reputed to have had a special affection for the English Church.

Honorius I

Campania; 27 October 625 to 12 October 638

Modelling himself on Pope St Gregory the Great, Honorius gave great support to the Christianisation of the Anglo-Saxons, inducing the Celts to accept the Roman liturgy and the date of Easter according to Roman practice. The crux of his pontificate was his role in the Byzantine Church's controversy over Monothelitism; in about 634, replying to a letter from Sergius, Patriarch of Constantinople, Honorius appears to give some support to the theory of 'one will' in

Christ. He was posthumously condemned for his reply, but modern scholars debate his real understanding of the matter.

Severinus

Rome; 28 May 640 to 2 August 640

Of aristocratic background, Severinus was elderly when elected in May 638. The emperor refused to confirm his election unless Severinus agreed to the teaching of Monothelitism that in Christ there was only one will. Severinus held firm to the orthodox teaching and had to wait two years, during which he was humiliated by the emperor's troops in Rome. They also ransacked and stole from the papal treasury. Severinus' health suffered as a result, and only months after his consecration (having apparently never accepted the emperor's terms), he died.

John IV

Dalmatia; 24 December 640 to 12 October 642

An archdeacon serving in Rome, when elected, John had to wait from August 640 to the December of that year for the approval of the Byzantine emperor. He vigorously combated Monothelitism (the teaching that proposed that Christ had only a divine will, rather than a human and divine one; as was the Orthodox teaching) and called a synod in Rome in 641 to condemn it. He also wrote to the Irish Church warning against the dangers of the British heresy of Pelagianism.

Theodore I

Greece; 24 November 642 to 14 May 649

The son of a bishop, also named Theodore, Theodore I was of a Greek family that had lived in Jerusalem. He devoted much of his energy to fighting Monothelitism; he had more success in the Western Church than in the East. He appears to have quarrelled with the

Patriarch of Constantinople and incurred the wrath of the Emperor Constans II (641–668), who decreed that there was to be no further debate on the teaching.

Martin I, St (martyr)

Todi, in Umbria; July 649 to 16 September 653
(in exile from 17 June 653)

A very independent and strong pontiff, Martin refused to seek the Emperor Constans' approval of his election, and not only re-opened the fight against Monothelitism, but also summoned the Lateran Council in 649, to condemn it. Furious that his authority had been flouted Constans ordered the arrest of Martin. The bedridden pope was dragged from his bed and transported to Constantinople, where he was condemned as a traitor, publicly flogged and sentenced to death. The emperor commuted the sentence to banishment in the Crimea, where Martin was humiliated with inhumane treatment and suffered terribly from the cold. His diocese of Rome ignored him, sent no aid and elected a successor when he was dispatched into exile.

Eugene I, St

Rome; 10 August 654 to 2 June 657

A Roman by birth, Eugene served all his life in Rome and was elected after Pope Martin I had been flogged and exiled. Martin, from his deathbed, wrote to acknowledge Eugene as his successor. Eugene continued Martin's policies, refusing to bow to Monothelitism and angering the emperor by refusing to recognise the Patriarch of Constantinople because of his heretical sympathies. The emperor threatened the same penalties as Martin endured, but Eugene died before any action against him could be taken.

Vitalian, St

Segni, Campania, Italy; 30 July 657 to 27 January 672

The focus of Vitalian's reign was upon damage limitation, after years of hostility, and working for a reconciliation with the Byzantine emperor. He was so successful that Constans II visited Rome where he was received with honour. Vitalian also strove to solve the problems thrown up by the heresy Monothelitism.

Adeodatus II

Rome; 11 April 672 to 17 June 676

Also known as Deusdedit II. A Roman by birth, Adeodatus joined the Benedictine Order, entering at a tender age. It is believed that he was elderly when elected pope. Little is known about his pontificate, except that he had many Roman churches restored that had fallen into disrepair.

Donus

Rome; 2 November 676 to 11 April 678

Donus was elderly when elected. His reign was unnoteworthy apart from the record that he was involved in compelling the Archbishop of Ravenna to give up his claim to be independent of Rome; he also restored some Roman churches.

Agatho, St

Sicily; 27 June 678 to 10 January 681

Believed to be very elderly when elected, Agatho was a well-educated Benedictine monk. He sent papal legates to the Sixth General Council (sometimes called the Trullan Council) at Constantinople, where Monothelitism was finally condemned. In preparation for this, Agatho held a Western synod to work out a doctrinal formula that was found to be acceptable to both the Western and Eastern Churches. He died before he was able to ratify the decrees of the Council.

Leo II, St

Sicily; 17 August 682 to July 683

Leo was elected while the Sixth General Council at Constantinople was sitting, and he was forced to wait six months to be consecrated. The emperor, Constantine IV, would not give his approval until Leo gave public censure to the unorthodox statements of his predecessor, Honorius I, on the will of Christ. Leo ratified the acts of the Council and advanced Church music, which was a personal interest.

Benedict II, St

Rome; 26 June 684 to 8 May 685

Benedict's election was not confirmed by the emperor for nearly a year. As a result Benedict worked for a change; this allowed the approval to come from the Byzantine emperor's representative at Ravenna. Future popes could thus avoid serious delays between their election and their consecration. Benedict restored several Roman churches and is reputed to have been humble and kind.

John V

Syria; 23 July 685 to 2 August 686.

As one of Pope Agatho's representatives at the Third Council of Constantinople (680–681) John was well known and respected. Bad health made his pontificate ineffectual but he is remembered for his love of the poor; little else is known of him.

Conon

Birthplace unknown; 21 October 686 to 21 September 687

Believed to be the son of a Thracian soldier, Conon was educated in Sicily. He appears to have been elected in old age, as a compromise candidate between two rival factions in Rome. Conon offered no leadership and his passing resulted in two anti-popes (Theodore and Paschal) competing with one another.

Sergius I, St

Palermo; 15 December 687 to 8 September 701

Sergius came from a Syrian family and served under two popes. There was electoral turmoil on the death of Pope Conon and Sergius, correctly elected, had to compete with two anti-popes (Paschal and Theodore). Considered one of the most influential of seventh-century popes, Sergius resisted moves to make Constantinople an equal See to that of Rome. He resisted the attempt of the Byzantine emperor, Justinian II, to exert control over the Church and also refused to endorse the decrees of an Eastern Council (692). He showed an interest in English affairs, baptising Caedwalla, King of Wessex (689); he also consecrated Willibrord Bishop of the Frisians and ordered St Wilfred to be restored to his See of York (c.700). Sergius is further credited with the introduction of the *Agnus Dei* ('Lamb of God') into the Latin Mass.

700–1050
A Christian Europe
under siege from Viking
and Islamic invaders

Timeline 700–1050

711   Muslim armies begin the invasion of Spain and Portugal.

716   The English monk Boniface begins missionary work in the Germanic lands.

732   The French king, Charles, defeats the invading Muslim armies at the battle of Poitiers.

781   Evidence found of Christian missionary work in China.

800   The French king, Charlemagne, is crowned Holy Roman Emperor by Pope Leo III.

830   Missionaries begin to spread Christianity throughout Scandinavia.

863   A major schism develops between the Pope in Rome and the Patriarch of Constantinople. Missionary work begins in Slavic countries.

871   King Alfred the Great encourages English Christianity.

909   A monastery is founded at Cluny, France. The Cluniac order soon spreads throughout Europe.

988   Vladimir, Prince of Kiev, is baptised into the Eastern (Orthodox) Church. Russia is converted *en masse* to Orthodox Christianity.

1000   Muslims persecute the Egyptian Coptic Church.

1009   Trouble in the Holy Land: the Muslims destroy the Church of the Holy Sepulchre.

1031   Muslim rule in Spain suffers a major defeat – the Catholic kingdom of Aragon is founded.

The evangelisation of Europe

This was the true Middle Ages in Europe. The remains of Roman civilisation had truly collapsed under repeated invasions from barbarian Germanic tribes, and the Saracens had taken North Africa, the Holy Land and much of the eastern Mediterranean, and by 716 had occupied Spain and were threatening to sweep through France.

The culture, economy and education that the Roman Empire had brought to Europe collapsed – few people were educated, few could read or write Latin. The violent, unpredictable nature of European society meant that trade routes (both waterways and the famed Roman roads) became dangerous and fell into disuse, and as a result the economy collapsed. Money all but went out of use, the middle classes disappeared and towns were abandoned. Europe became a manorial society where the population divided into landowners who owned manors or fiefs, the clergy and the peasants. Landowners ran large estates, owning the land, property and the lives of the people living on it. The peasants lived as subsistence farmers, working their own plots of land as tenants of their lord, acting as his unpaid labour force for the lord's farms, and paying taxes in kind for services such as having corn ground. The lord owned all the game, so meat was scarce, and there was little in the way of clean water or hygiene. As a result, people were poor, malnourished and frequently in ill health. Few people lived into their forties, and life was indeed short, nasty and brutish. The clergy served the Church and mirrored the rest of society, with many attached to large, rich churches or monasteries, but with some local priests living a life every bit as impoverished as the peasants around them.

Despite the chaos of the Middle Ages, order began to emerge with strong royal families rising first in France, then in Germany. In both cases these kings formed strategic allegiances with the papacy, and the kings of these dynasties saw themselves as priest kings, with their earthly rule mirroring God's rule in heaven. Forming such alliances both strengthened and compromised the papacy. An alliance with a powerful king gave the pope an ally in a time of crisis, and with a king accepting Christianity, the pope of the day had a certain amount of power over the king's actions – even a king feared excommunication from the Church.

In the tenth and eleventh centuries the papacy went through a period of genuine crisis with decadent, politically active popes compromising the standing of the papacy, leading to their exile in Avignon and the emergence of competing popes and anti-popes.

But despite the Vatican's problems, the Church in this period continued its conquest of western Europe. Britain now exported its vigorous hybrid of Celtic and Roman Christianity back to mainland Europe and its monks were instrumental in Christianising the once barbarian Germanic tribes. The eighth century started badly for European Christianity as Arabs, upholding the new and vigorous religion of Islam, had conquered Spain and Portugal by 716, and advanced north into France, where their armies under Abdur Rahman were beaten by Charles Martel, the Frankish king. The Franks went on to conquer and unite much of western Europe. Since the Frankish kings became papal allies, where the French armies conquered, Christian missionaries followed in their wake. In this period, Christianity did another of its remarkable survival and conquest acts – the Vikings invaded, raided and settled western Europe almost at will, but by the end of this period they, too, had come under the influence of the Christian missionaries, and abandoned their traditional gods. By the end of the tenth century, the Kings of Norway, Sweden and Denmark were followers of the Roman Church. Some historians consider 700–1100 to be the age of the Vikings, but it is also undoubtedly the age when Christianity conquered western Europe.

The history of the period shows that western Europe owes a great debt to Christianity, since the Church allowed culture and education to survive this brutal, turbulent time. As civil society declined, the Church became the main force for education, leadership and civilisation in western Europe. Church leaders began to administer civil power and justice, and the cathedrals and monasteries were the main European centres of education, preserving the use of spoken and written Latin, and copying and preserving ancient Greek and Latin manuscripts. The Church set up schools and used its buildings as hospitals and accommodation for travellers – it provided some relief in what must have been a difficult time to be alive in Europe.

The Papal States

For almost 1,100 years the pope was not merely head of the growing Catholic Church – he was a wealthy landowner whose estates covered large areas of central Italy.

The Papal States, as they became known, were handed to Pope Stephen III by the Frankish ruler, Pepin the Short, in 754 and augmented by the Treaty of Pavia in 756. This came about as a result of some astute power politics by Pope Stephen. Much of northern Italy was under the control of the kings of Lombardy, with whom the Pope disagreed. He did not trust them, and indeed feared them, so he appealed to Pepin for military help. Pepin, anxious to please the Pope and form a powerful alliance obliged, invading and defeating the kings of Lombardy, then nominally handing the territory over to the Pope. However, while the territories were the Pope's in name, Pepin was the de facto ruler. The Papal States eventually covered the areas of Italy now known as the Marche, Umbria, Emilia–Romagna and the Lazio region surrounding Rome.

The popes' abilities to rule their States varied with the politics of the time. Their rule survived the growth in local feudal lords in the early Middle Ages, and such was the strength of the papacy that the Papal States also withstood dispute with the Holy Roman Emperors from Germany between the 1150s and 1300s. During this time the German emperors had seized much of northern Italy, and were pressing for more influence in Rome and the politics of the papacy, including the right to veto the election of a pope.

Despite the pope supposedly ruling the Papal States, he was not often able to do so, and between 1200 and 1400 powerful local families or commune governments were the real powers in the land. The papal grip on his States was weakened still further when the papacy transferred its home and power base from Rome to Avignon in France between 1309 and 1377.

With the emergence of the Renaissance, and the humanist threat that it represented to the Church, the Renaissance popes worked hard to establish the papacy as a secular political force in central Italy, but they failed to make their Renaissance statesmanship work: although papal in name, by the start of the seventeenth century the Papal States could be considered part of (at the time) fragmented, disorganised Italy. Later popes attempted to continue this policy of bringing the Papal States back under Vatican control, but they met with as little success as their Renaissance predecessors.

The next major upheaval came when Napoleon swept through Italy and confiscated the Papal States, first from Pope Pius VI in 1798 then from Pius VII in 1808. The latter lived to see the lands returned after Napoleon's defeat at Waterloo in 1815.

However, the Papal States had become an unruly place during the years of Napoleonic control – liberal and anti-clerical sentiment had grown, and in the short-lived reign of Pius VIII (1828–1830) the Papal States revolted against authoritarian religious rule. Pope Pius IX (1846–1878), one of the great popes of the modern times (who introduced the doctrine of the Virgin Mary's sinlessness and that of Papal infallibility) suffered the same indignity with a further revolution in 1849.

Italian nationalistic politics finally put an end to the pope's unhappy time as a large-scale landowner: the movement for Italian unification (the Risorgimento) was underway. The Papal States effectively cut the Italian peninsula in half, and only continued to exist because foreign governments insisted on the Vatican's right to keep control of the lands.

However, the papal territories of Umbria, Marche and Emilia voted to abandon their papal landlord and join the growing Risorgimento. Then, in 1870, the French troops who had been propping up what remained of the Papal States around Rome fled. The Italians occupied Rome in triumph, and declared it the capital city of a united Italy.

Pope Pius IX would not accept the loss of his lands, and for the fifty-nine years successive popes (Leo XIII (1878–1903), St Pius X (1903–14), Benedict XV (1914–22), Pius XI (1922–39) considered themselves prisoners in the Vatican. This (perhaps over-dramatised) state continued until Pius XI negotiated the Vatican's independence as an independent city state in the Lateran Treaty of 1929.

The split between the Roman and Byzantine Church

While Western Christianity was coping with rising Frankish and German kings and Viking invasions, the Christians of Byzantium had their own internal and external problems.

In the seventh century the Byzantine Empire had twice repelled Saracen attempts to conquer Constantinople, but having saved their capital city they had lost much of the Eastern Empire to the Muslims, so the Byzantine Empire now took in what we know as Turkey, Greece, parts of southern Italy and the Balkan coast (the former Yugoslavia). Christianity in Byzantium was starting to develop along different lines to Roman Christianity, particularly in its methods of worship, and the

St Bede

St Bede was one of the most valuable witnesses we had to the Middle Ages. He was born in 673, and became a monk at a time when monastic life in Britain was flourishing. Strengthened and invigorated with monks from Ireland, the monasteries in Scotland and the north of England became great centres of spirituality, missionary activity and learning.

Bede lived in the monasteries of Jarrow and Wearmouth on the north-east coast of England, and became a meticulous recorder of British Christianity, writing his History of the English Church and People, which was first published in 731. While clearly influenced by his Christianity, it is nonetheless a valuable historical document that provides much information about a time in history where a turbulent, impoverished, uneducated and often violent society meant that accurate written records of the time are rare and valuable.

Bede was a thoughtful, educated man, who translated the Bible into Anglo Saxon and issued widely read commentaries on the Scriptures. He also helped spread the use of the Anno Domini Calendar which had been started in 527 by Dionysius Exiguus.

He was one of the most powerful influences in the vigorous Northumbrian Anglo Saxon Church, and was a powerful influence on the monk Alcuin of York, who in turn went on to be a spiritual advisor to Charlemagne, the powerful and long-lived Frankish king and a powerful ally of the Pope. Bede was recognised for his holiness with the title 'The Venerable Bede' long before his canonisation to sainthood.

tension between the Roman and Byzantine Churches began to ease the two apart.

The Byzantine Church became strongly attached to the veneration of icons – images of saints or holy men which were reputed to have special powers, such as intercession with God, protection or healing. This reverence for icons was encouraged by the emperors of Byzantium, to the point that worshippers began to confuse the icons with the holiness of the people they represented. This was idolatry, the very sin for which God punished the Israelites in the desert, and in 726 the Byzantine emperor Leo condemned the worshipping of icons, a move that became known as 'iconoclasm' – a word derived from the Greek meaning the 'breaking of icons'. This met with hostility from the Christians in Byzantium, and there was widespread rioting, but despite this in 730 Leo demanded the destruction of all icons, both those displayed in public and those that formed an extensive part of the ornamentation in churches and were a part of Byzantine masses.

This split Byzantine society and infuriated the pope, who condemned the destruction of icons. Undaunted, the emperor of Byzantium convened a synod of his bishops who supported their emperor's line, saying that worshipping icons was committing the sin of idolatry, and affirming that all remaining icons should be destroyed.

It is in some respects incredible that whether or not an icon – simply a painting of God, or of a holy man or woman – could create such chaos, but it got worse. Supporters of icon worship were vigorously persecuted. Tens of thousands fled from Constantinople, and those supporters of icon worship who remained were arrested, excommunicated and sometimes mutilated before being sent into exile.

The argument over the right to worship icons raged into the ninth century, with Emperor Theophilus stating that to worship an icon meant death or exile. Official support for iconoclasm persisted until a synod of bishops once again announced a toleration of icons, and for political reasons (he was unpopular at the time, and needed the support of the clergy to stay in favour) the emperor agreed. A major rift in Orthodox Christianity was healed, and Orthodox Christians celebrate this day as the Feast of Orthodoxy on the first Sunday of Lent.

However, the dispute over the veneration of icons was to have longer-lasting and more profound consequences – it drove a wedge between the pope in Rome and the Church in Constantinople. Eastern and Western Christianity also differed in their interpretations of the Creed, and the nature of God, and these, added to the rancour caused by the icon controversy, led to the 1054 schism between Orthodox and Catholic Christianity.

Vikings – the scourge of the Middle Ages

One of the most significant influences on the development of Europe in the period 700-1050 was the presence of enemies on the borders of Middle Ages Europe. The Saracen invaders were routed from France in 732, but Europe seemed to have no defence against the Norsemen who seemed able to raid Britain and mainland Europe at will. These raiders became known as Vikings, derived from their own term for piracy, which to Norsemen was going a-viking.

The natives of Scandinavia were suffering from a population boom that put pressure on the availability of land and resources, and being a seafaring nation they began to look across the seas for lands to raid. They had a warlike disposition and were excellent shipbuilders and navigators.

During the years 700–1100 they terrorised Europe, using raiding parties or invasion fleets. The monastery at Lindisfarne was looted in 745, and Viking pirates swept through the British Isles and Ireland, settling the town that became Dublin. They were a particularly unpleasant, merciless brand of invader who believed in sparing neither women nor children; what they could not steal, they burnt. Viking raiders found the churches and monasteries of the period attractive targets, since they frequently contained gold altar fittings, books with ornate, jewel-encrusted covers and ornaments made from precious metals.

By the ninth century, the Vikings had turned their attention to France, Italy, Spain, Belgium and the Netherlands, all lands where the Roman Church was beginning to gain influence. The Viking raids were so feared that prayers would be said, asking God to 'protect us from the fury of the Norsemen'.

Judging by the Viking success in invading large portions of Europe these prayers went unanswered: the Vikings continued to plunder, kill and burn almost at will. Vikings left their mark on European society in the names of the days of the week – Wednesday, Thursday and Friday are all named after the main Viking gods: Odin, god of battle, Thor, god of the sky and Freya, goddess of the land and love.

The Vikings settled in large areas of England, and after besieging Paris in the early tenth century, settled in northern France (William the Conquerer, who invaded England in 1066, was the descendent of Viking settlers). In so doing, they came into contact with Christian missionaries, and before long Christianity had repeated another of its remarkable conquests, displacing the old Viking gods.

By this time, the Vikings had created a stable, prosperous society in Scandinavia and had secured the trade routes into what became Russia. Christianity once again conquered the conquerors, and extended its influence north into Scandinavia and east into Russia.

The papacy and The Holy Roman Empire

With the collapse of the Carolingian Empire, France was divided into states ruled by competing feudal lords. In what became Germany, local lords squabbled with the king until Otto I managed to subdue his rebellious nobility and consolidate his authority. He also paid attention to the Church in Germany, and when Pope John XII (955–963) realised that he needed political and military support against turbulent Roman politics, he turned to Otto I. This suited Otto, since like the Frankish kings he approved of the idea of his reign on earth reflecting God's reign in heaven – he saw himself as a priest king and an alliance with the pope strengthened Otto's rule. At the time, the northern Italians were causing the pope problems, and Otto invaded northern Italy, temporarily removing a potential crisis for the pope. The pope crowned Otto as emperor of a new Holy Roman Empire.

Otto repaid Pope John XII's trust by demanding that henceforth Otto or his successor should have a veto over who became Pope. Pope John disagreed, was tried by a synod, and ejected from the position of pope. A layman was appointed pope; in order for this to happen, he went through all his holy orders in a single day, ending with his consecration as Pope Leo VIII. This caused a problem for the Church, in that an outside power now claimed a say in who became the pope – given the influence of the Church throughout Europe, who became Pope was as much a political as a religious matter. Otto's insistence on his and his successor's right to have a say on papal succession laid the papacy open to more than one pope being nominated. Now there could be popes and anti-popes.

In crowning Otto I, Emperor of the Holy Roman Empire, the pope re-introduced the idea of a western European empire. The Empire, which was in effect a loose confederation of German and north Italian states, lasted until 1806.

The conversion of Russia

Around the mid ninth century, the Byzantine emperor Michael III received an irresistible request from Prince Rastislav of Moravia. Would the emperor send some missionaries to convert his Slavic population to Christianity?

The Slavs were descended from a race that had migrated from

Asia to eastern Europe, and can be considered the ancestors of the Czechslovakians. Some had settled in Macedonia, part of the Byzantine Empire. The Patriarch of Constantinople made an inspired choice in his evangelists – a pair of Greek brothers called Cyril and Methodius who had Slavic neighbours and had learned to speak the Slavic language.

Slavic was an unwritten language, so before setting off to evangelise the Slavs, Cyril and Methodius invented an alphabet so that the Slavic language could be written. As a result, they could translate the Bible, prayers and the liturgy for their mission to the Slavs. Their script was called Glagolithic, which evolved into the Cyrillic script, now used throughout Russia and parts of eastern Europe.

Cyril and Methodius (who became known as the Apostles to the Slavs) spent three successful years spreading Christianity through the Slavs of Moravia, but their efforts were partly in vain, since invading Magyars (who had also helped destroy the Christian Carolingian Empire of France) plundered Moravia.

This Byzantine-derived Orthodox Christianity spread to Bulgaria, and then to Romania. In 998, according to legend, Vladimir, the pagan prince of Kiev in Russia, decided to adapt one of the major world faiths for his people, and sent his emissaries to evaluate Islam, Judaism and Roman Christianity. Evidently, the reports he received failed to impress the prince.

However, Vladimir's envoy went to mass in the Hagia Sophia in Constantinople, then the largest church building in the world with its gold, splendour, singing and incense, and later reported that he couldn't tell whether he was on earth or in heaven. Vladimir was impressed, and ordered the mass baptism of the Russians according to the Orthodox rite.

Vladimir's son Yaroslav the Wise continued his father's policy, allowing the Byzantine Church in Constantinople to run the Russian Church, and in Kiev he built a cathedral and named it after St Sophia, the church in Constantinople that had so impressed his father and prompted the mass baptism of Russia.

When the Orthodox and Roman Churches split in 1054, the Russians took the Orthodox side, and were taught to despise Roman Catholics as heretics.

Reform of the clergy

The developing Church did not simply have problems with kings and invaders – the behaviour of the clergy occasionally left something to be desired, and Church synods of this period often condemned poor behaviour by priests and monks.

There was concern about priests having relationships with women, getting drunk, hunting and carrying weapons, and eventually a bishop in Metz issued a set of behavioural rules for his cathedral clergy. The need for unimpeachable behaviour spread, and the Benedictine monks of Cluny in France started a powerful reform movement that did much to counter the abuses of the Church, especially simony, the selling of indulgences, relics and even Church posts.

Selling indulgences came about as a result of the belief that after death the forgiven soul spent time in purgatory prior to entry into heaven. An indulgence, bought for money, was a way of lessening your soul's time in purgatory, and in the uneducated Middle Ages, where the Church exerted such influence on society, the population believed in the effectiveness of such spiritual cures – and paid.

The reforms had a limited effect, but the same problems continued to plague the Church and in 1518 it was the continuing sale of indulgences and pardons that prompted the monk Martin Luther to write the Ninety-five Theses, a document that ignited the Protestant Reformation.

The papacy and the Carolingian Empire

In the eighth century Western Europe was a fragmented, feudal society where landlords ruled manors and there was little notion of nationhood. The Carolingian kings founded an empire that ruled from the mid 700s to the mid 800s. In 732 King Charles Martel defeated the Saracen armies at Poitiers in France, and having seen the Muslim invaders off French soil, turned to the conquest of France, defeating the Frankish landowners and annexing their lands.

He was succeeded by his son Pepin the Short, who continued the expansion of the Frankish kingdom and founded the Papal States.

Then in 786 Charlemagne became the Frankish king, and he expanded the kingdom into northern Spain, Germany and the Baltic states.

It was the first time that Europe had been united since the collapse of the Roman Empire, and the papacy, by now experienced in coming to terms with kings and princes, went into a strategic alliance with the Frankish kings.

The Franks were to have a massive influence on the actions of the papacy, the ability of a missionary Church to convert Europe and on the shape of Europe for centuries to come: the Frankish kings regarded themselves as warrior kings with a priestly aspect, and were in many respects natural allies for the popes in Rome. The pope's nearest neighbours were the kings of the Lombardy region, and they disagreed over the possession of much territory in central and northern Italy. The Church of the time had ambitions as a sovereign power in its own right (see Papal States).

As a means of thwarting the kings of Lombardy, Pope Gregory III appealed to the Franks to help against the ambitious and often ruthless Lombard rulers. By way of persuasion he sent the keys to St Peter's tomb, no mean gesture from a Pope. Gregory III died, and it was his successor Zachary (741–752) who reaped the rewards: Pepin invaded northern Italy from his native France and crushed the Lombards, handing the lands he won over to papal rule.

The pope was in debt to the king of the Franks. When Pepin died, his son Charles (known as Charlemagne) became king, and again he came to the aid of a beleaguered pope to repel a further Lombard invasion in 773. He visited Rome, and the magnificence of the city confirmed his allegiance to the cause of Christianity. The Franks effectively became the secular arm of the papacy, and where the Franks conquered, Christian missionaries followed.

At the time, the papacy was in low odour: in 799 Leo III was accused of adultery, perjury and selling papal blessing and indulgences. He was dragged into the street and beaten. Saved, Pope Leo asserted his innocence and made an astute political move: he invited the Frankish King Charles to Rome and, on Christmas Day 800, crowned him Emperor of Rome as he rose to his feet during a Mass in St Peter's Basilica.

Charlemagne died in 814. By the time of his death he had created a Christian empire that covered most of France, Germany, the Netherlands and Belgium, Germany, the Czech Republic, northern Yugoslavia and Croatia, and some of northern Spain, and he was really

_ Papal States. It was an empire run by the allied powers
.sh nobility and the pope but it was surrounded by enemies.
.ıngian Empire came under repeated attack by Magyar tribes
what we now know as Hungary), Saracen invaders and the
.ıgs. By the start of the tenth century, the Carolingian Empire had
.lapsed, and the papacy had to look elsewhere for political and military
support.

St Boniface and the conversion of Germany

The Germanic tribes had been prime agents in the downfall of the
Roman Empire. They were also a significant part of the reason that
Middle Ages Europe was such an impoverished place – a society cannot
thrive during the uncertainly and turbulence of war.

During the early eighth century, missionaries from Ireland and
Britain moved into Europe. They first revived Christianity in Gaul
where with the support of the Carolingian rulers they spread Christianity throughout what is now France. From there, the barbarian
lands of Germany were open to the missionaries in the wake of the
territorial gains made by the Frankish armies.

An Anglo Saxon monk called Wynfrith (680–754) was
summoned to Rome and consecrated as 'Bishop of the German Church'.
The German Church hardly existed at that time – a few Celtic
missionaries had made it into Germany in the 600s, but their work
had not really taken hold. Celtic Christianity was excellent at missionary
work, but it did not have the ability to build on its successes.

Wynfrith, who took the name Boniface with his consecration,
took the Roman Church's sense of organisation and authority into
Germany with him, and brought the recently barbarian German states
into the growing European Christian commonwealth. He founded the
large, influential monastery at Fulda, and ended his days as Archbishop
of Mainz. He died a martyr's death, shielding himself with a Bible as
he was attacked and killed.

THE POPES
701–1054

John VI

Greece; 30 October 701 to 11 January 705

John, of whom little is known before his election, pursued the policies of Sergius, but took care not to antagonise Constantinople, although Byzantine influence on the Italian peninsula was on the wane. In the political turmoil of the period John gave protection to victims of the conflicts and paid bribes to release hostages taken in battle.

John VII

Greece; 1 March 705 to 18 October 707

Son of Plato, a Byzantine official of the Imperial court, John turned to advantage the good relations he had with the Lombards, receiving back papal property stolen by them. He had the Benedictine monastery of Subiaco restored. The emperor, Justinian II, back in power, demanded papal approval of the acts of the Eastern Council of 692. John vacillated (for which he has been accused of cowardice), returning the documents to Constantinople without comment.

Sisinnius

Syria; 15 January 708 to 4 February 708

Imperial approval was delayed and Sisinnius, elderly and ill when elected (October 707), was not consecrated until January 708. He died suddenly a few weeks later, not well enough to have achieved anything.

Constantine

Syria; 25 March 708 to 9 April 715

From a Syrian family, Constantine inherited the problem of the endorsement of the acts of the Council of 692 (see Sergius II and John VII). The Byzantine emperor, Justinian II, invited Constantine to Constantinople to resolve the impasse; Constantine was warmly welcomed – Justinian kissed the foot of the pope – and negotiations were successful. The murder of the emperor (711) nearly unravelled the agreement but his Monothelite successor was also murdered and Anastasius II, the new emperor, continued Justinian's policies.

Gregory II, St

Rome; 19 May 715 to 11 February 731

Gregory came from a Roman family. He became the papal librarian and proved to be a good diplomat when sent by Pope Constantine to negotiate with Emperor Justinian II. Highly respected, he proved to be one of the best pontiffs of the eighth century. Gregory clashed with Emperor Leo III when, at the beginning of the Iconoclast Controversy, (the struggle over the veneration of icons) Leo demanded the destruction of all icons. He also led resistance in Italy to the heavy taxation demands of the emperor. He courageously and diplomatically avoided conflict with the Lombards, persuading Liutprand, king of the Lombards to lift the siege of Rome. Gregory was energetic in recruiting and sending missionaries into northern Europe; he consecrated St Boniface (d.754).

Gregory III, St

Syria; 18 March 731 to November 741

A Roman crowd surrounded Gregory at the funeral of Pope Gregory II and chose him as their bishop; he was elected immediately by acclamation. He proved to be the last pope who would seek approval for his election from the emperor. Gregory resolutely resisted the edict of Emperor Leo III that all icons and images were to be destroyed (see Gregory II); the emperor responded by occupying papal lands. Diplomatically Gregory did not assist the Lombards in their war with Leo III and regained the emperor's favour, without giving in on iconoclasm. The Lombards remained a threat to Rome and Gregory appealed to the Franks for assistance; this was not forthcoming but it did open avenues for future co-operation.

Zachary, St

Greece; 10 December 741 to 22 March 752

Also known as Zacharias. Of a Greek family, born in Calabria, Zachary proved to be the last Greek pope. A gifted diplomat, he made peace with the Lombards, who had been long-standing enemies, and convinced them not to invade the territory of Ravenna (which belonged to the Byzantine emperor). This action brought the gratitude and respect of the emperor, Constantine V. Zachary supported the claim of Pepin III to the Frankish throne, which brought the warm gratitude of the Franks.

Stephen (II)

Rome; 23 March 752 to 26 March 752

A Roman priest, Stephen had a stroke and died three days after his election. As he was never consecrated, the canon law of the time dictated that he should not be considered 'Bishop of Rome'; so he was not listed. When the rules changed in the sixteenth century he was recognised as Stephen II and listed. However in 1961 his name was dropped from the official list as recorded in *Annuario Pontificio*. Hence his successors of the same name were given a dual numbering system.

Stephen III (or II according to official lists)

Rome; 26 March 752 to 26 April 757

Unanimously elected after the sudden death of Stephen II. Stephen turned to the Franks for protection from the Lombards. He crossed the Alps (754) to plead for King Pepin's support. The Frankish armies captured large tracts of land, including Ravenna, and gave these lands to the papacy (known in history as the Donation of Pepin). Hence the Papal States.

Paul I, St

Rome; 29 May 757 to 28 June 767

Paul was the younger brother of Stephen who had died so soon after his election. A papal administrator before his election, Paul used his talents to great benefit, installing the foundations of the management of the Papal States that would last for centuries. He was skilful also in managing the precarious relations between the Franks, the Lombards and the Byzantine emperor. Paul continued his predecessors' opposition to the icono-clastic policy prevailing in the East. His death resulted in a contest for the papal throne, which produced two anti-popes, Constantine and Philip.

Stephen III (IV)

Sicily; 7 August 768 to 24 January 772

Stephen emerged victorious from the anarchy which was caused by two anti-popes, Constantine and Philip. His triumph was due to the bloodthirsty methods of a certain papal notary, Christopher. The Lombard king, Desiderius, cunningly contrived to get Stephen to abandon the support of the Franks and Charlemagne, and accept the Lombards as allies. The pro-Franks in Rome, including Christopher, were murdered by the Lombards. Stephen realised too late what he had done; he died before the resulting war between the Franks and the Lombards broke upon Italy.

Hadrian I

Rome; 1 February 772 to 25 December 795

Renowned as a preacher, from an aristocratic background, Hadrian was elected after serving under Popes Paul I and Stephen. Confronted by the troubles caused by the Lombards in Italy, he invited the young Frankish king, Charlemagne to invade Italy. This was the beginning of a working relationship and rapport with the emperor. Their relationship symbolised the mediæval ideal of State and Church working together. Hadrian was responsible for much building work in Rome, including several churches and the city walls.

Leo III, St

Rome; 26 December (27) 795 to 12 June 816

Long in the service of the preceding popes, Leo was elected with an unanimous vote. An able administrator he soon upset the Roman aristocracy who hired thugs to attack him and even attempted to gouge out his eyes and cut out his tongue. He was brutalised and shut up in a monastery but escaped and took refuge with the Frankish king, Charlemagne. With the support of Charlemagne and his troops, Leo was returned to Rome; and all charges against him – perjury and adultery – were investigated and dismissed. On Christmas Day 800, Leo surprised Charlemagne by crowning him Emperor in the West. By this action Leo broke the ancient bond with the Byzantine emperors and introduced the custom of the pope crowning the Holy Roman Emperors.

Stephen IV (V)

Rome; 22 June 816 to 24 January 817

Stephen's short reign was marked only by his crowning, at Reims, of the Emperor Louis the Pious, (October 816). He thus cemented the emperor–pope relationship which was to prove to be mutually beneficial.

Paschal I, St

Rome; 25 January 817 to 11 February 824

Abbot of St Stephen's monastery, Rome, at the time of his election, Paschal's consecration was hastily arranged because of suspected opposition from the emperor, Louis. However at the notification of Paschal's consecration Louis welcomed it and granted certain privileges to the pope. Paschal crowned Louis' son, Lothair, as co-emperor in 823. Friction and violence followed from Lothair and the Franks became intensely disliked in Rome. Paschal distanced himself from Roman sentiment but this aroused the hatred of the Romans and, at his death, they prevented the pope's body being buried in St Peter's.

Eugene II

Rome; February 824 to August 827

Eugene, an archpriest of Rome, was the favoured candidate of the Roman nobility, who wanted a different style of pontificate from that of Paschal. Eugene welcomed co-emperor Lothair to Rome and accepted that popes should, in future, take an oath of loyalty to the emperor. However, he demonstrated his spiritual authority by calling a Synod in 826 to introduce several reforming measures. He also would not bow to the pressure of the emperor to accept iconoclasm, which had resurfaced in the West. Eugene persisted in proclaiming that the veneration of images was permissible.

Valentine

Rome; August 827 to September 827

The Liber Pontificalis states that Valentine was unanimously elected and had been in papal service. He only survived for little over a month and nothing else is known of his pontificate.

Gregory IV

Rome; 827 to January 844

Gregory was serving as a cardinal priest at the Basilica of St Mark when he was reluctantly chosen to succeed Valentine. Gregory gave support to co-emperor Lothair in his disputes with his father, Louis, and his brothers, Pepin and Louis the German. He travelled with Lothair to meet the German bishops; they confronted Gregory and charged him with disloyalty, reminding him of his oath of loyalty to Emperor Louis. Gregory protested that he was only working for peace in the Empire. Too late Gregory discovered that he had been used by Lothair, who briefly managed to depose his father. After his restoration (834) Louis continued his friendship with Gregory, but at Louis' death (840) the Empire was torn by a civil war and Gregory's best efforts to restore peace achieved nothing. Gregory introduced the Feast of All Saints.

Sergius II

Rome; January 844 to 27 January 847

Elderly when elected, Sergius was the choice of the Roman nobility; the other classes chose an anti-pope, John, but he was quickly seen off by the aristocracy's troops. The Emperor Lothair I was furious that he had not been asked for his approval and threatened to send an army to invade Rome. Sergius pacified Lothair, adroitly reaffirming imperial rights without swearing fealty to the emperor. Sergius' brother, Benedict, hindered the pope's work and simony was rampant. When a Saracen force marched on Rome from Ostia and sacked the city, despoiling the tombs of St Peter and St Paul, the populace declared that it was a sign of God's displeasure with Sergius.

Leo IV, St

Rome; 10 April 847 to 17 July 855

A Benedictine monk who became a cardinal priest working in papal service, Leo did not seek imperial approval for his election, excusing himself on the grounds of the constant threat of further attacks from the Saracens (see Sergius II). This was the major concern of his pontificate. Leo had massive fortifications and walls built around Rome and the Vatican; he also organised a military alliance that launched a powerful fleet against the Saracens, beating them off Ostia in 849.

Benedict III

Rome; 29 September (July) 855 to 17 April 858

Benedict had been a cardinal priest and was the second choice of the electors (the first choice, the later Hadrian II, declining the position); the imperial party in Rome pushed forward their own candidate, Anastasius Bibliothecarus, and the anti-pope had Benedict imprisoned. The people of Rome rose up and in the face of violence the imperial candidate and his supporters withdrew. Benedict's chief preoccupation was with the restoration of the churches destroyed in the sacking of Rome (see Sergius II).

Nicholas I, St (the Great)

Rome; 24 April 858 to 13 November 867

After many years in papal service, Nicholas was elected and proved to be one of the most forceful personalities and a strong advocate of papal rights and authority. He was justly famed for his courage and forthrightness in dealing with kings and emperors. His support for the illegally deposed Ignatius, Patriarch of Constantinople, led eventually to the Photian Schism; he upheld the dignity of marriage against King Lothiar of Lorraine and King Charles the Bold of Burgundy. He sent missionaries to Scandinavia and Bulgaria. Nicholas was held in high regard for his personal integrity, care of the poor and the pursuit of reform among the clergy.

Hadrian II

Rome; 14 December 867 to December 872

His Roman noble family had already produced two popes – Stephen IV and Sergius II – and Hadrian had been married before his ordination. Rising in the papal service to cardinal priest under Gregory IV, Hadrian had twice before been elected, but declined the post each time. Wanting to bring peace to a violent Rome, the aged Hadrian accepted on the third occasion. He did not succeed and proved to be weak and vacillating; gradually giving away all the gains and successes achieved by Nicholas I. He watched while Bulgaria slipped from Roman to Greek control; and Rome was sacked, once more, by the Duke Lambert of Spoletto.

John VIII

Rome; 14 December 872 to 16 December 882

A relatively young man when elected (he was fifty-two), John had served with distinction under the two previous popes. He was energetic in confronting the violent crises of the time, the biggest menace being the Saracens, who raided the Papal States from their bases in southern Italy. He organised a papal fleet and built a defensive wall around St Paul's Basilica; his efforts to get a military alliance organised to combat the Saracen threat failed. In the same hope John crowned Charles the Bald, Emperor (875) but the emperor died and his rival imprisoned him. John escaped and sought help from Constantinople; for this he was required to recognise Photius as patriarch. He gave support to the missionary work of St Methodius and approved the use of the Slavonic language in the liturgy. The pontificate ended in tragedy when John was murdered poisoned and clubbed to death by members of his own entourage. He was the first pope to be assassinated.

Marinus I

Tuscany; 16 December 882 to 15 May 884

In the service of the popes from an early age, Marinus was an experienced diplomat. Feuding and vendettas in Rome followed the murder of his predecessor. He appears to have used his diplomatic skills well after his election. Little is known of his short pontificate.

Hadrian III, St

Rome; 17 May 884 to September 885

Little is known of this pontiff or his reign. He appears to have become involved in the bitter feuding, rampant in Rome at the time. While on his way to meet with Emperor Charles III at Worms, he died suddenly and in suspicious circumstances.

Stephen V (VI)

Rome; September 885 to 14 September 891

Renowned for his sanctity, Stephen was unanimously elected, but immediately had political problems. The Carolingian Empire, founded by Charlemagne, was breaking up and could not give Stephen the assistance he needed with a severe famine and the Saracen raids on papal territories. The western princes Stephen appealed to were unreliable and he turned to the ambitious Guy III of Spoleto. Stephen forbade the use of the Slavic liturgy in Moravia, which resulted in the loss of the region to the Latin Church.

Formosus

Portus; 6 October 891 to 4 April 896

After his appointment as Bishop of Porto (864) Formosus entered papal service and proved to be a very able missionary and diplomat. He was a key player in attempts to repair relationships with Constantinople after the Photius shambles. His considerable abilities

attracted envy and enemies and he was deposed as bishop and excommunicated under Pope John VIII. In 878 Formosus was pardoned and continued in personal service of Marinus and Stephen V. Although elderly at his election Formosus was still a formidable pontiff. He promoted friendly relations with the Eastern Church, trying to heal the schism which had developed; his attempts to deal with the evil effects of the political ambitions of Guy (Guido) of Spoleto and his son Lambert, led him to seek an alliance with Arnulf, king of the East Franks. Formosus crowned Arnulf as the Holy Roman Emperor; thus he won the eternal enmity of the Spoleto family. The alliance failed and Formosus died hated virulently by his enemies. His death was not the end of his history. (See Stephen VII.)

Boniface VI

Rome; April 896 to April 896

At this low point in Papal history, Boniface, who had an unsavoury past, was elected. He only lasted for fifteen days; his sudden death, in the climate of the time, has suggested to commentators that he may well have been murdered.

Stephen VI (VII)

Rome; May 896 to August 897

Candidate of the powerful Spoleto family (see Formosus) Stephen's election was followed by a brutal period of retribution against those who had supported Pope Formosus. The bloodbath only ended when Stephen, at the insistence of the Spoleto family, summoned the infamous Cadaver Synod (897) to try the decomposing corpse of Pope Formosus, which was exhumed, dressed in pontifical vestments and tied to a chair for the trial. After mutilation the corpse was thrown into the Tiber. The Roman populace were so disgusted by the behaviour of Stephen that they rose up in revolt and demanded that he be deposed. The Spoletans imprisoned Stephen and had him strangled.

Romanus

Gallese, Italy; August 897 to November 897

Little is known of this pontiff. He was probably a candidate proposed by the all-powerful Spoleto Family (see Formosus and Stephen VI). One source of the time suggests that he was deposed by the Formosan Party and that he later became a monk, but no reliable information is available.

Theodore II

Rome; December 897 to December 897

Theodore's reign was even shorter than that of Romanus, lasting only twenty days. It is said that he had the corpse of Formosus (see Stephen V) which had been fished out of the Tiber, buried with dignity. The acts of the infamous Cadaver Synod were annulled. How and when he died is not known.

John IX

Tivoli, Italy; January 898 to January 900

A former Benedictine monk, John owed his election to the influence of Lambert of Spoleto who was keen to undo the harm done by his family in the three previous pontificates. John was determined to rehabilitate the work and memory of Pope Formosus (see Stephen VI or VII) and to this end he summoned synods at Rome and Ravenna. At these Pope Stephen was condemned for holding the Cadaver Synod (897) and all the acts of that Synod were destroyed.

Benedict IV

Rome; January 900 to July 903

King Lambert's sudden death threw Rome into turmoil; those for and against Formosus fought one another, while the new pope, Benedict, who was pro-Formosus, tried for peace. There were further troubles over the successor to Lambert and Benedict appears to have backed the wrong candidate. He excommunicated Baldwin II, Count of Flanders, for the murder of the Archbishop of Reims. Little else is known of Benedict's reign.

Leo V

Ardea; July 903 to September 903

Due no doubt to the confusion and turmoil of Rome at the time, the electors chose not a member of an aristocratic family but a humble parish priest with a reputation for holiness. Leo had to face an anti-pope, Christopher, who had him deposed and thrown into prison. Shortly afterwards Christopher joined him, having been removed by Sergius III. It is believed that both Leo and Christopher were strangled in prison early in 904, on the orders of Sergius.

Sergius III

Rome; 29 January 904 to 14 April 911

Sergius had been elected pope before, in December 897, but had to give way to John IX who had imperial support. If Sergius was guilty of the deaths of Leo V and the anti-pope Christopher (see Leo V), as it is believed, it was the opening act of a depressing pontificate that marks a dark and dangerous era for the papacy. Sergius declared that his reign had begun in 897 and that all the acts (including ordinations and consecrations) of the previous three popes were illegitimate and null and void. When opposed in any action he appealed to his sponsors, the powerful Theophylact family, by whose daughter, Marozia, his enemies claimed, he had a son, the future John XI. Although his life was immoral, in matters of doctrine he was entirely orthodox.

Anastasius III

Rome; April 911 to June 913

Little is known of this Bishop of Rome; as the Theophylact family were dominating Rome and the papacy at this time, it is safe to assume that Anastasius was their appointee.

Lando

Sabina, Lombardy; July 913 to February 914

Other than that Lando came from a wealthy Lombardy family, nothing else is known about him or his pontificate, which is believed to have lasted only just over six months.

John X

Romagna; March 914 to May 928

While serving as Archbishop of Ravenna, John, sponsored by the Theophylact family, was elected. His main objective was to defeat the Saracens who were constantly raiding the southern half of Italy. Friends with the ruling powers, John organised an alliance, including the Byzantines, with whom he was trying to improve relations; this was victorious over the Saracens in 915. He rebuilt the Lateran Palace. However, relations with the Roman nobility, especially the Theophylacts, deteriorated and they had John imprisoned in the Castel Sant'Angelo, deposed and murdered.

Leo VI

Rome; May 928 to December 928

While the deposed John languished in prison, Leo, an elderly cardinal priest of Santa Susanna, was elected courtesy of the Theophylact family, who controlled Rome at this time. Leo died after a few months; it is believed that he too was murdered.

Stephen VII (VIII)

Rome; December 928 to February 931

Stephen, a cardinal priest, owed his elevation to the
See of Rome to Marozia, the powerful matron who led
the Theophylact family. Marozia, the supposed mistress
of Pope Sergius III, completely dominated Stephen,
who achieved nothing of note in his reign. The Roman
populace believed that Marozia was only waiting for
the time when her son, John, who many believed was
also the son of Pope Sergius III, could be elevated to
the papacy.

John XI

Rome; February 931 to December 935

Due to his family's influence John was already a cardinal
in his twenties; his mother, the infamous Marozia,
leader of the Theophylact family, arranged his election,
with the expectation that she would further her
ambitions through him. (Whether John was the
illegitimate son of Pope Sergius III has never been
established; it was certainly popular belief.) John's half-
brother, Alberic II, the ruler of Rome, was enraged
when John presided over the unlawful marriage of his
mother to her brother-in-law, Hugh of Provence.
Alberic had his mother and John imprisoned. Apart
from approving the Cluniac reforms, which were
halting the decline in monastic discipline, John achieved
nothing of note after his release from prison.

Leo VII

Rome; 3 January 936 to 13 July 939

One of the four popes who was elected at the behest of
Alberic II, Leo was controlled by his patron. Although
not permitted any political power he was encouraged
to work for monastic reform, giving substantial support
to Odo of Cluny. One contemporary writer described
Leo as being 'kind and wise'.

Stephen VIII (IX)

Rome; 14 July 939 to October 942

Stephen owed his election to Alberic II, who controlled him. Stephen, like his predecessor, poured his energies into monastic reform throughout Europe. His premature death, 'mutilated by certain Romans', according to Martin of Oppau, a contemporary writer, was almost certainly due to his falling out of favour with Alberic.

Marinus II

Rome; 30 October 942 to May 946

Almost nothing is known of Marinus, also nominated by Alberic. He would appear to have been under the same control as his two predecessors.

Agapitus II

Rome; 10 May 946 to December 955

Also known as Agapetus. Agapitus was another of Alberic II's appointees. He showed more independence than his immediate predecessors, working with the emperor, Otto I, to evangelise northern Europe. Agapitus enjoyed the reputation of being a holy and virtuous pontiff. On his deathbed Alberic compelled Agapitus, the Roman clergy and the nobility to swear that they would elect his illegitimate son Octavian as Agapitus's successor. This they did.

John XII (Octavius)

Tusculum; 16 December 963 to 14 May 964

The illegitimate son of Alberic II, Octavian, who was only 18 years of age, when elected, took the name John and was the second pope to change his name on election, the first being John II. His private life was a great scandal; his lechery turned the Lateran Palace, so contemporaries report, into a brothel. He showed no interest in spiritual matters and is said to have called upon the pagan gods to help him win at dice! However, he had a talent for government in an unstable Italy. To protect the Papal States he called upon the help of the German king, Otto I, who saw himself as the new Charlemagne. In return John crowned him emperor in 962. The two allies fell out and Otto, who felt betrayed, marched on Rome. John fled and the emperor set up an anti-pope, Leo VIII. A revolt in Rome (early in 964) ousted Leo and brought John back At twenty-seven John died suddenly and mysteriously; it is alleged that he had a stroke while in an adulterous union!

Leo VIII

Rome; 4 December 963 to 1 March 965

At this juncture there is no little confusion. John XII had been deposed by Emperor Otto I and Leo was installed. John returned and ousted Leo. Shortly afterwards John died suddenly. Was John's deposition valid? Was Leo an anti-pope, or was Benedict V, who was elected by John's supporters at the death of John? The emperor refused to accept Benedict and returned to Rome. He deposed Benedict and restored Leo, who was never accepted by the Roman people, and took Benedict off with him to Germany. He died in Hamburg in 966. Leo died in Rome in March 965.

Benedict V

Rome; 22 May 964 to 4 July 966

See Leo VIII.

John XIII

Rome; 1 October 965 to 6 September 972

John was elected through the influence of Emperor Otto I and remained dependent upon him. He was never accepted by the people of Rome who, when the emperor withdrew, deposed John and drove him into exile. In November 966 he was restored by Otto and his reign remained peaceful. John received back from the emperor territories that were earlier lost to the Papal States. He crowned Otto II co-emperor in 967, and remained independent in ecclesiastical matters.

Benedict VI

Rome; 19 January 973 to June 974

Elected late in 972 Benedict was not consecrated until January 973; the emperor Otto I died shortly afterwards. In the following turmoil, with Otto II preoccupied with troubles in northern Europe, the powerful Crescenti family, which controlled Rome, imprisoned Benedict in Castel Sant'Angelo. He was strangled there, two months later, on the orders of the anti-pope Boniface VII, the appointee of the Crescenti family.

Benedict VII

Rome; October 974 to 10 July 983

While the anti-pope, Boniface VII, claimed the papal throne, his claim was not upheld by the emperor's representative, Count Sicco, who approved the election of Benedict. He was a member of the Roman nobility and a relative of the famous Alberic II (see the popes of the early 900s). In 980 Boniface returned to Rome and drove Benedict out. With the help of imperial troops Benedict returned; he worked with the emperor to eliminate simony and his reign ended in peace.

John XIV

Pavia; December 983 to 20 August 984

Born in Pavia, Peter Canepanova was bishop of his native city when he was chosen by Emperor Otto II to succeed Benedict VII. He changed his name as it was not thought appropriate to use the Apostle's name. Unfortunately Otto II died almost immediately after John's election and he became the target of the

Crescenti family. Boniface (see Benedict VII) returned and John was deposed and imprisoned in the Castel Sant'Angelo; he was left to starve to death. Boniface VII then ruled until July 985, When he died he was so hated for his bloodthirsty record that the Roman populace dragged his naked body through the streets and mutilated it.

John XV
Rome; August 985 to March 996

A cardinal of St Vitale, John was elected through the influence of the Crescenti family. His ability to rule was hindered at every turn by his patrons, which John found so unbearable in 995 that he fled from Rome to Sutri and sought the help of Emperor Otto III. John died before the emperor could get to Rome. He had some success abroad, for example negotiating a peace between England and Normandy in 991. John was able to make various liturgical changes and his principal claim to fame is conducting the first recorded canonisation of a saint: St Ulrich of Augsburg.

Gregory V
Saxony; May 996 to 18 February 999

Bruno of Carinthis, who took the name Gregory, was the second German pope, a relative of Otto III, the new emperor. Only in his twenties, Gregory worked well with the emperor at first but problems developed and Gregory lost Otto's protection. The Roman nobility resented having a foreigner as their bishop and Gregory was forced to leave Rome and took refuge in Lombardy. This gave his enemies the chance to elect and install an anti-pope, John XVI. The emperor, with his army, restored Gregory to Rome and viciously punished his enemies, including the anti-pope. Gregory did not live long after his restoration.

Sylvester II

Auvergne; 2 April 999 to 12 May 1003

Benedictine scholar and the first French pope, Sylvester came to the papacy from being a much respected Archbishop of Ravenna. He proved to be a champion of papal rights and prerogatives and worked with Emperor Otto to rid the Church of simony and other abuses. He promoted missionary work in Poland and Hungary. Sylvester was not well liked by the Roman nobility who drove him out of the city in 1001. When the emperor died, the following year, Sylvester was permitted to return.

John XVII

Rome; June 1003 to December 1003

John XVI was an anti-pope but somehow became included in the numbering. Giovanni Siccone took the name John on election, which was almost certainly due to the influence of the powerful Roman family, the Crescenti. Little else is known about him.

John XVIII (Giovanni Fasano)

Rome, January 1004 to July 1009

Giovanni Fasano owed his election to the powerful Crescenti family who controlled Rome at this time, some believe that he was a family member. Little is known of his life except that he appears to have abdicated because he ended his days as a monk, probably in 1009.

Sergius IV

Rome; 31 July 1009 to 12 May 1012

Little is known of Sergius save that he appears to have introduced the custom, although he was not the first, of a change of name at election (he was originally Peter). His death was sudden and in suspicious circumstances, just a week before that of his patron, John II Crescentius of the powerful Crescenti family. The new power in Rome, the Tusculani family, then secured the papal throne for their candidate.

Benedict VIII (Theophylactus)

Tusculum; 18 May 1012 to 9 April 1024

A power struggle in Rome swept the Cresenti family away to be replaced by the Tusculani. Benedict, formerly Theophylactus, was a member of that family and some have viewed the sudden death of his predecessor with suspicion. Benedict spent much time in armour, and on horseback, leading his troops into battle against the Saracens. After Benedict crowned the German king, Henry II, emperor (1014) in Rome, pope and emperor worked together to defeat Byzantine incursions in Italy. At Ravenna in 1022 Benedict and Henry called a synod and enacted reforms, denouncing simony and promoting celibacy.

John XIX (Romanus):

Tusculum; April 1024 to 1032

Romanus, of the Tusculani family, was Benedict VIII's brother; he bribed his way into the See of Rome. A layman when elected, John's scandalous lifestyle won him few friends although he was able to maintain peace in Rome. The new emperor, Conrad II, who John crowned, showed him no regard or respect.

Benedict IX (Theophylactus)

10 April 1032 to 1044

Benedict was the only pope to reign three times. As nephew of John XIX, he kept the papacy in the Tusculani family. He was totally corrupt, scandalous and violent; he only kept the papal throne by force of arms. The Crescenti family used the scandals and with the help of a Roman mob drove Benedict out and installed their own man, John of Sabina.

Sylvester III (John)

Rome; January 1045 to February 1045

Bishop of Sabina, within Crescenti territory, John was elected to replace the unworthy Benedict; however, aided by the Tusculani family, Benedict returned and Sylvester was sent back to his bishopric at Sabina. An attempt to have him charged with crimes and imprisoned failed. He is believed to have died in 1063.

Benedict IX (second time)

10 April 1045 to 1 May 1045

Benedict only lasted two months this time. He is believed to have sold his position to his godfather, a priest named Giovanni Graziano, who became Gregory VI.

Gregory VI (Giovanni Graziano)

Rome; 5 May 1045 to 20 December 1046

Godfather of Benedict IX, Giovanni appears to have been a good priest who was trying to free the papacy of corruption; however, a very large sum of money was exchanged before Benedict abdicated. Benedict had stepped down because he wanted to marry, and when he tired of this he reclaimed the papal throne. There were now three popes, Sylvester III, Benedict IX and Gregory, each with supporters. The emperor, Henry III, of Germany, called the Synod of Sutri (December 1046) to sort out the muddle. All were persuaded to step down and the emperor, clearly trying to rescue the papacy from the thralls of the Roman nobility, had his nominee, Suidger, a German bishop, elected.

Clement II (Suidger)

Saxony; 25 December 1046 to 9 October 1047

Bishop of Bamberg, and of the Saxon nobility, Suidger took the name Clement and launched immediately into a reform of the Church, convening a synod in Rome (January 1047) to reform the Church, particularly to rid it of simony. Progress was slow, and before any action was possible Clement died suddenly, in suspicious circumstances; research has shown that he was poisoned. The Roman nobility immediately brought Benedict IX back (for a third time).

Benedict IX (a third time)

8 November 1047 to 17 July 1048 (d.c. 1055)

The emperor, Henry III, was furious at Benedict's return and had him removed by force of arms. Benedict was held in a secure place from which he issued condemnations of the next two popes.

Damasus II (Poppo)

Bavaria; 17 July 1048 to 9 August 1048

Bishop of Brixen, Poppo was the second German pontiff, nominated (and not elected) by the emperor, Henry III. He continued his efforts to protect the papacy from the ambitions of the Roman nobility. As bishop and advisor Poppo had assisted Henry when he was forced to deal with the three claimants to the papal throne (see Gregory VI). Damasus only lasted twenty-three days as pope; it was rumoured that he had been poisoned, but this claim has never been substantiated.

Leo IX, St (Bruno)

Alsace; 12 February 1049 to 19 April 1054

Bruno of Egisheim was nominated by the emperor, Henry III, because he was famed for his reforming zeal. After election he devoted himself to the reform of the Church; he was assisted by St Peter Damien and Hildebrand (later Pope Gregory VII). Leo called several reforming synods and took the unusual step of touring Europe to promote celibacy and papal supremacy and to combat simony. A highly respected and acclaimed pontiff, he made one fatal error. In 1053 he led a poorly equipped army against the Normans, who were ravaging southern Italy, and was defeated and imprisoned for nine months. The defeat also worsened relations with Michael Cerularius, Patriarch of Constantinople, who threw off papal allegiance; (Cerularius' motto was 'I will not serve'); mutual excommunications followed, and the final breach between Rome and Constantinople. Leo died shortly after his release from captivity. The sanctity of his life was acknowledged, the first papal saint for 170 years.

1050–1400
Dark Ages for Europe
and the Church

Timeline 1050–1400

1054 Roman and Byzantine Christianity split as the Pope and Patriarch of Constantinople exchange letters of anathema.

1059 Cardinals become solely responsible for the election of new popes.

1095 Pope Urban II institutes the First Crusade.

1098 The Cistercian order is founded.

1099 The Crusaders wrest Jerusalem from Muslim control.

1143 The Koran is translated into Latin, allowing the Christian study of the Muslim holy book.

1146 Bernard, a Cistercian monk from Citeaux, preaches in favour of a second Crusade to the Holy Land.

1170 Thomas à Becket, Archbishop of Canterbury, is murdered on the orders of the King of England.

1187 Saladin, a talented Arab military leader, captures Jerusalem from the Crusaders.

1189 The Third Crusade begins.

1204 The Fourth Crusade invades and sacks Constantinople.

1216 The Dominican order is established.

1223 Pope Honorius III approves the Rule of the Franciscan Order.

1232 Pope Gregory IX founds the Inquisition.

1244 The Muslims lose control of Jerusalem.

1261 Crusaders are thrown out of Constantinople by the Byzantine Emperor.

1274 The Council of Lyons, attempts to reunify the Roman Church and that of Constantinople. It fails.

1302 Pope Boniface VIII declares that papal power is superior to that of kings.

1305 The papacy is exiled to Avignon in France.

1330 William of Ockham, an English Franciscan friar, dares to publicly criticise the papacy.

1348 Europe is devastated by the 'Black Death', an epidemic of bubonic plague.

1375 Englishman John Wyclif publishes attacks on priestly wealth and papal authority.

Introduction

By the mid eleventh century most of western Europe was Christian. Orthodox Christianity had spread into Russia, but Roman Catholic influence had spread into Bohemia, Poland and Hungary.

From the poverty of the early Middle Ages, 1050–1400 in Europe represents what historians have named the high Middle Ages. European society stabilised and an economic recovery began to change life in Europe. Peace meant trade, and the land routes and waterways that had fallen into disuse were reopened. Along these trade routes towns began to grow around sites such as monasteries or castles. Travellers and merchants would break their journeys in these fledgling towns, and with that came the demand for goods and services. Peasant farmers were able to leave the land in search of employment as tradesmen, developing crafts and moving to the towns. Agricultural methods improved, and international sea trade developed, with large fleets of ships based in Venice, Pisa and Genoa trading throughout the Mediterranean, bringing not only goods from the rest of the world but also new ideas about farming and industries.

The feudal system of government began to break down as people deserted the land for the growing towns. Living in a town was in many ways an improvement over being a peasant, but the early towns were crowded, disease-ridden, dangerous places.

With the improvement of trade, money came back into use. Previously a lord of the manor would pay for a political or military service by granting his servant land (a fief), but in the high Middle Ages lords could pay with money. But the age of the lords was also beginning to wane, and the powerful nation-states of England and France began to develop as kings subdued their nobility.

French influence spread with William the Conqueror's invasion of Britain in 1066. This invasion had the approval of Pope Alexander II, since it allowed him to spread the growing clerical reform movement to Britain. Christianity had by now spread throughout Europe and the popes were as keen to assert their power as they had been in 597 when Gregory first spoke about a Christian commonwealth.

Given that the Church had been the main civilising, unifying factor in the dark days of the early Middle Ages, the papacy was keen to have its influence continue now that times were getting better. The popes of the time expected their word to be law, since they were God's representatives on earth, and felt that their rule exceeded that of kings.

Part of the process of church reform that started in this period was an insistence that only clergy should have a say in the election of future popes, and that clergy should be independent of the local landowner's or king's bidding.

Inevitably, this caused friction between kings and the Church hierarchy, but the Church's influence now ran so deep in society that even kings were afraid of incurring the Church's displeasure, since the Church held the ultimate sanction of excommunication.

For instance, in 1205 Pope Innocent III excommunicated King John of England over a dispute as to who should become Archbishop of Canterbury, and the same pope publicly forced King Philip of France to take back the wife he had dismissed (with the agreement of his tame local bishops) in favour of another woman.

With the growth and enrichment of society, the Church also flourished, and throughout Europe cathedrals were built with the help of donations from the local population. Cathedrals became ever larger and more elaborate. Originally built as the headquarters of a bishop and his household, cathedrals also became a visible presence of the Church's importance to the community, and were often places of shelter, meeting, trade and for the sick to be treated.

The Church also began to organise education in Europe. As society stabilised, schools were opened by the Church and the earliest universities opened in Oxford, Paris and at Padua in Italy. With increasing overseas travel, Greek and Roman ideas that had been lost to Europe in the chaos of the early Middle Ages, returned and Church thinkers had to grapple with ideas such as whether the philosophy of the Greeks, particularly Aristotle, could be reconciled with Christian thought.

This was both a great and a shameful time for the Church . The monastic movement did tremendous work to settle and enrich the life of western Europe, and people such as St Francis of Assisi developed a new, simple way of engaging ordinary people into the spiritual life of Christianity. The papacy, however, became deeply involved in power politics, and in this period instituted first the Crusades, then the Inquisition.

This period saw a collapse in the ways of the early Middle Ages, where the Church was able to exert its influence over an uneducated population stuck in its primitive living on the land. Towns had grown in size and influence, education was more widespread and ideas were coming into Europe from abroad. Pope Boniface VIII (1294–1303) fell into dispute with the kings of England and France, which ended in the pope excommunicating the king of France and the king retaliating by attempting to kidnap the pope, after which the papacy came under direct French control with the election of the Archbishop of Bordeaux to the papacy, and the removal of papal administration from Rome to Avignon.

The fortunes of Europe also faltered, and from 1300–1400 a series of crises once again caused stagnation in the continent. The bubonic plague, also called the Black Death, ravaged Europe between 1347 and 1352, killing between one quarter and one third of the population. The collapse of the certainties of feudalism led peasants to revolt against their lords, and in towns workers rebelled against the merchants who exploited them.

The Crusades

The Crusades must represent one of the most ambitious, spectacular, genocidal, ill-conceived enterprises in human – let alone religious – history. And they were started by a pope, in this case Pope Gregory VII (1073–1085). When Pope Gregory ascended the throne of Peter, Europe was in a state of turmoil. The pope was having a war of words with Henry, the Holy Roman Emperor of the time, and each condemned the other, saying that they had no authority. It was a war of words between the Roman Catholic Church and the earthly power represented by a king and emperor. The Church won, and most of the powerful lords and landowners of Europe submitted to the authority of the pope. This was the primer for the Crusades, since large armies became available to a pope should he take it into his head to invent such a thing as a holy war.

In 1095, Pope Urban II (1088-1099) did just this, as a response to the fact that the relatively new religion of Islam had outraged Christendom by capturing much of the Holy Land, including the sites of Christ's birth, death and resurrection. Even now Muslim Turks were pushing west out of Iraq, capturing the eastern part of the Byzantine Empire and threatening Constantinople, the second city of Christianity.

Pope Urban received a worried request for help from the Emperor of Byzantium, and in November 1095 summoned a Grand Council at Clermont in France, and gave full papal backing to the Byzantine plea for help in fighting the marauding Muslim Turks. Using the power of the papacy to put God's stamp of approval on the announcement, he announced a Crusade where all Christian warriors should rally to their Christian brethren in the east. The Turks would be routed in God's name, and this army of God would then go on to liberate Jerusalem. His audience received the call enthusiastically.

The Crusaders, he said, should fight under the cross of Christ, and anyone who took part would be paid both on earth, with money, and in heaven, since his sins would be forgiven merely by participating in the Crusade. In 1095, this was a powerful promise to make. A great many Crusaders would find out just how good the papal promises were – 80 percent of them would die on Pope Urban's awfully big adventure, but on the way they would carve a trail of bloody, murderous devastation through Byzantium and the Middle East, with a further diversionary murderous excursion to southern France to obliterate the Cathars.

Following a papal tour of France whipping up support for the Crusade, knights from France and England answered the call, and began heading to the Byzantine Empire to confront the Moslem 'infidels'. This shows to some extent the problems caused when religious and territorial motives clash. The Crusaders were ordered to kill Moslems in Christ's name, yet these 'infidels' held Christ in high esteem as a prophet.

The Crusades got off to a vile start by murdering Jews in Germany and the modern Czech Republic as they passed through, despite the fact that the Jewish communities in many cities were under the protection of the local Bishop. No matter that Christ was a Jew – the Jews crucified him, so they were put to the sword.

The formal crusading army of knights were augmented by a deluded, pilgrimage-crazed individual called Peter the Hermit. Seeing Pope Urban's Crusade to liberate Jerusalem from Moslem occupation as his chance to fulfil a lifelong ambition to complete a pilgrimage to the Holy City, he gathered a huge army of peasants and set off for Jerusalem in the wake of the cross-bearing knights of the official crusade. What we now know as the troubled country of Yugoslavia was, in 1096, part of the equally troubled Byzantine Empire. It was Christian, and subject to papal rule, but that did not stop Peter the Hermit's disorganised rabble pillaging one town (Semiln) and burning Belgrade down.

Both Peter the Hermit's rabble and the official Crusade now rampaged into Anatolia (modern-day Turkey), where a variety of heretical Christian sects flourished under a tolerant Islamic rule. Many Christians were slaughtered and their belongings stolen. Nicaea was raided, and the castle of Xerigordon captured by the Crusaders, then besieged by the Turks. The Crusaders surrendered and were given the chance to convert to Islam, or die.

Peter the Hermit's men then walked into a Turkish trap and some 20,000 were killed. The official Crusaders carried on their lamentable activities, capturing Nicaea, then advancing through Anatolia and across the Taurus Mountains to besiege and ultimately take Antioch in June 1098. One year later, they arrived at the walls of Jerusalem, then in the power of the Egyptians and thought to be impregnable by its governor. He was mistaken. The Crusaders built towers with which to scale the walls, processed barefoot around the city singing hymns and praying, and attacked. Jerusalem fell to the Christian Crusaders on 15 June 1099.

What followed was a massacre, as Moslems and Jews, men, women and children were slaughtered without mercy. As one Crusader observed, 'Such a slaughter of pagans no-one has ever heard of.' It included Crusaders disembowelling the dead in search of swallowed gold coins.

The news of the glorious recapture of Jerusalem for the Christian faith was sent to the pope, but he died before it arrived. Pope Gregory VII, whose European power games made this butchery possible is a saint, whereas Urban II, who actually founded the Crusade, is merely Blessed. The Eastern seaboard of the Mediterranean became Crusader States, nominally under the pope's rule but actually governed by a squabbling coalition of Crusader lords.

The Moslem nations themselves were a fairly disunited lot, and it was not until 1126 that Imad ed Din Zengi united sufficient Moslem forces to mount a serious counter -attack on the Crusader states. He did this with some success until he was killed in 1146. He began the Islamic counter crusade, fighting one Holy War with another, and giving the world the word *jihad*.

In 1146, fired by the success of the first Crusade, Bernard of the monastery of Clairvaux raised a second Crusade of largely German and Frankish forces. Making their way to the Holy Land was fairly uneventful in Crusade terms – just a couple of towns burned down. By May 1148, the Second Crusade was ready for action against the Moslem city of Damascus. It was a glittering prize, since it occupied a prominent place in the Bible, and it would be a strategically significant capture.

The Christians fought well, but made a crucial tactical mistake. They were routed, and the Second Crusade was a bloody humiliation.

The occupying Crusader forces were subject to increasing attacks as the Islamic world unified under Nur-ed-Din, and later the famous Saladin, who expelled the occupying Christians from Jerusalem in July 1187. Unlike the Crusader's invasion of Jerusalem, there was no murder. Saladin ransomed many of the population, freeing those too poor to pay and giving donations to Jerusalem women widowed in the recent battles. The Christian Patriarch of Jerusalem behaved in a most unchristian fashion – he paid his 10 dinar ransom and fled Jerusalem, taking with him wagonloads of treasure and leaving his flock to be sent into slavery.

The papal response to the fall of Jerusalem came from Pope Clement III (1187–91) who in 1189 declared a third Crusade to once again retake Jerusalem. This Crusade attracted some of the great European kings and heads of state: Frederick Barbarossa, the Holy Roman Emperor, went in person, drowning on the way when he jumped into a river to cool off. The Holy Roman Emperor's body was pickled in vinegar to allow him to complete the journey, but he went off and had to be buried en route. King Philip Augustus of France voyaged the 1,800 miles from Genoa to Tyre with a Crusading army, as did Richard the Lionheart, king of England, a country he heartily loathed.

The Crusading army spent two years capturing the city of Acre from Saladin's forces, then marched on Jerusalem to achieve the crowning glory of the Crusade. Richard the Lionheart failed. After a final battle outside the walls of the city of Jaffa, Richard and Saladin signed a truce. The Crusaders could keep the coast, but the Moslems under Saladin kept Jerusalem and, with a generosity not evident in their Christian enemies, kept the Holy City open to pilgrims.

Pope Innocent III (1198–1216) left the Catholic Church with some tremendous legacies – the Franciscans were established under his rule, and the Dominicans flourished. But he also had a Crusade-fixation and announced a fourth Crusade to free Jerusalem. It became yet another miserable episode of internal conflict in the Crusader leadership. A Crusading army 11,000 strong set sail from Venice in November 1202, in a fleet of ships provided by the Venetians – the region's strongest maritime power. Instead of sailing straight for the Holy Land to do Innocent's bidding and turf the Moslems out, the Crusade became an instrument of Venice's territorial ambition and went instead to the Hungarian city of Zara, which the Doge of Venice wanted. The local bishop was armed with a letter of protection from the pope, but the Crusaders laid siege to the city, bombarded it into submission with catapults over five days, then pillaged it.

The pope, furious, excommunicated the entire Crusade; then, realising such a move would stop his bid to rescue the Holy Land, he un-excommunicated them.

The Crusade to the Holy Land then fell on Constantinople, once the second city of Christianity. The essentially French and Venetian Crusaders detested the rulers of Constantinople because they were Greek and represented the last remnants of the old Roman Empire. In April 1203, the Crusaders, having tried to extort massive levies from the emperor of Constantinople, invaded and sacked the city. Rape and murder followed, from which neither nuns nor children were safe. It had been a cry for help from Constantinople that had started whole Crusades movement in 1095.

So ended the Crusades to the Holy Lands. They ended with the Eastern Church in Constantinople crushed and subjugated to the French and Italian-dominated Church of the West. It left a trail of slaughter, rape and disgrace throughout what we now know as Greece, Hungary, Turkey, Syria and the Holy Land. It provoked the Islamic notion of *jihad* – holy war. And Jerusalem was still in the hands of 'infidel' Moslems.

The Albigensian Crusades

Having failed in the Holy Lands, Innocent III, who also had a fixation about heretics closer to home, sought to crush the growing southern French Cathar community. The Cathars were anathema to Innocent. Despite living in the wealthy south of France, they were unworldly, believing the material world to be inherently evil. They believed in poverty, chastity, pacifism and simplicity. They rejected the notion of a pope, or the special powers of clergy to administer the sacraments.

When Innocent III declared what became known as the Albigensian Crusade, he directed the barons of northern France to conduct a genocidal attack on the Cathars of the south. The idea was not salvation or conversion, but annihilation. When the Cathar town of Béziers was attacked in July 1208, every resident was killed. A bishop in attendance was reported to have told soldiers who asked how to discriminate Christians from Cathar heretics, 'Kill them all. God will decide.'

Cathar resistance ended with the siege of the fort of Montsegur in 1229, when the last remnants of the Cathars were trapped in a mountaintop Pyrenean fort. Following their version of Easter, they surrendered to Innocent's Crusaders and refused to recant their heresy. They were herded into a building, which was set ablaze.

The fifth and final Crusade to the Holy Lands

While exterminating the Cathars, Innocent in 1213 called for a further Crusade. He did so in order to establish a powerful grip over Europe's lords and their armies. A knight on Crusade duty was under papal duty, and to ensure this happened Innocent stated that anyone taking part in a Crusade would have his sins forgiven, and so would anyone who funded a Crusader. The implication of this was clear: Pope Innocent allowed Christians to buy themselves forgiveness, and so entrance to heaven. Innocent died in 1216. His papal reign, for its day and the technology available, must rival the holocausts unleashed by Stalin or Hitler for brutality and mercilessness.

Still, his legacy was the Fifth Crusade to free Jerusalem. As with the Fourth Crusade, the Fifth was diverted from its goal, Jerusalem. Instead it attacked Damietta in Egypt, despite the fact that al-Kamil, the Moslem ruler, was on friendly terms with local Christians. But the Crusaders went to Crusade, so they fought al-Kamil, and lost heavily. He could probably have wiped them out, but instead he offered to restore Jerusalem to Christian control. However, the pig-headed Crusaders were there not merely to regain Jerusalem, but to destroy heretics. Moslems were heretics, the Crusaders thought, so the battle-scarred, exhausted Crusaders marched on Cairo, the Egyptian capital. Stupidly, they camped overnight on a Nile flood plain, so al-Kamil, his patience finally worn out by these violent, unreasonable Crusaders, demolished his flood defences and drowned the lot.

Jerusalem finally did return to western, but not Christian, hands when Frederick II defied Pope Gregory IX and set off to recapture the city. Since he defied the pope, he was excommunicated, which was deeply ironic since he talked his way into Jerusalem in 1229 without shedding any Crusader or Moslem blood. Frederick II returned home to a different Crusade: the man who had liberated Jerusalem found that the pope had declared a Crusade against him.

Antipopes

Throughout the history of the papacy there have been occasions where there were more popes than vacancies for the job. During the early Church, the method of appointing a new pope was vague, often a political process and open to dispute and to inconclusive results. Sometimes the consequence would be a pope, and a pretender to the papal throne, the anti-pope.

Antipopes emerged for a variety of causes. Sometimes, it was personal rivalry, often the power politics of the day was a significant factor; and the most obvious cause was the fine theological differences that often caused not only multiple popes, but also intrigue and murder.

By the fourteenth century the College of Cardinals played a large part in the election of the popes. During the Papacy's exile in Avignon (1309–1377) the power base in the College of Cardinals moved from Italian to French. When in 1377 Gregory XI returned the papacy to its former home in Rome, the French College of Cardinals took this loss hard, and elected an anti-pope to the vacant papal palace in Avignon. This caused the Great Western Schism, in which the Church had no fewer than three people claiming to be pope – Gregory's conventional papacy in Rome, that of Gregory XI (1370–1378), with a competing anti-pope in Avignon, then a second anti-pope established by the Council of Pisa. The Great Schism lasted until the election of Pope Martin V in 1417.

Although the records as to the early Church are vague, Pope Callistus was certainly challenged by an aspirant anti-pope, Hippolytus. There are incidences of anti-popes also in the fourth, fifth and seventh centuries where elections were stalemated or the pope fell to a secular coup, with a more politically pliant anti-pope rival being installed in the exiled pope's place. Pope Liberius was exiled in 355, when the Arian emperor installed his placeman Archdeacon Felix into the Bishopric of Rome. Pope Felix II was displaced, considered an anti-pope, and Liberius continued to reign until 366.

Avignon

Political pressure forced the papacy from its traditional Roman home between the years of 1309 and 1377. As we have seen earlier in this book, it was decided early in the Church's history that the Bishop of Rome should be *papa*, the father of the Church. So for this turbulent period of the papacy, the Bishop of Rome was resident in the southern French town of Avignon. The Avignon popes were:

Clement V	(1305–14)
John XXII	(1316–34)
Benedict XII	(1334–42)
Clement VI	(1342–52)
Innocent VI	(1352–62)
Blessed Urban V	(1362–70)
Gregory XI	(1370–78)

The Avignon period saw a change in the complexion of the papacy – all of the seven popes were French, and the vast majority of the College of Cardinals were French, too. Rome was in turmoil when Clement V ascended to the papal throne, and it was at the invitation of King Philip VI of France that the Papacy left a troubled Rome. Avignon was at the time owned by papal placemen, but it was bought outright for 80,000 gold florins by the hedonistic Pope Clement VI.

Clement lived very well. There were massive papal parties, and persistent rumours of prostitutes frequenting the papal palace and of the pope having a long-term affair with his own niece. Yet despite his extravagant tastes, Clement showed he was not entirely a dilettante. In 1348 he spent his personal wealth alleviating the outbreak of bubonic plague that struck Avignon, and when the people of Avignon blamed the local Jewish community, Clement's direct intervention on their behalf saved them from probable death.

Neither England nor Germany were happy with the papacy's residency in Avignon – it represented a strengthening of France's political power by being so closely associated with the authority vested in the leadership of the Church. To save the papacy further damage in the eyes of the English and Germans, Pope Gregory XI moved the papacy from Avignon back to its traditional home in Rome. The strain broke his health and he died the following year.

The beginning of universities

The period 1050-1400 heralded the beginning of university education. The Latin term *universitas* was used to describe a guild of students and teachers, where the students would pay their tutors for instruction in grammar, logic, rhetoric, arithmetic, geometry, astronomy and music. These seven 'liberal arts' were inherited from the classical Roman and Greek ideas of what was necessary for a man to be considered educated.

After four years studying the seven liberal arts, there would be a further two-year period of study, resulting in gaining a Master of Arts degree, which in turn allowed the graduate to teach the seven liberal arts. From here, a student could go on to specialise in medicine, law or theology.

The early universities were established with a charter from the pope, but later they were accredited by the local authorities. The universities of this period were at Bologna, Salerno and Padua in Italy; Paris, Toulouse and Montpelier in France; Oxford and Cambridge in England and Salamanca in Spain. Universities developed as institutions when, instead of renting separate properties, colleges were built so that students and tutors could live and study together. The universities started as exclusively religious establishments, but with the Renaissance, education became more secular and professional.

While the universities were educating people in the seven liberal arts and starting to produce lawyers and doctors, Church thinkers were deep into a theological argument called scholasticism. At the time, the intellectual bedrock of western civilisation was Greek philosophy, particularly that of Aristotle. Christianity was the dominant social force in Europe, and this prompted many of the greatest thinkers of the time to engage in an ultimately futile struggle to reconcile Greek philosophy and Christianity.

St Francis of Assisi

Francis of Assisi was born in 1182, son of a wealthy cloth merchant. He was a fortunate child and teenager, wanting for nothing and reputedly enjoying an indulgent youth and teenage years.

His ambition was to become a knight, and his father was happy to encourage his son into such a worthy profession, but Francis' life took a surprising turn when he experienced a remarkable conversion. Experiencing visions where he was called upon to serve Christ, he rejected his wealthy life in favour of a life of poverty, preaching and service.

Francis gave up his rich lifestyle, sold his possessions to provide money to give to the poor, clothed himself in a rough brown robe and travelled throughout central Italy looking after lepers and preaching. He soon attracted like-minded followers, and the kernel of the order now known as the Franciscans was formed. He received a vision from the crucified Christ, in which he was instructed to 'rebuild my Church', an order that Francis initially took rather literally, starting to renovate a derelict chapel in the valley below Assisi.

As the numbers of followers grew, so did an identity. The Franciscans gladly embraced poverty, living off alms and donations. The brothers dressed in the same rough brown robes, and the movement grew to the point where St Francis visited Rome to seek papal approval. This was the time of Pope Innocent III, perhaps one of the most powerful popes ever – he could compel kings to do his bidding, he raised armies and instigated the Crusades. Innocent was not used to receiving petitions from beggars from central Italy, and refused Francis' request. But that night, the pope dreamed that his basilica, St John Lateran, was collapsing; before it fell, Francis appeared, stopped the collapse and saved the Church. The pope granted Francis an audience and permitted him to establish the Franciscan Order, which Francis called the Friars Minor.

At a time when the Church was an ostentatiously rich, politically powerful organisation, the Friars Minor caused some bewilderment. Their style was a more joyous form of Christianity than that practised by the monks closeted in their monasteries or the clergy who pandered to the local landowners. Francis and his friars went straight to the areas of most need, the poor and sick, and did their work there.

Francis' example attracted another rich Assisi resident, Clare, who founded the Poor Clares, an enclosed order of contemplative nuns also living the Franciscan ideal of prayer and poverty.

Francis' life became the stuff of legend. In the Umbrian town of Gubbio, the residents were being terrorised by a man-eating wolf, and during one of Francis' preaching visits, he summoned the wolf and struck a bargain. If the residents fed the wolf, it should leave the townspeople alone. The wolf agreed, and sealed the bargain with a paw-shake, now the town's crest. He is also famed for his sermon to the birds. One version of this story is that, while he was preaching, a flock of birds settled in a nearby tree to listen. Another is that, faced with a crowd uninterested in his message, he left the crowd and went instead to preach to the birds.

Francis took his mission to spread the Word of God seriously and completely fearlessly, travelling to Syria, Morocco and Egypt in an attempt to convert their Muslim rulers These same rulers were being heavily demonised by western Christians at the time – this was the age of the Crusades. That Francis went at all was a mark of his courage, and that he was not killed for proselytising says much about the power of his personality.

As the order grew, politics intervened and he had to put the running of the Friars Minor into the hands of administrative-minded brothers. Upset at what they did to his original ideas, he withdrew into the Tuscan countryside, living in a grotto on Mount Alvernia, where he received the stigmata, wounds similar to those of Christ's crucifixion wounds.

In 1226, Francis died at the small chapel he had started to rebuild at the very start of his mission. He died (or, as he put it, 'welcomed Brother Death') lying naked on the ground. The original humble chapel and the site of his death now sit under the dome of an enormous Italian basilica, and Francis, whose nickname was *il Povorello* (the little poor man) was buried beneath not one but two grand basilicas in Assisi, a town which has become a centre of pilgrimage for millions every year.

The Jews in Europe

Early Christian Rome recorded a large Jewish population, and by the high Middle Ages there were communities of Jews throughout Europe. As Western Christianity gained its ascendancy in Europe and popes vigorously pursued the conversion of Europe and the creation of a Christian commonwealth, an antipathy developed to other faiths.

The Muslims were demonised for obvious reasons: they had occupied the Holy Land and North Africa and brought a new, vigorous religion to a previously Christian part of the world. While there was evidence that the Muslim conquerors tolerated both Christian and Jewish religious practice under their rule, the pope nonetheless condemned them.

The European Jews, too, suffered papal hostility and the consequences that brought. In the Fourth Lateral Council Pope Innocent proclaimed that Jews should be forced to wear special badges and be excluded from general society. This confirmed and strengthened the growing prejudice against Jews: there were attacks on Jews in European towns and cities throughout the twelfth and thirteenth centuries, and in 1290 the Jewish population was expelled from England. They did not return for more than 350 years.

The Crusaders who were dispatched to the Holy Land to liberate it from the Muslims began their Crusades with sporadic acts of violence against Jewish communities on their route.

The Hundred Years War

The Hundred Years War raged through France from 1337 to 1453, and was an important contributory factor in the stagnation of Europe towards the end of the fourteenth century.

It was not a hundred years of constant war, but was marked by bouts of conflict interspersed by shaky peace treaties. The English at the time had territories in France, and the French kings resented the English presence on French soil. The French also sought to restrain English wool-trading in Belgium, and there were disputes over sailing and fishing rights in the English Channel.

The war was fought on French soil by invading English armies, and the English won a series of battles at Crécy (1346), Poitiers (1356) and Agincourt (1415), after which the English king, Henry V, was made heir to the throne of France. However, after Henry died, the French revolted at the idea of an English king of France, and by 1453 had ejected the English from France with the exception of the province of Calais, which remained English until 1558.

THE POPES
1055–1404

Victor II (Gebhard)

Swabia; 13 April 1055 to 28 July 1057

Consecrated Bishop of Eichstatt at twenty-four years of age, Gebhard Dollnstein-Hirschberg, was a leading advisor to the Emperor Henry III. At the death of Leo IX delegates from Rome arrived at the imperial court, requesting that Henry nominate Gebhard as the next pope. For five months Gebhard refused, but eventually he accepted and became an effective reforming pope like his predecessor. The Normans were still a problem in southern Italy and Victor relied upon the emperor for assistance. On his deathbed Henry entrusted his five-year-old son into Victor's care. With great diplomatic skill he secured his succession and negotiated a lasting peace in the empire, in Victor's name.

Stephen IX (X) (Frederick)

Lorraine; 3 August 1057 to 29 March 1058

Abbot of the famous Benedictine monastery of Monte Cassino, and cardinal, Frederick of Lorraine was another reforming pope in what later came to be known as the Gregorian Reform. He drew around him reforming advisors like St Peter Damien and Hildebrand; the latter he favoured as his successor.

Nicholas II (Gerard)

Burgundy; 24 January 1059 to 27 July 1061

The electors were waiting for the return of Hildebrand (see Leo IX) from a mission in Germany when a minority group elected Benedict X. This was declared unlawful, and to correct the situation Gerard, Bishop of Florence, was elected. The anti-pope, Benedict, fled

Rome. After his coronation Nicholas summoned the Lateran Council, which decreed strict rules to govern the election of all popes. Cardinal bishops would choose and that choice would be submitted to the Roman clergy and people. Nicholas condemned clerical marriage and lay investiture; the latter, and his alliance with the Normans, upset relationships with the German people.

Alexander II (Anselmo of Baggio)

1 October 1061 to 21 April 1073

Using the new rules of the Lateran Council (1059) Anselm, who had been working with St Peter Damien and Hildebrand for Church reform, was elected by the cardinal bishops. The German emperor, Henry IV, had not been consulted and the Germans nominated an anti-pope, Honorius II. While the latter had the support of the Emperor, Alexander, in Rome, ignored him and pushed ahead with Church reforms. Supported in his claim to the papacy by a Norman army, in 1066 Alexander gave his blessing to William the Conqueror and his plans to invade England.

Gregory VII, St (Hildebrand)

Tuscany; 30 June 1073 to 25 May 1085

One of the most famed of the reforming popes of the Middle Ages, Gregory's name has been given to the whole reform movement of this time. Originally named Hildebrand he came from a humble family in Tuscany. After being educated in Rome he was appointed chaplain to Pope Gregory VI. On the death of that pope Hildebrand joined a monastery. Summoned to Rome by Pope Leo IX, he served the three following popes for thirty years, resisting any suggestion that he should be elevated to the papacy. He could not resist his election, by popular acclaim, on the death of Alexander II. Gregory then worked tirelessly for the reform and moral revival of the Church. He used synods in Rome to issue reforming decrees and outlawed the practice of lay investiture. This brought him into direct confrontation with the European princes and particularly Emperor Henry IV. The emperor's attempt to get Gregory deposed resulted in his excommunication, and eventual public penance. The conflict continued; Henry IV installed an anti-pope Clement III, and the emperor invaded Rome. Gregory, unbending to the last, was ejected from the city by the Romans. He went first to Monte Cassino, then Salerno, where he died. His dying words are reported as, 'I have loved justice, so I die in exile.'

Victor III (Daufari or Desiderius)

Benevento; 24 May 1086 to 16 September 1087

Desiderius became a Benedictine at an early age. He moved to the great Benedictine monastery of Monte Cassino, where he was elected abbot in April 1058. He proved to be one of the greatest abbots that community has ever had. He made it a centre of learning and radically rebuilt the monastery. His fame led to his elevation as cardinal and Pope Nicholas II gave him great authority to appoint bishops and abbots in southern Italy. He was at Gregory VII's side when he died, and the papacy was virtually forced upon him by the cardinals. He became embroiled in problems with an anti-pope (Clement III) and the emperor; Victor fled back to Monte Cassino from the frustrations caused by trying to work with the cardinals. Brought back to Rome he survived only a year, dying during a synod at Benevento.

Urban II, Bl. (Odo of Lagery)

France; 12 March 1088 to 29 July 1099

The anti-pope, Clement III, was still in control of Rome and the controversy over investiture was still festering when Odo of Lagery was elected and took the name Urban. Renowned for his intelligence, eloquence and piety Urban continued the reforms of his predecessors. He was only able to regain control of Rome in 1093.

He called the reforming Councils of Melfi (1089) and Clermont (1095) and is best remembered for calling for the First Crusade. Jerusalem fell to the Crusaders two weeks before Urban died.

Paschal II (Ranierius)

Ravenna; 13 August 1099 to 21 January 1118

A monk from an early age, Ranierus took the name Paschal on election and pledged to continue the work of Urban II; however, the issue of lay investiture dominated his reign. In conflict with the Emperor Henry V, Paschal supported his son, Henry VI, in his claim to the throne. This alliance, and agreements reached, proved worthless and the young king forced his will upon Paschal after capturing him and sixteen cardinals. Paschal gave in, after threats of torture and death, on lay investiture and crowned Henry emperor. The ensuing turmoil led to Paschal hiding away in the Castel Sant'Angelo after excommunicating the emperor for his insulting violence. Paschal was also challenged, for various reasons, by no fewer than four anti-popes (Clement III, Theoderic, Adalbert and Silvester IV) during his pontificate.

Gelasius II (John of Gaeta)

Gaeta; 24 January 1118 to 28 January 1119

John of Gaeta was a monk of Monte Cassino whose talents were recognised by Pope Urban II; he served for nearly thirty distinguished years as chancellor to the papacy. John shared Pope Paschal's imprisonment. He was unanimously elected and was reluctantly persuaded to accept the papacy. The election was without the approval of the emperor Henry who had Gelasius insulted and imprisoned. The pope escaped from Rome and fled to the monastery of Cluny, in France, where he died. Henry VI meanwhile installed an anti-pope, Gregory VIII, in Rome.

Callistus II (Guido of Burgundy)

Burgundy; 9 February 1119 to 13 December 1124

Related to many of the royal houses of Europe, Guido
was elected as a strong opponent of lay investiture. As
Archbishop of Vienne and papal legate he had shown
his willingness to take on the emperor, Henry V. His
first efforts as pope failed but subsequent negotiations
led to the famous Concordat of Worms (1122) which
resolved the issue. The Concordat was later ratified at
the Lateran Council of 1123. On his return to Rome
(he had been elected and consecrated at Vienne, France)
Callistus acted resolutely over the anti-pope, Gregory
VIII, who was packed off to a monastery.

Honorius II (Lamberto Scanabecchi)

Imola, Italy; 15 December 1124 to 13 February 1130

After assisting Pope Callistus by playing a prominent
role in the negotiations over lay investiture, Lamberto
was virtually thrust upon the papal throne by the
military might of the Frangipani family. The cardinals
had meanwhile elected another candidate. In the
subsequent confusion both candidates offered to step
down, but the cardinals endorsed the choice of
Lamberto. Serving worthily Honorius continued
Church reforms and approved the new Religious Order
of the Knights Templar. He was unsuccessful in
opposing the rise of Norman power in southern Italy.

Innocent II (Gregorio Papareschi)

Rome; 14 February 1130 to 24 September 1143

The powerful Frangipani family were once again (see
Honorius II) responsible for turmoil and confusion at
the election of Gregorio Papareschi, who was chosen
by a small minority of cardinals, the moment Honorius
II was dead. The majority elected Anacletus II. Innocent
travelled to France where he received the support of
St Bernard of Clairvaux, King Lothair II of Germany
and King Louis VI of France. Anacletus was declared

an anti-pope and although Innocent had the support of Lothair (whom he crowned emperor in Rome) and the imperial army, the situation was not settled until Anacletus died in 1138. His successor, the anti-pope Victor IV, was persuaded by St Bernard to resign.

Celestine II (Guido di Citta del Castello)
Umbria; 26 September 1143 to 8 March 1144

Of aristocratic background, Guido was elderly when elected. He had served as a papal legate and was a long-time friend of Peter Abelard. In his short reign he lifted an interdict placed by his predecessor on King Louis VII of France and attempted to thwart the ambitions of the Norman king of Sicily, Roger II, in southern Italy.

Lucius II (Gherardo Caccianemici)
Bologna; 12 March 1144 to 1 February 1145

Soon after election Lucius, who had spent much of his life in papal service, was confronted in Rome by a new secular political group claiming authority in opposition to his own. An appeal for military assistance to the Norman king, Roger II, and the German king, Conrad III, fell on deaf ears. Lucius, armed as a soldier, personally led a force against the insurgents; there was a heavy loss of life and the pope was seriously wounded. He died not long after from his injuries.

Eugene III, Bl (Bernardo Paganelli)
Pisa; 18 February 1145 to 8 July 1153

A surprise choice of the cardinals, meeting outside Rome (see Lucius II) Bernardo was the Cistercian abbot of SS. Vincent and Anastasius, outside Rome. Even St Bernard of Clairvaux (1090–1153), his mentor, was amazed that so inexperienced a monk should be chosen. However, he proved to be a very able pope. Eugene tried to negotiate with the commune ruling Rome,

but with no lasting success and he was barred from the city. He is best known for preaching, getting St Bernard to preach the Second Crusade, his promotion of Church reforms and the excommunication (1148) of an extreme reformer, Arnold of Brescia. Eugene formed an alliance with Frederick Barbarossa, the Western emperor (1152––1190) but he died before the emperor could get to Rome to assist him with the political situation there.

Anastasius IV (Corrado di Suburrra)

Rome; 12 July 1153 to 3 December 1154

Corrado had been Pope Innocent II's vicar to Rome while the anti-pope, Anacletus II, was in control there. He was elderly at his election, but because he was familiar with Rome and relationships there the republican group controlling Rome accepted him. He restored the Pantheon and the Lateran and improved papal relations with Germany and England.

Hadrian IV (Nicholas Breakspear)

St Albans, England; 4 December 1154 to 1 September 1159

Also known as Adrian. The only Englishman to become pope, Nicholas Breakspear (born c.1110) came from St Albans but was educated in France. He entered the Augustinian monastery of St Rufus, near Avignon, where he became abbot in 1137. While he was on a trip to Rome, Pope Eugenius III retained him in the papal service and elevated him to cardinal (c.1150). In 1154 he was unanimously elected pope and entered into a stormy relationship with the emperor, Frederick Barbarossa, whom he crowned in 1155. There was a very jaundiced view of the Irish throughout Europe at this time; Hadrian formed an alliance with the unscrupulous Normans, and by the bull *Laudabiliter* (1156) granted Ireland to the English king, Henry II. The pontificate ended in acrimony and an alienated empire.

Alexander III, (Orlando Bandinelli)

Siena; 7 September 1159 to 30 August 1181

One of the foremost legal experts of his age, Bandinelli rose rapidly in the Church to become Cardinal Chancellor, in 1153, and close advisor to Pope Hadrian IV. In that position he vigorously opposed the growing power of the emperor, Frederick Barbarossa. At Hadrian's death the majority of the cardinals voted for Alexander; the imperial favourite, Cardinal Octaviano, tried to seize the papacy. This was the beginning of a succession of anti-popes – Victor IV (not the one of 1138); Paschal III and Callistus III – as the emperor tried to impose his will. Alexander also had to deal with the emergency of major heresies, the Waldensians and the Albigensians. He continued to vigorously defend papal authority, including his support for Thomas Becket against Henry II of England.

Lucius III (Ubaldo Allucingoli)

Lucca; 1 September 1181 to 25 September 1185

An elderly Cistercian monk, whom Pope Hadrian IV had appointed Cardinal Bishop of Ostia, Lucius tried to negotiate peace with the emperor, Frederick Barbarossa, but without lasting success. He did, however, persuade the emperor to set out on the Third Crusade. Lucius was too old, weak and vacillating to achieve much.

Urban III (Umberto Crivelli)

Milan; 25 November 1185 to 20 October 1187

Umberto, who was Cardinal Archbishop of Milan at Pope Lucius III's death, was swiftly and unanimously elected to prevent the interference of the emperor, Frederick Barbarossa. Urban III resolutely resisted and quarrelled with Frederick, who was so enraged that he sent his son, Henry, to capture the Papal States. Urban set out for Venice where he intended excommunicating the emperor; however he died on the journey.

Gregory VIII (Alberto de Morra)

Benevento; 21 October 1187 to 17 December 1187

Alberto de Morra had successfully served several popes as Chancellor of the Church (1172–1178) and papal legate when chosen to follow Urban III. It is believed that he was elected because he was on good terms with the emperor, Frederick Barbarossa, and his son, Henry. Relations were immediately improved with the emperor. Clerical reforms continued, but Gregory's principal interest was the summoning of another Crusade, after hearing of the fall of Jerusalem to Saladin. He died at Pisa, while attempting to reconcile the Pisans and the Genoese, as a first step to the launching of a fleet to sail to the Holy Land. He was buried in Pisa's cathedral.

Clement III (Paolo Scolari)

Rome; 19 December 1187 to March 1191

The Roman republicans, who had barred Rome to the popes, admitted Clement after his election at Pisa (see Gregory VIII). Good relations were restored. He was not so successful in the more general tortuous political scene in Italy, as he attempted to keep the balance between the imperialist claims and the Norman kingdom of Sicily. Clement did all he could to encourage the progress of the Third Crusade and won the support not only of the emperor (who drowned on it), but of Richard the Lionheart of England and King Philip II of France. The Crusade was, however, a disappointing failure.

Celestine III (Giacinto Bobo)

Rome; 30 March 1191 to 8 January 1198

Giacinto Bobo (or Bobone) was elected pope when he was eighty-five years of age, after being a cardinal for forty-seven years. Like his predecessor, Celestine attempted to keep the balance between the imperial claims in Italy and those of the Norman king, Tancred, in Sicily. He was a friend and defender of Peter Abelard and also of Thomas à Becket. Celestine was known for his moderation and patience which was sorely tested in his relations with Emperor Henry VI, who oppressed the Church in Germany and imprisoned King Richard the Lionheart of England. He gave recognition to the Templars, the Teutonic Knights and the Knights Hospitallers.

Innocent III (Lotario of Segni)

Anagni, Italy; 8 Jan 1198 to 16 July 1216

One of the most important popes of the Middle Ages, Lotario was of aristocratic family and the nephew of Pope Clement III. Famed for his intellect and erudition, he proved, after his election, that he was a consummate diplomat. He sorted out the political factions in Rome, reasserted authority over the Papal States and restored relationships with the Kingdom of Sicily. He excommunicated King John of England and placed the country under an Interdict, until John accepted papal authority. However, Innocent was more interested in spiritual matters and authority, declaring himself 'the Vicar of Christ', laying stress upon his spiritual authority. He reformed the Curia and supported the new mendicant Orders, the Dominicans and the Franciscans. He promoted the Fourth Crusade, (1202-1204) but abhorred the sacking of Constantinople by the Crusaders. There were darker events: the authorised crusade against the heretic Cathars in France and the decree of the Fourth Lateran Council (1215) summoned by Innocent, ordering Muslims and Jews to wear a badge to distinguish them from Christians. His death came unexpectedly while he was preaching and preparing for a fifth Crusade.

Honorius III (Cencio Savelli)

Rome; 18 July 1216 to 18 March 1227

Although aged at election, Cencio Savelli was famed for his administrative talents; he was unanimously elected. Honorius took for his two main aims Church

reform and the promotion of the Fifth Crusade, but
his principal interest was in the Crusade. He had been
tutor to the young Frederick II, and he imposed the
Crusade upon a reluctant emperor, who had other
political ambitions. Honorius's erudition was demonstrated in a number of seminal works, including the
first compilation of canon law.

Gregory IX (Ugolino, Count of Segni)

Anagni; 19 March 1227 to 22 August 1241

A distinguished theologian and canon lawyer, Ugolino
had also served as a papal legate. In character and
determination Gregory was very like Innocent III; he
excommunicated the emperor, Frederick II, for not
setting out on the Sixth Crusade. Frederick retaliated
by rousing up the Roman populace against Gregory.
The emperor and Gregory were temporarily reconciled
after Frederick had led a successful Crusade; more
conflict followed when Frederick tried to make himself
the master of the whole of Italy. Gregory gave the
Dominicans authority to search out and arrange punishment for heretics, through the Court of Inquisition.
Gregory died with the Emperor Frederick's army
surrounding Rome.

Celestine IV (Goffredo Castiglioni)

Milan; 25th October 1241 to 10 November 1241

The most unusual of conclaves followed the death of
Gregory IX; with only ten cardinals available (two
languished in the emperor's prisons) the electors could
not agree. Matteo Orsini, the virtual dictator of Rome,
had them locked up in a squalid old palace, where the
conditions were so appalling the English cardinal died;
after two months they chose an old Milanese cardinal,
Goffredo Castiglioni. As Celestine IV he lasted sev-
enteen days. Then the cardinals took more leisurely
eighteen months to choose the next pope.

Innocent IV (Sinibaldo Fieschi)
Genoa; 25 June 1243 to 7 December 1254

After an interregnum of nearly two years, the brilliant canon lawyer, Cardinal Fieschi, was elected. Thought of as a friend of the emperor, Frederick II, Innocent soon assumed a tough stance against him; and his reign was full of more bitter conflict. Driven from Rome, Innocent fled to France, where he excommunicated the emperor on charges of heresy and sacrilege at the Council of Lyons. Frederick's death brought no respite for Innocent, who was then involved in the imperial succession squabble. Innocent was criticised at the time for heavy taxation in the Papal States, and nepotism.

Alexander IV (Rinaldo, Count of Segni)
Anagni; 12 December 1254 to 25 May 1261

As a cardinal, Rinaldo was closely associated with the Franciscans. He was elected at Naples where Innocent IV had died. A man of prayer, but indecisive, Alexander made several political mistakes. First he excommunicated Manfred, the illegitimate son of the former emperor, Frederick; then he undermined the claim of the legitimate heir to the German throne, the infant Conradin. He tried to give the Kingdom of Sicily to Henry III of England's son, Edmund; that misfired and Manfred went on the rampage and took first Sicily and then the greater part of central Italy. Alexander was forced to reside at Viterbo and when Germany was left without effective government his interference caused greater problems. When Alexander died there were only eight cardinals for a conclave.

Urban IV (Jacques Pantaleon)
Troyes, France; 29 August 1261 to 2 October 1264

Jacques Pantaleon was not one of the eight cardinals left, inadequately, by Alexander IV; he was the Patriarch of Jerusalem, and providentially was in Viterbo when the cardinals were looking for a successor. It was a good choice, for Urban increased the number of cardinals; and offered Sicily to Charles of Anjou, who later brought about the downfall of the Hohenstaufen dynasty of Holy Roman Emperors. Urban also replenished the papal coffers. Not all Urbans' good intentions were realised for Manfred caused him to flee to Perugia, when hostilities were resumed; Urban died there.

Clement IV (Guy Foulques)

Saint-Gilles-sur-Rhône, France; 5 February 1265 to 29 November 1268

Guy Foulques, a French lawyer, became a priest after his wife's death; he rose swiftly to cardinal and papal legate. A long conclave of four months, without Guy's presence, ended in his surprise election on his arrival at Perugia. Wishing to rid the papacy and Italy of the powerful interference of the German armies, Clement appealed to the French king, Charles of Anjou. In February 1266 first Manfred and then Conradin of Germany were defeated. Clement realised too late that the French merely replaced the Germans in the power struggle. Clement inherited from Urban IV an attempt to resolve the schism with the East; but Clement, prompted by Charles of Anjou, demanded too stringent political conditions and the offer of Michael Palae-ologus, the Eastern emperor, was withdrawn. Clement spent most of his reign at Viterbo, where he died and was buried.

Gregory X, Bl. (Teobaldo Visconti)

Piacenza; 1 September 1271 to 10 Jan 1276

The conclave that followed Clement IV's death was the most bizarre in history. The cardinals bickered for nearly three years; at last they were locked in the papal palace (at Viterbo), the roof was removed and food was reduced, to force them to take action. They deputed six cardinals to make a choice. The Archdeacon of Liege, a well known lay man, Teobaldo Visconti, on Crusade in the Holy Land, was utterly surprised to be elected. His pontificate revealed that he was committed to mounting another Crusade and improving relations with the Eastern Church; and at the Council of Lyons (1274–175) a short reunion was achieved. His major contribution was legislation to prevent any further delayed and disgraceful conclaves.

Innocent V, Bl. (Pierre of Tarentaise)

Savoy; 21 January 1276 to 22 June 1276

The first Dominican to be elected, Innocent had acquired a considerable reputation as a scholar, working with Albert the Great and St Thomas Aquinas. He had been appointed Archbishop of Lyons (1271) by Gregory X and then cardinal (1273). His brief reign focused upon trying to maintain the tenuous reunion between the Western and Eastern Churches and balancing the political ambitions of France and Germany in Italy.

Hadrian V (Ottobono Fieschi)

Genoa; 11 July 1276 to 8 August 1276

Ottobono Fieschi distinguished himself as Pope Clement III's legate in England sorting out the problems between King Henry III and his barons. Charles of Anjou brought pressure to bear on the cardinals in conclave when there was an inordinate delay. The only act of Hadrian after his election was to suspend the rules on the conduct of conclaves as set out by Gregory X. Already ill when elected, he died before his consecration.

John XXI (Pedro Juliao)

Lisbon, Portugal; 8 September 1276 to 20 May 1277

(No John XX through an error over the Roman numbering)

A medical doctor and renowned scholar, Pedro Juliao's election came out of a conclave that at first refused to abide by the new papal rules of procedure – so more chaos. He was not interested in the administrative or political roles of the papacy and left these to Cardinal Orsini. John had a special private study built for himself at the papal palace at Viterbo, where he continued his scholarly work. He died suddenly when the ceiling of the study collapsed and crushed him.

Nicholas III (Giovanni Gaetano)

Rome; 25 November 1277 to 22 August 1280

Giovanni Gaetano, Cardinal Orsini, had effectively been pope for the nine months of John XXIs reign (see John XXI) but it took the seven cardinals in conclave a further six months to elect him. Gaetano had had an illustrious career and, a cardinal for nearly thirty years, he had served under eight pontiffs. His election did not please Charles of Anjou, whose power Nicholas was determined to curb. While supporting the reunion with the Eastern Church his terms and conditions endangered its continuance. His nepotism was frowned upon as he appointed three new cardinals from the Orsini family. Nicholas undertook major building work on St Peter's Basilica and the Vatican palace. He also built a summer palace for himself at Viterbo; where he died of a stroke.

Martin IV (Simon de Brie)

Brie, France; 22 February 1281 to 28 March 1285

(A mistake occurred over names. Martin IV should be Martin II)

Six months of intrigue and turmoil eventually resulted in Charles of Anjou's candidate, Simon de Brie, being elected. He had only served the Church in France and was seen by all to be Charles' puppet throughout his reign, favouring French interests and undoing the political balancing act of Nicholas III. Unable to enter Rome because the Romans would not accept him, Martin was crowned at Orvieto. The tenuous reunion with the Eastern Church died when Martin excommunicated the Byzantine emperor Michael VIII and backed Charles of Anjou's military ambitions against Constantinople.

Honorius IV (Giacomo Savelli)

Rome; 2 April 1285 to 3 April 1287

Giacomo Savelli, grand-nephew of Honorius III, was elected swiftly and unanimously. He continued the political policies of Martin IV, having been a friend of Charles of Anjou, the sovereignty of Sicily being the principal issue. His reign was noted for his support of the Franciscans and Dominicans, giving them control of the Inquisition. Honorius appointed only one cardinal, and following his death the wrangling between the cardinals went on for nearly a year.

Nicholas IV (Girolamo Masci)

Lisciano, Italy; 22 February 1288 to 4 April 1292

General of the Franciscan Order, Girolamo Masci had served several popes. After a deadlock that lasted eleven months, during which six cardinals died, the remaining nine elected Girolamo, who at first refused the papacy. His political policies were erratic and centred upon the sovereignty of Sicily. The last Crusader stronghold, Acre, fell in the Holy Land and Nicholas called for another crusade; but no one listened. Nicholas was more successful in sponsoring missionary work in China and Africa. There followed two years and three months while the cardinals argued over Nicholas' successor. Outbreaks of violence in Rome eventually prompted an usual solution; they chose a famous saintly hermit.

Celestine V, St, (Pietro del Morrone)

Molise, Italy; 5 July 1294 to 13 December 1294

One of the most tragic of the popes, Pietro del Morrone was a Benedictine monk who sought greater austerity and solitude as a hermit. He attracted a group of followers who, after his election, became known as 'Celestines'. The cardinals were bitterly divided at the time of his election, and chose not a cardinal but this well-known eighty-year-old hermit. He was an immediate disaster. Recognising his incapacity he resigned after a few months. His successor, Boniface, fearing he would be used as a pawn by the enemies of the Holy See, had him imprisoned, where he died in 1296. He was canonised in 1313 by Pope Clement V.

Boniface VIII (Benedetto Caetani)
Anagni; 24 December 1294 to 11 October 1303

Following a variety of posts in the papal service, including papal legate to France (1288–1292), Cardinal Caetani advised Celestine V on his resignation and was elected in his place. He is remembered for his arrogance and fiery temper, and also his imperious demands for Papal authority, his bull *Unam Sanctam* (1302) claimed not only spiritual but also complete temporal authority over every human being. Patron of the arts, Boniface promoted learning, founding the University of Rome in 1303. He quarrelled with King Philip IV of France over taxation that funded the Hundred Years' War between France and England. More disastrously he waged a long-running vendetta with the Colonna family. They tried to have Boniface's election declared void and he retaliated by imprisoning the resigned Pope Celestine V. Matters reached a head when, at Anagni, his enemies personally attacked and severely abused him. Rescued by supporters, Boniface never recovered from his experience and died shortly afterwards.

Benedict XI Bl. (Niccolo Boccasino)
Treviso, Italy; 22 October 1303 to 7 July 1304

Niccolo Boccasino was the Cardinal Master General of the Dominican Order at his election. He was one of the two cardinals who stood by Boniface VIII during his ordeal at Anagni (see Boniface VIII). He sought the perpetrators, Guillaume de Nogaret and Sciarra Colonna, and brought them to trial, but lifted the censures placed upon Philip IV of France and the two cardinals of the Colonna family who had plotted against Boniface VIII. His short pontificate ended when Benedict died suddenly at Perugia; some sources say that he was poisoned, others that he died of dysentery.

Clement V (Bertrand de Got)

France; 5 June 1305 to 20 April 1314

After eleven months of dissension between pro-French and anti-French cardinals, they chose the life-long friend of King Philip IV of France, Bertrand de Got, who was Archbishop of Bordeaux and not a cardinal. Clement, immediately under the influence of Philip, chose to be crowned at Lyons and eventually took up residence with the Dominicans at Avignon, France (where the papacy stayed for seventy years). Clement never set foot in his diocese of Rome. He appointed a large number of French cardinals to outnumber the Italians, and gave in to King Philip's insistence that he absolve those responsible for the humiliating attack on Boniface VIII. Likewise Clement weakly supported Philip's campaign to destroy the Knights Templar, using the Council of Vienne (1311–1312) to do this. Clement was so deeply into nepotism that he made five members of his family cardinals. His actions had caused much scandal in the Church by the time of his death.

John XXII (Jacques Deuse)

Cahors; 7 August 1316 to 4 December 1334

The conclave following the death of Clement V took two years and three months to find a successor. Jacques Deuse, the elderly Bishop of Avignon and a cardinal, was a compromise choice. John XXII was not expected to live long but his energy and ability surprised everyone. He consolidated the presence of the papacy at Avignon, improved considerably its financial stability, re-organised the Curia, and promoted missionary endeavours around the world. Despite being austere and simple in lifestyle, he indulged in nepotism. His biggest problem was the rift in the Franciscan Order between the Conventuals and the austere Spirituals, who were against holding possessions. John offended Louis IV, king of Germany, who tried to call a Council to depose him; when this failed Louis set up an anti-pope, Nicholas V, who was a Spiritual. John's last years were shrouded in controversy and mystery; some accusing him of teaching heresy. He repented on his deathbed of any misunderstanding his teaching had caused.

Benedict XII (Jacques Fournier)

France; 20 December 1334 to 25 April 1342

The third pope to live at Avignon, Benedict devoted himself to the reform of the Church and its Religious Orders. He himself had been a Cistercian monk, graduating in theology at Paris, and rising from abbot to bishop and cardinal in 1327. His ability as a theologian recommended him to his fellow cardinals, and as pope he immediately settled a theological dispute, caused by John XXII about the Beatific Vision (direct supernatural knowledge or vision of God) and set about a rigorous reform of the Religious Orders. This met with fierce opposition and most of his reforming work was undone after his death.

Clement VI (Pierre Roger)

France; 7 May 1342 to 6 December 1352

Pierre Roger, a former Benedictine and Cardinal Archbishop of Rouen, was the favoured choice of King Philip IV, who had been unhappy with the austerity and reforms of Benedict XII. Clement VI quickly undid those reforms and set up a grand princely court at Avignon, enlarging the papal palace and purchasing the city from Queen Joanna of Naples. He was comfort-loving but not morally corrupt, as his detractors maintained. Politically Clement had few successes; his attempts to intervene in the Hundred Years War came to nothing, but his enmity with Emperor Louis IV led to the latter's excommunication and replacement by Charles IV of Bohemia. Clement was popular with the people for his kind generosity and courage; when the plague decimated Avignon (1348) he gave large sums of money to combat the disease, put himself at personal risk and protected the local Jewish community from persecution when they were blamed for the plague.

Innocent VI (Etienne Aubert)

France; 18 December 1352 to 12 September 1362

After an illustrious ecclesiastical career Etienne Aubert, Cardinal Bishop of Clermont, was elected after a two-day conclave. He ended the luxurious court established by his predecessor and set out to reform the Curia at Avignon, which had attempted to curtail papal power. Innocent tried to end the Hundred Years War between France and England and only achieved a ten-year respite (Treaty of Bretigny, 1360). He attempted to regain order and control in the Papal States and considered returning the papacy to Rome.

Urban V, Bl. (Guillaume de Grimoard)

France, 28 September 1362 to 17 December 1370

A saintly Benedictine and Abbot of the Abbey of St Victor, Marseilles, Guillaume de Grimoard was not a cardinal when elected. As pope he continued wearing his black habit and maintained his frugal way of life as pope. His reign was noted for peace in Europe and reform. He curbed the extravagant lifestyle of many of the higher clergy and spent the money on supporting poor students. He founded universities at Vienne and Cracow. His two major concerns were to return the papacy to Rome and to improve relations with the Eastern Church. Risking the displeasure of the French king and cardinals, Urban returned to a dilapidated Rome in 1367, and welcomed the Byzantine emperor,

John V, there in 1369. His hopes of a reunion with the Eastern Church were not fulfilled and revolts in the Papal States drove him back to Avignon, to the papal administration. He died, while at Mass, three months later.

Gregory XI (Pierre de Beaufort)

France; 30 December 1370 to 26 March 1378

The last of the French popes and the one to end the Avignon papacy, Pierre de Beaufort was elected within two days of Urban VI's death. Nephew of Pope Clement VI, he had been raised to the cardinalate by his uncle; like his predecessor, whose policies he shared; he was deeply religious. Gregory's main objective was to return the papacy to Rome, but his ambition was thwarted by Florence rousing the Papal States against him. He directed the War of the Eight Saints (1375-1378) ending in the Peace of Tivoli. Constantly urged by St Catherine of Siena to return to Rome, he did so on 17 January 1377. The next month a massacre at Cesena, ordered by the papal legate, infuriated the Roman populace who drove Gregory from the Eternal City to Anagni. He died there a disappointed man.

Urban VI (Bartolomeo Prignano)

Naples; 8 April 1378 to 15 October 1389

This reign brought the start of the Great Schism. The seeds had been sown during the six preceding reigns, when ninety French cardinals had been created as against fourteen Italian and six from other nations. With the political tensions in Rome and Italy, and the conflict over where the papacy should be, Avignon or Rome, the cardinals wanted to have a swift decision. However, the Roman mob stormed the conclave and demanded an Italian pope (as did the Italian cardinals). In haste Bartolomeo Prignano, an archbishop in charge of the papal chancery, was elected. Urban, wanting to reform the luxurious way of life of the cardinals, immediately alienated them by his violent and intemperate behaviour. He refused to heed the advice of St Catherine of Siena, who was a supporter. The French cardinals gathered at Anagni and declared Urban's election invalid, as it had been conducted under threat. With the support of King Charles V of France they elected Robert of Geneva as Clement VII. Both sides gathered allies and nations decided for either Urban or Clement. Urban set up his Curia, with twenty-nine new cardinals, at Rome and Clement at Avignon. So Christendom was split into two opposing camps. Urban alienated everyone, even imprisoning and torturing six of his cardinals believing that they were conspiring against him; although St Catherine of Siena remained loyal, most people believed that he was unbalanced, and he was widely hated as a despot. Embarking on a campaign to capture Naples, in revolt against him, he was heavily defeated. His passing, very likely a result of poisoning, was not mourned.

Boniface IX (Pietro Tomacelli)

Naples; 2 November 1389 to 1 October 1404

Elevated to the cardinalate by Urban VI, Pietro Tomacelli was not noted for sanctity or scholarship, but was a stable man of considerable charm and a tactful diplomat, a combination of qualities believed necessary to rectify the mess left by his predecessor. Boniface proved to be arrogant and uncompromising. He was more interested in furthering the prestige of the papacy than resolving the Schism. He dismissed overtures from the anti-pope, Clement VII, and his successor, Benedict XIII. At first enjoying good relations with the Romans, he was forced out of the city when he acted as an absolute monarch and left for Perugia. At great expense he regained control of Naples. Boniface was shameless in pursuing a lucrative policy of simony and introduced the sale of indulgences. His policy of tenaciously maintaining the legitimate papacy had a positive effect but it dragged out the Schism.

1400–1600
Reformation,
Counter Reformation
and exploration

Timeline 1400–1600

1414 Start of the Council of Constance. The Council states that its deliberations are more powerful than papal edicts. It also executes church reformer Jan Huss.

1438 The Council of Ferrara fails to reunify the Churches of Rome and Constantinople.

1453 Constantinople is taken by invading Turks.

1479 The Spanish Inquisition is established.

1492 Portugal starts Europe's race for exploring new lands.

1506 The construction begins of St Peter's Basilica in Rome. Pope Julius II lays a foundation stone.

1510 A visit to Rome appals Martin Luther.

1517 Luther publishes his objections to the trade in pardons in Wittenberg, Germany.

1521 Luther is excommunicated at the Diet of Worms. The Protestant Reformation begins.

1522 Ignatius of Loyola drafts his Spiritual Exercises.

1534 Henry VIII of England passes the Act of Supremacy, supplanting the Pope as Head of the Church in England.

1540 The Jesuits are founded with the approval of Pope Paul III.

1545 The Council of Trent begins. Attempts to reconcile Roman Catholicism and the growing Protestant movement fail.

1557 The Vatican publishes an index of prohibited books.

1570 Pope Pius V states that Catholics in Protestant Britain owe no allegiance to Queen Elizabeth I.

1577 The Lutheran Confession formalises its doctrine in The Formula of Concord.

1588 An attempted invasion of Protestant England by Catholic Spain fails when the Spanish Armada is defeated.

1598 The Edict of Nantes allows rights for French Protestants.

Introduction

The Europe of 1400–1600 was far from settled. On its eastern borders the Ottoman Turks were an ever-present threat. The Ottomans captured the Byzantine capital of Constantinople in 1452, and from their bases along the coast of what is now Yugoslavia regularly raided Italy to carry off women for their ruler's harem, and the threat of the Turkish replaced Vikings as the terror of Europe.

Europe was also reeling from the bubonic plague, which had first broken out in 1347 and continued to erupt throughout the fifteenth, sixteenth and seventeenth centuries. It was an appalling epidemic, which is thought to have killed one third of the population of Europe, and the effects of such a devastating disease affected the whole of European life, since peasants, rulers and clergy alike fell to plague.

In these circumstances, a population frightened by the threat of Turkish invasion and the fear of death by plague looked for someone to blame, and the rich, reputedly corrupt Church attracted its share. The Turks and the plague were God's judgement on the worldly Church of Rome.

Then, as now, the good work done by the Church went unreported and the bad news was passed around and no doubt embellished and exaggerated. Many reports of the time tell of corrupt and debauched clergy, and the papacy did itself few favours by starting the fifteenth century with first two, then three men claiming to be pope and a Great Schism affecting the hierarchy in Rome. However, it was the sale of Church posts and of indulgences that represented the worst of Church corruption and most incensed those who wanted the Church to reform.

A corrupt clergy, a scared European population, the invention of printing and a renewal movement in Europe – the Renaissance, which brought Greek and Roman humanist thinking into European society, a way of thought not entirely in keeping with the teachings of the Church – all this meant that the European stage was set for a huge upheaval in the Reformation. Europe was also changing politically, with strong royal houses developing in England, France and Spain, and with centres of trade developing in northern Germany and the Low Countries of the Netherlands and Belgium.

In the Middle Ages, the pope had been able to come to terms with Europe's kings and emperors, keeping them as allies by diplomacy and if necessary by threat of excommunication. By the sixteenth century the developing nation-states of Europe were building an identity and a consciousness that did not look to the pope for support as much as the Saxon, Frankish and Germanic kingdoms had in the past. In 1512, the Fifth Lateran Council was of the opinion that the Roman Catholic Church's position was unassailable: one participant told the Council, 'No-one contradicts, no-one opposes.' But five years later Martin Luther started the Reformation, which caused the second great split in Christianity.

In this period, Europe also became a more outward-looking population, and with the growth in trade and the economy, the demand for resources rose and the age of exploration began. Developments in ship design and building allowed sailors to make journeys that were previously beyond them, and the adventurers went to discover the New World – the Americas.

Europe started this period unstable, threatened by plague and Turks. Throughout the fifteenth and sixteenth centuries several factors conspired to plunge Europe into successive wars – wars that were made worse by the introduction of gunpowder and firearms into Europe.

The Protestant Reformation

The simple story of the Reformation movement is that it started on All Saints Day, 31 October 1517, when Martin Luther, an Augustinian monk nailed his Ninety-five Theses to the door of the church in Wittenberg. His Ninety-five Theses were a condemnation of the Roman Catholic Church's practice of selling indulgences, and with this Luther started a religious and political movement that led to a substantial section of Christian Europe splitting from the authority of the pope and forming the Protestant confession of churches.

The pressure for the papacy and clergy to reform had been growing for some time, but repeated efforts to bring about change had failed. Germany in the fourteenth and fifteenth centuries developed a school of pre-Reformation thought that moulded Luther's thinking, but there was also a Europe-wide readiness for Church reform, informed by a growth in humanist thought .

Martin Luther lived from 1483-1546. He joined the Augustinian Order in 1505 and became a priest in 1507. By 1512 he was a doctor

Printing and the Gutenberg Bible

The fifteenth century brought about one of the most significant inventions in the world – modern printing. Until then, texts had been passed on by hand copying, which was slow, inefficient and prone to errors creeping in.

Around 1440, Johann Gutenberg, then living in Mainz, Germany, began to experiment with metal type, inventing a system of blocks of metal with raised words or letters which could be arranged in racks to form words, sentences and pages. The surfaces of the letters were inked and pressed against a sheet of paper, leaving a printed impression of the text. Where previously one copyist would labour over a page using a quill or pen repeatedly dipped in ink, now a printer could rapidly produce many identical, correct copies of a page.

The first book to be printed was a Bible printed by Gutenberg in the city of Mainz in 1456. Printing was initially a secretive craft, known only to a guild of printers living in Mainz, until the forces of European turbulence took a hand. Mainz was invaded and sacked in 1462, and as a result much of the population fled, including the printers, who established themselves elsewhere. The craft of printing spread throughout Europe, arriving in Rome in 1467 and in London in 1476.

Printing made books available to the public on a scale that had never been known before, and with knowledge came the ability to evaluate and criticise. Critics of the Church could have their ideas put into print, and in many ways the invention of the printing press was one of the factors that primed Europe for Luther's reformation.

of theology at the University of Wittenberg, and a working parish priest. As a priest, he saw his parishioners travelling to buy indulgences – scraps of paper supposedly signed by the pope that promised the purchaser remission from punishment for their sins, and for those of their dead relatives.

The Ninety-five Theses – by no means intended as a revolutionary document – stirred dissenting interest throughout Europe. Luther had also developed other theological differences with the Catholic Church. The Church proclaimed that the faithful could be saved by good works and through intercession, and that the pope had the authority to interpret the Scriptures and 'open the gates of paradise'. Luther disagreed, feeling that through the Scriptures the believer formed a direct relationship with Christ, and that this was sufficient to ensure salvation – this became known as 'justification by faith'.

The Church objected, and in 1517 Luther was reported to the pope, and was summoned to Rome. The Church at the time had an active Inquisition, and in 1415 had ordered the Czech reformer Jan Hus burned at the stake. Luther fled rather than risk Rome, and his beliefs became even stronger, until in 1519 he publicly declared the pope and his Councils to be fallible.

The pope issued a papal bull threatening to excommunicate Luther, and Luther responded by burning the document. He was excommunicated in 1521.

In that year, he appeared before the Imperial Court (the Diet) in the German town of Worms, where he was charged to recant his writings and sayings. He refused, unless anyone could disprove his ideas relying on the Scriptures for their authority, finishing his address to the Court with the words, 'Here I stand. I can do no other. God help me. Amen.' His life was at risk, and he was taken into protective custody by the sympathetic local ruler Frederick of Saxony. While in Wartburg Castle he turned his impressive mind to translating the New Testament from Greek into German, so giving more of the German population direct access to the Word of God.

When he re-entered society in 1522, a reform movement was gaining momentum in Germany, and in 1529 the emperor's court tried to block Luther's progress. A body of German princes stood to protest at the proposed legislation, and their actions gave rise to the term 'Protestant'. In a court in 1530, the fledgling Protestants made a statement of their beliefs to the court, which was rejected. Luther died in 1546, and by 1547 the first Catholic–Protestant war erupted in Germany, with the emperor imprisoning the Protestant leaders. By 1552, the Treaty of Passau recognised the legality of Protestantism. European Christianity had split into the Roman Catholic and Protestant confessions.

The reformation outside Germany

Switzerland, too, saw a Reformation, which broke out at the same time as Luther's. It was led by Huldreich Zwingli, a priest in the Zurich Great Minster, who like Luther rejected Church corruption and began preaching a more evangelical – Scriptural-based – style of faith. He was opposed by the local Catholic bishop, and at times his reforming tendencies were too extreme even for Luther. Zwingli ultimately lost the support of the local Catholic princes, who sent an army against Protestant Zurich, killing Zwingli in the Battle of Zurich. Like Luther, Zwingli married, breaking with the Catholic tradition of clerical celibacy.

John Calvin (1509–1564) was a very significant figure in early Protestantism. Born and educated in Catholic France, he heard Luther's teachings in Paris, renounced his Catholicism and went to live in exile in Basle, Switzerland, where in 1536 he published *The Institution of the Christian Religion,* a lucid statement and defence of Protestant beliefs. He was an intelligent man who spent much energy trying to settle various disagreements within the growing Protestant Church. In 1537 he moved to Geneva to give impetus to the Reformation there, founding the Geneva Academy, which became a focal point for training Protestant clergy.

In France, the Reformation started slowly, since early reformers were executed or exiled, but once French-speaking Switzerland accepted the teachings of Luther and Calvin, Protestantism began to grow in France, with records of a Calvinist congregation forming in Paris in 1555. The French did not accept Protestantism readily, and opposition from the Catholic establishment was violent, culminating in the St Bartholomew's Day Massacre in 1572, when many French Protestants were slaughtered in cold blood.

In 1589 the Protestant Henry VI became king, but under threat from Catholic Spain and French Catholic nobility he renounced his faith to save France a further bout of civil war. However, in 1598 he enshrined the right of Protestants to worship freely in the Edict of Nantes.

The Low Countries (the Netherlands and Belgium) were at the time ruled by Catholic Spain, and histories record that by as early as 1523 people were being killed for professing Lutheran beliefs. The Spanish King Philip II opposed the growth of Lutheranism, since it was strongly linked to a movement for political independence, and more than 100,000 Low Countries Lutherans were killed in the period

1565–1573. The reformers ultimately won, expelling the Spanish and rejecting Roman Catholicism.

Jan Hus (1374–1415) primed Bohemia (the modern-day Czech Republic) for the arrival of Luther's teaching. Hus was ordained in 1401 and taught at the University of Prague. He was an early Protestant in all but name – like Luther, he said only God can forgive sins, declared that the Church hierarchy should not try to establish Church rules that contradicted Scripture, and opposed the sale of indulgences. These beliefs put him in conflict with Rome, and he was summoned to the Council of Constance to defend his beliefs. Hus travelled to Constance under the protection of the emperor, but once he got there the Council arrested him, tried him and had him burned at the stake. His death aroused a wave of nationalistic, anti-Catholic feeling in Bohemia, and a Protestant Hussite Church was established which later became heavily influenced by the teachings of Luther and Calvin. Lutheran-inspired churches were established in Poland and Hungary, and by 1527, just ten years after Luther's first stand, Swedish law accepted the Reformed Church as the national religion. Denmark, too, embraced Protestantism in a turbulent period between 1524 and 1536, and the Reformation spread from Denmark to Norway in 1536, and to Iceland shortly afterwards.

The Reformation in England

England had its own pre-Reformation reformer in John Wyclif, who lived from around 1329 to 1384. He studied and taught philosophy at Oxford University, and developed many of the convictions that were subsequently espoused by Luther and the German reformers: that the lay members of the Church did not need a priest between them and God and that the Eucharist was a spiritual event, not a real transformation from bread and wine into the body and blood of Christ. Like European reformers he translated the Bible into the local language, and backed the government in stripping corrupt clergy of their property. As with other reformers, he incurred the Pope's displeasure, but he had powerful friends at home who protected him. Wyclif's ideas attracted followers who became known as Lollards, a group whose religious protests also became political, leading them to be suppressed after Wyclif's death, but Wyclif and his followers nonetheless opened the way for Luther's teachings.

England in the early sixteenth century already had undercurrents of anti-papal and anti-clergy sentiment, which were fuelled by smuggled imports of Luther's writings and English translations of the Bible. But the English Reformation was started when King Henry VIII asked papal permission to divorce Queen Catherine who had not managed to bear him a son and heir to the throne. The Tudor dynasty was relatively recent, and the king was anxious to perpetuate the line, so when the pope proved uncooperative, Henry proclaimed himself head of the Church of England in 1534, and free to sanction his own marriage arrangements.

Despite displacing the pope as head of the Church in England and embarking on a comprehensive destruction of monasteries, Henry remained in his religious practices essentially Catholic, although without any sense of obligation to the pope. It was not until Henry's son Edward VI (ruled 1547–1553) took the throne that the Reformation was introduced throughout the country in a systematic manner. King Edward's more thorough Reformation was assisted by Thomas Cranmer, the Archbishop of Canterbury, Nicholas Ridley and Hugh Latimer. But King Edward was sickly and died after only six years on the throne. His replacement, Queen Mary, was a Catholic, and set about restoring the old faith in her five year reign. She was intolerant of the new Protestants, and suppressed them vigorously, condemning about 200 to burn at the stake, including Cranmer, Latimer and Ridley. Many fled the country in fear of their lives.

With Mary's death came Queen Elizabeth I, who reigned from 1558 to 1603, and during this period she re-established Protestantism, sweeping the last of the Catholic clergy from the Church and replacing them with Protestants. As a result she faced opposition from the overtly Catholic powers of Spain and France, and risked potential insurrection at home, since the remaining Roman Catholics who lived in England were under papal orders to oppose her.

Scotland of the sixteenth century was almost still in the Middle Ages – deeply feudal with an indifferent Church still affected by ignorance and corruption. Patrick Hamilton, a student of Luther brought the Reformation to Scotland, and in 1528 was burned at the stake. John Knox (1505–1572) studied under John Calvin in Zurich, and when he returned to Scotland in 1558, launched the Scottish Reformation. By 1560 Scotland had accepted the Reformation and both England and Scotland were Protestant countries.

The sixteenth century had started with a wholly Catholic western

Europe, but by 1600 the Reformation had swept through central and northern Europe and Scandinavia. Nation-states with strong monarchies were developing, but with two contending branches of Christianity now competing in Europe, the Reformation produced new sources of European conflict.

The Catholic Reformation

To a Catholic Church hierarchy that was so sure of itself that, in 1512, at the Fifth Lateran Council, there was a declaration that no-one opposed the Church, the Reformation must have come as a surprise. Even though Pope Clement VII (1523–1534) tried to reform the papacy, his efforts were ineffectual. Many in the hierarchy of the Church had a vested interest in the corruption continuing, and Clement, although well intentioned, was under great political pressures.

Reforming popes followed in Paul III (1534–1549) and Paul IV (1559–1565), who inaugurated a series of changes in the way the hierarchy and papal administration worked, removing some of the more obvious corruption. But the Protestant Reformation was sweeping not Rome but Europe, and if the Church was to counter the rising tide of Protestantism, it needed a spiritual renewal, which came when Paul III gave Ignatius of Loyola permission to found and develop the Jesuits in 1540. The Jesuits did a great deal to counter the Protestant Reformation, winning back converts to Catholicism in France, Germany and the Low Countries.

Paul III also inaugurated the Council of Trent in 1545, which met in three sessions between 1545 and 1563 – a meeting that was to clarify Catholic doctrines and practice, by reaffirming the literal fact of transubstantiation, the existence of purgatory and the use of indulgences. The council upheld celibacy for the clergy and bolstered the authority of the pope.

Remarkably for such a time, three delegations of Protestants attended the Council of Trent since there was lingering hope that the Roman Catholic Church might root out its allegiance to its Middle Ages heritage and reform from within along more Protestant lines.

It did not happen. The Roman Catholic Church came out of the Council of Trent with its dogma and practices more defined and distinct from Protestant hopes than ever. The Roman Catholics were strengthened, and had a growing army of spiritual troops (the Jesuits) ready to counter Protestantism. The Protestants were a distinct, competing religion, and before long a series of religious wars erupted throughout Europe.

The Jesuits

In 1540 Pope Paul III approved a new order of Catholic priests, the Jesuits. The order was founded and inspired by Ignatius, a nobleman from Loyola in northern Spain. During his early life as a soldier, he was severely wounded when a cannonball struck his legs, and during his long convalescence Ignatius experienced a remarkable conversion and dedicated his life to the service of God.

He spent ten years in study, then in 1535, with six similarly dedicated friends, took vows of poverty and celibacy before seeking the approval of the pope. As a former soldier, he ran the Jesuits on the basis of complete obedience to the head of the order and to the pope. Jesuits were to propagate the faith of the Roman Catholic Church by whatever means they could – recruits were rigorously screened for unorthodox beliefs, and had to have the dedication and intellectual rigour to stand training lasting more than ten years.

By the time of Ignatius' death in 1556, the order had grown from six to 1,500, and despite its rigorous selection criteria was spreading fast. The Jesuits' activity centred around educating young Catholics, countering the Protestant Reformation and undertaking missionary work abroad.

Jesuits would accompany Spanish and Portuguese explorers when they sailed for America or the Indies, and many of the Catholic communities outside Europe started through Jesuit missionary work. Francis Xavier (1506–1552) earned the name 'the Apostle to the Indies and Japan'. By this time, Jesuits were working in South America, India and Africa, and throughout Protestant northern Europe.

Such was the reputation of the Jesuits that in Reformation England it was specifically mentioned that being Jesuit was a capital offence, and many were martyred. In the seventeenth and eighteenth centuries, Jesuit schools were one of the most significant forces in European education.

The order hit a low point in 1773 when the French and Spanish forced Pope Clement XIV to order its suppression, and barely survived until its restoration in 1814 under Pius VII.

The age of exploration

Europe had emerged from the Middle Ages a more sophisticated society, one that generated a demand for products not available in Europe – silks, jewels and spices. But the overland and sea routes to the Middle East were not open to free trade – the city state of Venice had the monopoly on the Mediterranean sea routes, and the Mongol and Turkish domination of routes through the Middle East to Asia meant that European states who wanted trade with Asia had to find their own ocean route not involving the Mediterranean.

The great seafaring explorers of the sixteenth century came from Spain and Portugal, where shipwrights were building caravels, a new more seaworthy design of ship capable of withstanding ocean voyages. The first expeditions were sponsored by Prince Henry of Portugal. His aim was to find the sources of African gold used by Muslim traders, and to make converts to Christianity. His expeditions to the West African coast found metallic gold and an altogether new form of wealth – the indigenous Africans, who were captured and transported back to Portugal, marking the start of the European slave trade, a trade that increased in importance as America was colonised and the demand for slave labour grew.

In August 1492, Christopher Columbus set sail from Spain on a westward voyage, again with the intention of finding a trade route to 'the Indies'- the spice-rich south-east Asian countries. The idea of a westward sea route was something of a legend, so it was a brave act for Columbus to sail westward into an unknown ocean. He made a landfall in the Bahamas. Modern Europe had discovered America, and in a series of voyages between 1493 and 1504, explored the Bahamas and coasts of Central and South America. England was not far behind, with King Henry VII employing the Italian navigator John Cabot to cross the Atlantic. Cabot made landfall on the shores of North America, starting the English exploration and exploitation of America.

America owes its name to Amerigo Vespucci, an Italian who sailed America's east coast from 1499 to 1502, and called the new continent 'the New World'. The Europeans were still not sure of the extent of America, but it was clearly large and open for settlement and colonial exploitation. By the early sixteenth century they had worked out that the land mass of America lay between them and the Asian countries of the Pacific.

In 1517, Ferdinand Magellan set out from Spain, determined to find 'the Indies' by way of South America. En route, his convoy of five ships called at Argentina, then sailed through the world's most difficult waters into the Pacific Ocean, and on to the Philippines, where Magellan was killed. His surviving ship arrived back in Spain in 1522, having made the first ever voyage around the world.

By the early 1520s, the Spanish began to explore the interior of Central and South America, taking with them Catholic priests, firearms, horses and western diseases. This was a potent mix – the South American Indians had no defence against either the firearms or diseases such as smallpox, and the Spaniards began a rapid conquest of Central and South America. The missionaries went with them, and conquest and conversion went hand in hand. Missionaries began to accompany Spanish explorers on their voyages – it was clearly a missionary duty to convert heathens to the faith of Rome and the Roman Catholic Church had lost much of its European territory to the Protestant Reformation. Missionary zeal in accompanying the explorers allowed new territory to be claimed, and the missionaries' behaviour often acted as a civilising influence on the explorers and conquerors from Spain and France. They did not, however, prevent the destruction of many Central and South American civilisations at the hands of the Conquistadors.

By 1540, the Spaniards had crossed into North America and settled some parts of the south, but North America was principally explored and settled by English explorers, with the French establishing a presence in modern-day Canada, and although by 1600 the Spaniards had tried to claim all of America as their sovereign territory, the Protestant English were well established along its fertile, productive eastern coast. America, the New World, was open to anyone brave enough to risk a voyage across the stormy North Atlantic.

Western Europeans had colonised the Americas, established colonies in Africa and were now able to sail into the Pacific Ocean, to the Indies and the Orient – and where the explorers sailed, the Roman Catholic missionaries sailed with them. The Protestant Reformation failed to make progress in Spain and Portugal, so when these nations became the leading maritime explorers it was Catholicism that followed in their wake and was, as a result, spread around the globe in the sixteenth and seventeenth centuries.

Puritans and the Pilgrim Fathers

The Reformation in England did not produce a uniform kind of Protestantism, and for one group Queen Elizabeth's brand of Protestantism was too moderate. To the Puritans (as they became known) the Church of England still retained too many of the trappings of Catholicism. Their objections included the Church of England clergy still using vestments, the continued existence of bishops, and the congregation kneeling for communion. The Puritans worked first within, then outside the Church of England to produce a more austere form of English Protestant Christianity, more like that practised by John Calvin in Switzerland.

Both Queen Elizabeth and her successor King James refused the Puritans' demands, and the Puritans finally broke with the Church of England, setting up their rival congregations in Norwich. England at the time was a place where religious dissent was not tolerated, and the Puritans suffered such persecution that many fled to the Netherlands, where they were allowed freedom of worship. In 1620 Puritans led by the English exile John Robinson sailed from Leiden in Holland in the *Mayflower*, made a landfall at Plymouth, then sailed for America where they founded a Puritan colony in New England.

Humanism and the Renaissance

One of the important strands of European history to 1400 was the tension between the Church leaders in Rome and nations – the pope repeatedly insisted that the Church was a supreme body, and often used secular alliances or the Church's own powers to crush dissent.

Yet by the late 1300s, a new school of thought was developing that ran counter to much Church teaching – humanism. Humanist artists and scholars looked more to human achievements than the Church for their inspiration, and through rediscovering and studying the texts and histories of ancient Greece and Rome they hoped to bring Europe out of the cultural mire of the Middle Ages into a newer, more progressive cultural and artistic climate.

Humanists were not anti-religious, but felt that a training in classical subjects such as rhetoric, grammar, poetry and history would make educated Christians more complete. They were responsible for moving knowledge out of the monasteries and into the streets, where a recovering European society was once again ready to learn.

The plague

Disease is one of the most significant but under-recognised factors in human history, and in the Middle Ages and Renaissance Europe bubonic plague cut a swathe across the continent.

Bubonic plague is caused by a bacterium, *Yrsinia pestis*. It spreads when a flea sucks blood from an infected rat, then feeds on a human, infecting them in turn. Symptoms can develop almost immediately, or the infected person can carry the infection for two month before the disease erupts.

An infected person would suffer swellings of the lymph glands in the neck, armpit and groin (these 'buboes' were the first sign that a person was infected) and go on to develop aches throughout the body and high fever. In the Middle Ages and the Renaissance there was no cure, and the disease had a high mortality rate. An infected person could be dead within five days.

The social conditions of the Middle Ages and the Renaissance caused perfect breeding grounds for plague. Trading ships brought plague-carrying rats from the eastern Mediterranean, and when they landed, the rats would move into the densely packed ports, allowing infected fleas to jump on to human hosts to feed, and so infect them. In Europe from 1300–1500, the plague killed so rapidly that infected areas suffered a near breakdown of society – the dead were no longer buried in a Christian fashion, but dumped into mass burial pits.

In the Old Testament book of Samuel, a plague-like disease is reported in the city of Ashdod, and in 542 the Byzantine capital Constantinople was struck by an epidemic which killed half of the population. By 1400, the European epidemic had killed an estimated 40 million people throughout Europe.

In England, a house where an infected person was identified was marked with a cross on the door, and often an appeal for God to have mercy on all within. Plague-free towns and villages put themselves into quarantine, and throughout this period in Europe many settlements were abandoned, for when plague struck a village the population was either wiped out or so reduced that they fled.

Humanist thinking was crucial to the Renaissance, and informed both Catholic and Protestant Christians: Desiderius Erasmus, a Dutch humanist, was credited with having been a strong influence on Luther and the early Protestants. Thomas More, Chancellor to the English King Henry VIII, was both a vigorous humanist and a devout Roman Catholic – he opposed Henry's actions in setting up the Church of England and was beheaded in 1535.

The nobility of Europe were impressed with humanist thinking, and it became fashionable to give children a humanist education. Humanism allowed education to spread, giving the educated classes access to manuscripts and texts, and began a habit of intellectual criticism and debate about principles beyond Church teaching. Humanism spread beyond the borders of Italy into Germany, France and the Low Countries, and in many respects primed European minds for the Reformation.

More immediately, however, humanist thinking informed the Renaissance, a period of cultural revolution that began in Italy in the fourteenth century and spread through western Europe throughout the fifteenth and sixteenth centuries. 'Renaissance' is derived from the Latin for rebirth, and this was how Renaissance scholars and artists saw themselves – the classical Greek and Roman civilisations had been a great era, the Middle Ages a time of darkness, ignorance and brutality, and the Renaissance would bring a rebirth of the Roman and Greek virtues through humanistic study and applying the classical principles to arts, architecture and society.

Renaissance artists such as Leonardo da Vinci, Botticelli and Raphael moved art from exclusively religious imagery to portraying the human form, a trend mirrored in the Renaissance sculptures of Donatello and Michelangelo.

Architecture, too, changed in the Renaissance. Buildings were designed along Roman and Greek lines, moving away from the Gothic complexity of the Middle Ages – St Peter's Basilica in Rome was commissioned and designed as a Renaissance project.

As the Renaissance spread from Italy, one of its effects was a rise in interest in the nation-state, and the establishment of strong monarchies in France, Spain and England coincides with humanistic thought and the Renaissance. Intellectually, the period instituted a spirit of inquiry in western society that led to the growth in science in the eighteenth and nineteenth centuries, and a sense of human rather than exclusively religious control over society and human endeavour.

The Inquisitions

There were three distinct periods of Inquisition activity.:

1.   the mediaeval period, founded by Gregory IX (1227–1241) in the fourth year of his papacy.
2.   the Roman Inquisition, established in 1452 by Pope Paul III (1534–1549);
3.   the infamous Spanish Inquisition, started in 1478 by Pope Sixtus IV (1471–1484).

The Catholic Church was continuously beset by heretics, groups who differed in their interpretation of the Scriptures and rejected outright papal authority. From the earliest days of the Church in Rome, the earliest Christians fought theological battles with Gnostics, and by the eleventh century two major new heresies were threatening the Church's grip on Europe – the Waldensian heresy and the widespread, powerful Cathar heresy. Furthermore, the Church was concerned at the rise of Islam, and the continuing, stubborn presence of Jews throughout Europe.

The Inquisition was first established in 1231 to actively seek out and redeem or punish heretics. A kind of travelling religious court, the mediæval Inquisition would arrive in an area and start taking evidence from locals, priests and laity alike, on those suspected of heresy. A suspected heretic would be called before the inquisitor (a priest), and questioned. Witnesses to the suspect's heresy could be produced, and the suspect frequently did not know the charges being brought.

The Inquisition worsened when Pope Innocent IV (1352–1362) started his reign by authorising the use of torture to extract confessions from suspected heretics. The Inquisition's torturers were forbidden to draw blood in their attempts to persuade suspected heretics to confess their own heresies or to reveal the names of fellow heretics, but nonetheless became adept at forcing confessions from suspects.

Once a confession or guilty verdict had been obtained, the penalties could range from a penance of prayer through to imprisonment and forfeiting of property. People who refused to abandon their heretical ways or who had relapsed following absolution by the Inquisition were handed over to the secular authorities to be put to death in a ceremony called (in the Spanish Inquisition) the Auto da Fé.

At the Auto da Fé, a grand outdoor Mass was held where the

penitent heretics were publicly sentenced. The ones condemned to death had their heads shaved before being paraded before the congregation dressed in a shift with devils painted on it. Tied to a stake surrounded by firewood, they would be given a last chance to repent. If they finally repented of their heresy, they would be garrotted before the pyre was lit. Unrepentant heretics were burned alive.

The Spanish Inquisition was perhaps the most bloody. Its chief inquisitor was a Dominican monk, Tomas de Torquemada, whose use of torture and intimidation in finding heretics allowed him to send about 2,000 to the stake. A man could be denounced for failing to eat pork, or by a jealous business rival. The Spanish Inquisition set up outposts in the Spanish colonies of Peru and Mexico. Despite attempts by Joseph Bonaparte in 1808 to abolish the Inquisition, it persisted in Spain until 1834.

The Roman Inquisition was less vicious than its Spanish cousin, and its activity was limited to Italy, where Protestantism was seen as a growing threat. However, Protestantism failed to make any headway in Italy, and the Roman Inquisition faded as it had little Protestant heresy to seek out.

The Office of the Inquisition, however, remained as an instrument of papal authority, and its responsibility was ensuring the purity of the Catholic faith. It turned from an external religious police force to an internal one, and in 1908 Pope Pius X (1903–1914) sensibly dropped the word 'Inquisition' from the title of the office. Its successor, still concerned with the purity of the faith is called the Office of the Congregation for the Doctrine of the Faith.

THE POPES
1404–1605

Innocent VII (Cosma Migliorati)

Sulmona; 17 October 1404 to 6 November 1406

To resolve the Schism, the eight cardinals who met to select a successor to Boniface IX each took an oath that, if elected, they would abdicate if the anti-pope Benedict XIII would do the same. Once Cosma Migliorati, the Cardinal bishop of Bologna, had been elected, he reneged on his pre-election oath. He refused Benedict's request for a meeting. There was social and political upheaval in Rome, worsened by Innocent handing over responsibility to his nephew, Ludovico Migliorati. His violent methods – the murder of the city's leaders – led to a mob forcing Innocent and his court out of the city to Viterbo. He died of a stroke a few months later after returning to Rome.

Gregory XII (Angelo Correr)

Venice; 30 November 1406 to 4 July 1415

An eighty-year-old Venetian, Angelo Correr agreed, as all in the conclave did, to resign after election, with the anti-pope Benedict (see Innocent VII) agreeing to do the same, so that a solution to the Schism could be found. Gregory at first agreed but difficulties arose and then Benedict refused to step down. Gregory, contrary to an agreement, created four new cardinals (two of whom were his nephews); this caused a revolt among his cardinals. They summoned a Council at Pisa (1409) but neither Gregory nor Benedict would attend. The Council deposed both and elected a Franciscan as Alexander V. The scandal of three 'popes' was too much to bear and the Council of Constance (1414–1418), which Gregory recognised, convinced him to abdicate, in the interests of the Church; he was named Cardinal Bishop of Porto, where he died in 1417.

Martin V (Oddone Colonna)

Rome; 11 November 1417 to 23 February 1431

Oddone Colonna, who had helped to organise the Council of Pisa (see Gregory XII) was, at election, the first universally recognised pope for thirty-nine years. All other rivals had removed themselves or been deposed. Martin was a member of the powerful Colonna family, on whom he lavished lands and gifts. He reasserted papal authority, regaining, after a bloody struggle, control of the Papal States. He made overtures to the Eastern Church to seek reunion, but was rebuffed. Martin forcibly reaffirmed the authority of the papacy over any and every Council. Returning to Rome, he engaged in a large-scale restoration programme, particularly of St Peter's Basilica and the Lateran palace. Twice (in 1422 and 1429) he denounced anti-Semitic preaching. Martin summoned the Council of Basle but died before it could meet.

Eugene IV (Gabriele Condulmer)

Venice; 3 March 1431 to 23 February 1447

The reign of Eugene IV is notable for the brief reunion of the Western and Eastern Churches, a union sought by the Emperor John VIII Paleaologus, fearful of a Turkish invasion. Eugene was a nephew of Pope Gregory XI and he was elected because the cardinals thought he was sympathetic to Conciliarism. This was put to the test at the Council of Basle (1431–1449); Eugene opposed the cardinals there, who set about electing an anti-pope, Felix V. Eugene would not endorse the acts of the Council; he won political support and defeated Conciliarism by patiently winning the support of the majority of the cardinals. However, he made enemies of the Colonna family by taking back the lands given them by Martin V; they sought their revenge by stirring up armed revolt in the Papal States and Rome.

Nicholas V (Tommaso Parentucelli)

Sarzana; 6 March 1447 to 24 March 1455

Regarded as the first of the Renaissance popes, Nicholas V had been a papal legate and was Cardinal Bishop of Bologna at his election. Firmly upholding papal supremacy he won support from the new German king, Frederick III (the last Holy Roman emperor to be crowned in Rome). He brought to an end the stubborn resistance of the Basle rump council and accepted the submission of the anti-pope (see Eugene IV). An intellectual, he was most comfortable with scholars, artists and humanists. By his numerous bequests he founded the Vatican Library and supported artists like Fra Angelico. Despite this he was a genuinely humble pontiff, deeply disturbed by dissension, particularly by an assassination plot (1453) and the fall of Constantinople to the Ottoman Turks in 1453. Disappointed at the indifference of Western Christians, he died on 24 March 1455.

Callistus III (Alfonso Borgia)

Valencia; 8 April 1455 to 6 August 1458

The first of the Spanish Borgia popes, Alfonso had had an undistinguished ecclesiastical career and was considered a surprise choice. Although personally austere, he generously advanced the Borgia family's fortunes. His nepotism, e.g. giving preferment to his nephew, Rodrigo Borgia, the future Alexander VI caused much unrest. The other noteworthy occurrence was the Crusade that he summoned against the Turks. This had little success beyond capturing some Aegean islands and liberating Belgrade (1457). The heavy taxation to pay for this adventure caused widespread resentment. On his deathbed Callistus learnt that Rome had risen in insurrection and driven out all Spanish family members and supporters. Callistus died on the Feast of the Transfiguration, which he had introduced.

Pius II (Enea Silvio Piccolomini)

Siena; 19 August 1458 to 14 August 1464

Enea Silvio Piccolomini (born 1405), of an Italian aristocratic family, served three popes, and one anti-pope, before he was made a cardinal, and then pope in 1458. He had established a reputation as a humanist, a scholar, poet and astute politician. As pope he was driven by the vision of a united Christendom, which urged him to promote a Crusade against the Turks. He met with little interest and response from the European monarchs, but took the cross himself in June 1464; he died shortly afterwards, at Ancona, Italy, awaiting an armada of ships which never arrived.

Paul II (Pietro Barbo)

Venice; 19 Aug. 1464 to 26 July 1471

Destined for a career in business Pietro Barbo joined the clergy when his uncle became Pope Eugene IV. He rose rapidly and became a cardinal in 1440 at the age of twenty-two. Reputedly very vain, Pietro wanted to take the name Formosus (the Greek for 'handsome') but was dissuaded. He resisted the cardinals attempts to make his papal authority subject to the scrutiny of Councils. Totally opposed to any encouragement of art or literature from pagan sources, he however amassed vast collections of valuable jewels and objets d'art. He supported the Renaissance with the injection of large sums of money. The menace to Eastern Europe of the Ottoman Turks encouraged Paul to call the Christian nations to support a Crusade; but to no avail. He died suddenly of a stroke, much abused by the biased reporting of his enemies.

Sixtus IV (Francesco della Rovere)

Savona; 9 August 1471 to 12 August 1484

A renowned preacher and theologian, Francesco della Rovere was Master General of the Franciscan Order when elected. His election effected a remarkable

transformation from humble friar to one of the most worldly of pontiffs. He embarked upon an opulent lifestyle. Sixtus transformed Rome with lavish building projects and built the famed Sistine Chapel. He was shameless in his nepotism, elevating six nephews to the rank of cardinal. Two of these involved him in a scandalous and murderous attack on the Medici family of Florence, which led to the execution of his nephew, Cardinal Riario della Rovere, and a pointless war with first Florence and then Venice. Sixtus fruitlessly called for a Crusade against the Ottoman Turks. He launched the Spanish Inquisition, appointing the infamous Tomas de Torquemada as Grand Inquisitor. Sixtus also began the practice of selling plenary indulgences for cash to fund his building projects. His family members were so hated, at his death, that the mob, encouraged by the Orsini and Colonna families, looted their homes.

Innocent VIII (Giovanni Battista Cibo)

Genoa; 29 August 1484 to 25 July 1492

Two main factions struggled to secure the papacy for their candidate, one supporting Cardinal Giuliano della Rovere (the future Julius II) and the other Cardinal Rodrigo Borgia (the future Alexander VI); Giovanni Cibo was the compromise choice. He had been Bishop of Savona (1467) and cardinal under Sixtus. Innocent, who was charming but weak, continued the profligate lifestyle of his predecessor, but was more scandalous due to his acknowledged immoral background (he had several illegitimate children). Innocent was forever trying to raise money to finance his lifestyle; on one occasion he pawned the papal tiara to a Roman merchant! His foreign policies were totally directed by della Rovere, who had secured the See for him. For a large annual sum he gave sanctuary to the brother of Sultan Bayezid of the Ottoman Turks. His ineffectual reign caused a decline in control over the Papal States.

Alexander VI (Rodrigo Borgia)

Valencia; 11 August 1492 to 18 August 1503

Nephew of Pope Callistus III, Rodrigo became a cardinal at twenty-five and subsequently used his considerable abilities in the service of four popes, during which he amassed great wealth for himself through the accumulation of bishoprics and other benefices. He was vice chancellor of the Holy See for thirty-five years, while he lived an immoral life, fathering six sons and three daughters by several women. Rodrigo virtually 'bought' the long-desired papacy by the use of massive bribes. The reign had a promising beginning with civil order restored in Rome and reform of the Curia proposed, as well as a crusade, against the Ottomans. However Alexander's fondness for extravagant dissipation and the advancement of his family soon preoccupied him. His son Cesare became a cardinal at eighteen, and his eldest son, Juan, destined for the throne of Naples, was murdered, probably by Cesare. Charles VIII, a former friend, invaded Italy and threatened to have Alexander deposed. Another threat was the prophetic preaching of the Dominican friar, Savonarola (1452–1498); the Florentines disposed of him by trial, torture and execution. Alexander declared 1500 a Holy Year and instituted the idea of the 'Holy Door' in St Peter's. The offerings from the Holy Year pilgrims were fed straight into his son Cesare's violent and bloody military campaigns in the Papal States. His sudden death has been attributed to poisoning, but it may have been malaria. His many enemies among the powerful cardinals, encouraged slanderous reports of orgies, incest. etc. These exaggerations had foundation in a reign which had been arrogant, scandalous and shocking. The Holy Year pilgrims went home with disillusioned stories of the corruption rampant in the Holy City.

Pius III (Francesco Todeschini-Piccolomini)

Siena; 28 September 1503 to 18 October 1503

A man of acknowledged integrity, Todeschini-Piccolomini, after a glittering career as Archbishop of

Siena, cardinal (from the age of twenty-one) and Papal legate, seemed just the ideal candidate (although a compromise one). He took his name in memory of his uncle, Pius II, who had elevated him to cardinal. Eager to make the necessary Church reform Pius sought to call a General Council, but the sixty-four-year-old's failing health gave out; he died ten days after his coronation.

Julius II (Giulano della Rovere)

Savona; 31 October 1503 to 21 February 1513

Famed for two things, his warrior leadership of long wars and his patronage of some of the greatest artists and architects of the Renaissance, Cardinal della Rovere eventually became pope by bribery. Nephew of Sixtus IV and cardinal from the age of eighteen, he had planned for many years to be pope. Hated by Alexander VI, della Rovere had taken refuge during his reign with Charles VIII in France. Soon after election, Julius personally led his troops, in full armour, to regain control of the papal lands, lost under previous popes. He drove Cesare's armies (see Alexander VI) out of Italy and fought with, and then against the French; states and cities were returned to papal control. Julius founded the Holy League to defend the papacy. A great patron of the arts, he gave commissions to Michelangelo (the decoration of the Sistine Chapel), Bramante (the design of the new St Peter's) and Raphael (frescoes in the papal apartments). For funds Julius arranged for a massive sale of indulgences. He opened the Fifth Lateran Council (1512–1517) but died before it achieved anything of note. Nicknamed 'the Terrible' because of his temper and eagerness for war, his memory was also respected by Romans for his patronage of the Arts and the way he had liberated Italy from foreign domination.

Leo X (Giovanni de'Medici)

Florence; 9 March 1513 to 1 December 1521

Second son of Lorenzo de'Medici, the Magnificent, Giovanni grew up amid the splendour of the Medici courts. A cardinal at thirteen years of age, after a remarkable humanist education he travelled widely and eventually came into the service of Julius II. Elected at the age of thirty-seven, he first had to be ordained a priest, as he was still only a deacon. An extravagant sum was spent on the coronation celebrations and this set the tone for the pontificate. Personally moral and generous, Leo threw himself into a life of sumptuous living, a style which was emulated by the Roman cardinals. Artists and writers flocked to Rome seeking patronage. Leo was forced to take out massive loans and repaid these with the sale of indulgences and offices (in 1517 thirty new cardinals were created). A discovered assassination plot by a group of cardinals netted huge sums in ransom money. The rise of Martin Luther and his reform movement did not receive serious attention (Leo excommunicated the Augustinian friar in 1520) apart from declaring him a heretic. Leo awarded Henry VIII of England the title 'Defender of the Faith' for defending the Sacraments against Luther Vacillating in his foreign policy, he first formed an alliance with France, then an anti-French alliance with Germany. His sudden death was considered suspicious, but the symptoms could indicate malaria.

Hadrian VI (Adrian Florensz)

Utrecht; 9 January 1522 to 14 September 1523

A carpenter's son from the Netherlands and former tutor to the Emperor Charles V was a surprise choice but solved the problem for a divided conclave. The Romans were aghast at the appointment of an austere and devout Northerner; Charles V thought he could manipulate him and Francis I of France was fearful. Hadrian, with reforming zeal, tried to sweep away the customary papal favours, reduce the inflated staffing of the papal court and Curia, and stop commissions to artists, etc. These reforms, some too sweeping, were met by the hostility of the Curia. Trying to remain neutral between Germany and France, Hadrian's call for a Crusade against the Ottoman Turks fell on deaf ears. Although he understood the seriousness of Luther's reform movement, he responded inappropriately with condemnations and threats. Disappointed and disillusioned, Hadrian became ill and died; his passing was celebrated in the streets of Rome.

Clement VII (Giulio de' Medici)

Florence; 19 November 1523 to 25 September 1534

From the Medici family of Florence, Giulio was the illegitimate grandson of the famous Lorenzo the Magnificent. He rose through clerical circles to become the Archbishop of Florence and cardinal in 1513. Popular and respected as a shrewd advisor to the papacy, on election he soon proved to be unequal to the demands of the times. Clement was weak and vacillating; he became caught up in the ambitious struggles of the emperor, Charles V, and Francis I of France. When Rome was sacked in 1527, Clement fled for his life to the Castel Sant'Angelo; after surrendering to Charles V, he was humiliated with six months of imprisonment. At this time Henry VIII of England asked for an annulment of his marriage to Catherine of Aragon. Clement vacillated but finally, in 1533, declared Henry's marriage valid. Henry's Act of Supremacy, declaring the monarch of England to be the head of the English Church, followed. Clement's indecisiveness allowed the Protestant movement to sweep Europe. Very much a Renaissance pope, distracted by the luxuries of the papal court and with a love of the arts, Clement was personally of irreproachable character.

Paul III (Alessandro Farnese)

Rome; 13 October 1534 to 10 November 1549

Alessandro Farnese, from a Roman noble family, was the oldest and most experienced of the cardinals, and

known to be Clement VII's choice as his successor. He had been advanced in papal service by Pope Alexander VI, whose mistress was Alessandro's sister. Papal treasurer and cardinal (but not priest)in the Renaissance style before election, he had a mistress and four children. Paul's first cardinals were his two teenage grandsons and his nepotism was a byword. He lived in style and delighted the Romans with carnivals and street spectacles. Politically he was adroit, keeping a balance between France and Germany. He felt compelled to excommunicate Henry VIII of England over his divorce from Catherine of Aragon. Paul gave formal recognition to the Society of Jesus (the Jesuits). Recognising the danger of the Protestant Reformation he summoned a General Council, the Council of Trent (1545–1563). A patron of the arts, he gave commissions to Michelangelo and directed the continued construction of the new St Peter's. He died aged eighty-one.

Julius III (Giovanni Maia Ciocchi del Monte)

Rome; 7 February 1550 to 23 March 1555

Co-president and papal legate at the opening of the Council of Trent, Cardinal del Monte was a compromise candidate at the contentious conclave that elected him. While typically a Renaissance pope – he made Michelangelo principal architect of the new St Peter's – Julius was devoted to reform and his first act was to order the Council to reassemble; he was forced, for political reasons to suspend the sixteenth session. In 1553, when Mary Tudor became queen, he welcomed England back to the Church. Julius gave support to the Jesuits and founded the Collegium Germanicum to train priests to combat Protestantism in Germany. His reign was not without scandal when Julius took a young man, Innocenzo, from the streets into his household and made him a cardinal.

Marcellus II (Marcellus Servini)

Montepulciano; 9 April 1555 to 1 May 1555

Marcellus Servini had been tutor to Pope Paul III's nephew, and after five years he was raised to the cardinalate. Retaining his baptismal name, (with Hadrian VI, one of only two modern popes, who have done so), Marcellus was co-president of the Council of Trent and his reign began with high hopes for the reform movement. He was already ill when elected and his pontificate lasted only twenty-two days.

Paul IV (Giovanni Pietro Carafa)

Naples; 23 May 1555 to 18 August 1559

Due to the patronage of his uncle, Cardinal Oliviero, Giovanni rose swiftly through the ranks of the clergy to be cardinal (1536) and head of the Inquisition (1542); this post suited his rigid and austere life and he was known to be ruthless, fired by a merciless zeal. After election Pius was devoted to reform, but showed little confidence in the Council of Trent (suspended in 1552). No one was safe as all conduct was scrutinised; the respected Cardinal Morone was unjustly imprisoned for heresy. An Index of forbidden books was published. His reign was not free from nepotism: his nephew, Carlo Carafa, was raised to the cardinalate; he and other family members brought disgrace to the Carafa name and Paul IV stripped them of their privileges. At his death there was general rejoicing and the headquarters of the Inquisition were stormed and prisoners released.

Pius IV (Giovanni Angelo de'Medici)

Milan; 25th December 1559 to 9th December 1565

Giovanni de'Medici (not related to the famous Medici family of Florence) was a compromise candidate as the conclave was locked in indecision for four months. He immediately reversed all the policies of Paul IV and released Cardinal Morone. The Inquisition was reined in and the Index revised. He was a great favourite with the Romans, who warmed to his easy, affable ways. Pius's most noteworthy achievement was the reconvening of the Council of Trent. With Cardinal Morone's help he saw it through to its conclusion and ensured that its decrees were adopted. In this he had the invaluable assistance of his nephew and secretary, the saintly Cardinal Charles Borromeo.

Pius V, St (Michele Ghislieri)

Bosco; Italy; 7 January 1566 to 1 May 1572

Of humble origins, before his election Michele Ghislieri had been a Dominican inquisitor (1551) and later the Grand Inquisitor and Bishop of Nepi (1556). Severe and ascetic himself, he inaugurated, as pope, one of the most austere periods of the Catholic Church. He set about implementing in full the decisions of the Council of Trent. The Inquisition was given free rein, so that by the time of his death Protestantism had been totally eliminated from Italy. In politics Pius V was less successful. His excommunication of Elizabeth I of England alienated the English and triggered a vicious persecution of English Catholics. He quarrelled with Philip II of Spain, but successfully backed a Catholic league against the Turks, resulting in a famous victory at the Battle of Lepanto. His successors reaped the harvest of much of his work.

Gregory XIII (Ugo Boncampagni)

Bologna; 13 May 1572 to 10 April 1585

Son of a merchant of Bologna, Ugo Boncampagni received a good education and fathered a son. Undergoing a personal renewal he was ordained priest and then rose rapidly in the Church. He was created a cardinal by Pius IV and made papal legate to Spain. Following his election Gregory was determined to implement the decrees of the Council of Trent. He founded many seminaries, promoted education and encouraged missionary endeavours in the East. His reform of the calendar, using the more precise work of his astronomers, proclaimed in the encyclical *Inter Gravissimas* (1582), corrected the errors in the Julian Calendar (46 BC). Unfortunately the Papal States during this reign fell into disorder.

Sixtus V (Felice Peretti)

Grottamare; 24 April 1585 to 27 August 1590

A Franciscan from a humble background and renowned for his preaching, Felice Peretti, became head of the Inquisition in Venice and eventually procurator general of his Order and cardinal. His short five-year reign was a whirlwind of activity. Dedicated to restoring the Papal States, he earned the nickname 'the Iron Pope' by waging war and executing thousands of brigands who terrorised the people. With the same energy he enforced the decrees of the Council of Trent, sorted out papal finances, remodelled the Curia into the modern fifteen congregations, limited the number of cardinals to seventy; finished St Peter's Basilica and beautified Rome with wider streets, etc. Abroad he gave assistance to the Catholic population of Poland and gave support to the Spanish Armada as it set out for England. At his death the result of his wide-ranging activities was a populace grateful for a safer Italy and Rome and the creation of new jobs.

Urban VII (Giovanni Battista Castagna)

Rome; 15 September 1590 to 27 September 1590

Cardinal Castagna was the Inquisitor General of the Church and one of the most powerful men in Rome at the death of Sixtus V. He contracted malaria the day following his election and died before he could be crowned.

Gregory XIV (Niccolo Sfondrati)

Cremona; 5 December 1590 to 16 October 1591

Bishop of Cremona from the age of twenty-five, Niccolo Sfondrati took part in the Council of Trent and was elevated to the cardinalate by Pope Pius IV. A pious man, but an invalid at his election, his only achievement as pope was to bring help to the people of Rome during a famine and a plague.

Innocent IX (Giovanni Antonio Fachinetti)

Bologna; 29 October 1591 to 30 December 1591

While papal nuncio to Venice (1566–1572) Giovanni Fachinetti helped to negotiate the League that won the significant triumph of the Battle of Lepanto (1571). Patriarch of Jerusalem and later cardinal (1583), he was the favourite candidate to follow Gregory XIV. But he was eighty-one and in bad health; nothing of significance was achieved in his two months as pontiff.

Clement VIII (Ippolito Aldobrandini)

Florence; 30 January 1592 to 3 March 1605

Owing his preferment into papal service to St Pius V, after a long and distinguished career Cardinal Ippolito Aldobrandini was the leading candidate in the conclave that followed the death of Innocent IX. Known for his piety, Clement was an indefatigable reformer in the Counter-Reformation mould. He was a close friend of Philip Neri (later canonised in 1622) and he promoted the work of Francis de Sales (canonised in 1665) whom he appointed Bishop of Geneva; he elevated Robert Bellarmine to cardinal (canonised in 1930). A brilliant administrator, Clement energetically threw himself into every aspect of papal affairs. On the darker side he used the Inquisition to condemn and execute the philosopher Giordano Bruno, and raised nephews as young as fourteen, to the cardinalate. At his death he left a Church that was renewed, strong and confident.

1600–1700
Europe at War and
the growth of colonialism

Timeline 1600–1700

1601 Matteo Ricci, a Jesuit Missionary, travels to Peking to evangelise in China.

1611 The authorised King James Bible, printed in English, is published in London.

1614 Christianity is ruled illegal in Japan.

1618 Protestant revolts in Catholic Bohemia spark the Thirty Years War.

1620 *The Mayflower* carries Puritans from Holland and England to America.

1626 A Christian Church is established in Tibet.

1633 The Inquisition forces Galileo to recant his theory of the planets.

1637 Christianity persecuted to extinction in Japan.

1647 George Fox begins preaching, and establishes the Quakers.

1660 James II becomes King of England, and the Anglican faith is re-established.

1671 An Arabic translation of the Bible is published in Rome.

1682 William Penn, an American settler, founds Pennsylvania, intending it to be a place of religious tolerance.

1683 The siege of Vienna ends the Muslim Turkish invasion of Europe.

1685 Protestants are exiled from France by Louis XIV.

1689 Christian worship allowed in China.

1698 The Society for the Propagation of Christian Knowledge is founded in London.

Introduction

The 1600s saw a marked divide in European fortunes. Spain, England, the Netherlands and France had strong distinct national identities and colonial ambitions. They were confident seafaring nations which sent explorers to reinforce their existing colonies and to find new lands for exploration and exploitation. The urge to explore and colonise had several driving factors: trade was becoming increasingly important as the western European economy became more dynamic and sophisticated. Successful markets required a steady supply of commodities, more than Europe alone could furnish, so founding colonies in places such as America was a means of establishing supplies of raw materials for the future. All the exploring nations were keen to establish sources of spices, gems and precious metals, and cloths for trade at home. They were also keen to deny rivals territory and influence – Protestant England did not want Roman Catholic Spanish colonists moving north from Central America into North America.

In Europe the new discipline of experimental science emerged. Universities were growing in number, and secular philosophy was developing, leading to the Age of Reason, where a growing number of philosophers attacked the organised Church in general and the Roman Catholic Church especially. Age of Reason thinking held that organised religion favoured obedience to Church authority over the freedom of individuals, and that the obedience Catholic clergy gave to Rome weakened national sovereignty. The Age of Reason is held to be the beginning of modern philosophy.

The Reformation countries, notably Britain and the Netherlands, incubated the early pioneers in science, and in art and culture Baroque art and music dominated Europe, with Rome becoming the cultural and artistic capital of the world – a tribute to the cultural patronage still wielded by the Church.

But while science and art flourished, so did war: the seventeenth century was a time of conflict in Western Europe, a time of shifting allegiances as nations competed for territory, security and influence. The Germanic and Baltic states became embroiled in the Thirty Years War, a tragic and bloody conflict that ran from 1618 to 1648 and effectively kept the region out of the general scientific, social and economic advances that were driving an increasingly prosperous western European society. The Thirty Years War began as a conflict between Bohemian Protestants and Roman Catholics, but soon became a general war fought for the more usual warlike aims of territory and influence.

While Roman Catholicism and Protestantism struggled for supremacy in Europe, the Spaniards consolidated their grip on Central and South America, and the Franciscan and Jesuit missionaries who went with the Spanish explorers were extremely successful in seeding Roman Catholicism throughout the native South American Indian population. The Spaniards were rapacious conquerors, stripping treasure from native American kingdoms and taking American Indians into slavery. The missionaries were often the sole advocates for proper treatment of conquered native populations, and in this they received the support of Pope Gregory XV.

Catholicism had established a foothold in Japan, but in 1622 the Tokugawa dynasty came to power and instituted a period of Japanese isolationism. Christian missionaries were bloodily massacred and all Europeans either killed or evicted. The Japanese allowed only the Dutch to maintain a small trading post in the Japanese islands. Russian explorers struck eastwards into Siberia and Alaska, and the resurgent explorers from the prosperous Netherlands founded colonies in the East Indies, establishing a presence in Indonesia from where they explored the Pacific Ocean. Dutch navigators were the first Europeans to discover Australia, Tasmania and New Zealand, but made little headway in colonising any of these new lands.

The seventeenth century laid the foundations of the modern world in science, art, philosophy, exploration and commerce, and marked a significant diminution of the influence of the papacy in Europe. The Reformation had already removed the new Protestant countries from papal influence, and when the Thirty Years War ended with the Treaty of Westphalia in 1648, the Treaty stated that a nation's ruler could specify the religion of the kingdom. This chimed with the mood of growing European nationalism and the tendency of rulers to claim absolute power within their own borders.

1600s – Europe at war

The Reformation had threatened to tear Europe apart, but in 1555 the Roman Catholic and Lutheran factions in the Holy Roman Empire (which at the time comprised what we now know as Germany, Austria, northern Italy and the Czech Republic) agreed a truce with the Treaty of Augsburg, in which Lutherans had their right to worship accepted.

However, in subsequent years both Catholic and Protestant factions had broken the peace, and Europe had a growing number of Calvinist Protestants who began to agitate to have their rights to worship guaranteed in law.

The atmosphere in the Holy Roman Empire was already volatile when in 1618 a religious conflict sparked the Thirty Years War. The spark was in Bohemia (now the Czech Republic) where the Catholic archbishop ordered the destruction of a Protestant church. The anguished Protestants – who had received promises of religious freedom from their Catholic king, Ferdinand II – appealed to the Holy Roman Emperor Matthias, who sided with his Catholic archbishop and upheld the order to demolish the church.

The Bohemian Protestants revolted, and in a famous incident stormed Hradcany Castle and threw two Catholic councillors (and a loyal secretary who tried to rescue his employer) out of the castle windows. As one, Councillor Martiniz, was thrown, he was reported to have cried, 'Jesus, Mary, save me!' Whether by intervention or coincidence, there was a dung-heap in the moat below, and all three survived. The incident became famous as the Defenestration of Prague, and was credited with lighting the fuse of the Thirty Years War.

The Bohemian Protestants then deposed King Ferdinand and replaced him with Frederick, a German Protestant. In 1619, the deposed Ferdinand was elected Holy Roman Emperor, and from this position of power he recruited a large Catholic army and smashed the Protestant Bohemians at the Battle of White Mountain in 1620. Bohemia was annexed, and Catholicism enforced as the state religion.

Ferdinand's behaviour unnerved the Protestant rulers of northern Europe, and in 1625 King Christian IV of Denmark brought an army to northern Germany to curb Ferdinand's power. It was an ill-fated expedition, and over the following four years Frederick's army of soldiers from Catholic Germany supported by mercenary adventurers inflicted a series of defeats on the invading Danish armies. The Danes retreated from Saxony in 1629. Frederick was not magnanimous in victory – he signed the Edict of Restitution, which seized Protestant Church possessions and made them over to Catholics.

The Thirty Years War now took on a political dimension. King Gustavus Adolphus of Sweden was a Protestant, and concerned at the growing power of Ferdinand and his Holy Roman Empire. In 1630 Adolphus sent a 13,000-strong army to raise Ferdinand's siege of the German city of Magdeburg, and the Swedes became engaged in a four-year struggle. The Swedish army initially had the advantage – their army was well equipped and well disciplined, and it won the battles of Breitenfeld in 1631 and Lutzen in 1632, although the latter battle cost the Swedes the death of King Adolphus on the battlefield. In 1634, the military tide turned against the Swedes and they were defeated at the Battle of Nordlingen.

The war now became a territorial and political struggle. France was ruled by King Louis XIII, but he was a weak man and the real power behind the throne was Cardinal Richelieu. Although a Catholic, Richelieu was concerned at the power of the Catholic Holy Roman Empire, and in 1635 sent a French army into Germany. There they joined with a renewed Swedish army and for nine years the combined Franco-Swedish forces fought the armies of the Habsburg dynasty. A war-weary northern Europe sent delegations to a peace conference in 1644, and after four years of negotiations the war ended with the Peace of Westphalia in 1648.

The results of the Thirty Years War were profound. The Holy Roman Empire lost Alsace and Lorraine to the French, and ceded control of several important river estuaries (crucial to free trade) to the Swedes. The Thirty Years War was an early example of genocide, with entire populations slaughtered, and cities and towns wiped off the map. As in the war-torn times of the Middle Ages, art, science and commerce were stifled, and it took the Holy Roman Empire almost two centuries to recover.

The Peace of Westphalia did not mark the end of conflict in Europe: France and Spain were by this time at war, a conflict that lasted until 1659. Two of the great colonial powers, England and the Netherlands, had competing interests in exploration and maritime trade, and fought three mostly naval wars between 1652 and 1674.

France and England attacked the Dutch in 1670, who with help from the Germans and Spanish, resisted the English until they gave up and concluded a peace in 1674, after which the Dutch attacked and evicted the French invaders in 1678. One of the main characters in the Dutch defence was William, Prince of Orange. In 1689 he was crowned King William III of England (his wife Mary was from the English royal family) and with his ascent to the English throne England and the Netherlands declared war on France from 1689 to 1697.

But despite the wars that left almost none of western Europe untouched, England, France, the Netherlands and Spain maintained their exploration and colonisation of the rest of the world. Spain secured cultural dominance of Central and South America, and English and Dutch pioneers settled and explored North America while the French moved into Canada. The Dutch and English planted colonies and established trading posts in the Pacific and made discoveries around Australia and New Zealand that would be significant in future.

The nations of Europe managed to spend much of the seventeenth century at war, yet still export their culture far overseas, and secure overseas territories that would prove crucial in maintaining Europe's cultural and economic dominance in subsequent years.

Papal initiatives in the seventeenth century

Despite the growing strength of Protestant countries and the nationalistic independence of many European rulers, the pope could still issue decrees that affected the Catholic world. The Inquisition was powerful, and the threat of excommunication was a feared sanction.

Some papal proclamations were more profound than others. Just as the Church had set the date of Easter in 664, so in 1621 the then pope declared the first of January as the start of the new year. In 1624, Pope Urban VIII threatened excommunication to anyone who took snuff.

Recognising the growth in members of the Roman Catholic Church made possible by missionary activities in the sixteenth and seventeenth centuries, Pope Gregory XV founded the Congregation de Propaganda Fide to provide a framework for missionary activity among natives. The cardinals running this Church office showed surprising enlightenment in stating that local customs must be respected unless they outraged religion and morals, and that where possible local people must be recruited into the clergy.

Even though Catholic missionaries were still claiming new lands for the Church of Rome, the time of unquestioning submission to the Bishop of Rome was coming to an end.

Catholic France in the seventeenth century

The Catholic Counter-Reformation found a particularly profound expression in France, where it caused a genuine renewal of piety and spirituality. France, the largest country in western Europe, had many rural areas that suffered profound spiritual and financial poverty, and in the seventeenth century Vincent de Paul founded the Vincentians, an order of missionary priests devoted to serving the poor. He was assisted in this by Louise de Marillac, a nun who shared Vincent's devotion to the needs of the poor, and who like him was canonised to sainthood.

Work among the laity was complemented by a renewed interest in spirituality in the priesthood, and the this century saw the establishment of new religious institutes such as the French Oratory and the Congregation of Jesus and Mary.

However, the Vatican did not welcome all the manifestations of the French Catholic revival, since two new philosophies arose that caused the Vatican considerable disquiet – Jansenism and Gallicanism.

France had sided with German Protestants against the Catholic Habsburgs in the Thirty Years War, and following the end of the war in 1648, there was considerable tension between the hierarchy of the French Roman Catholic Church and the French monarchy. This existing tension was further heightened with the development of Gallicanism, a doctrine which stated that the authority of national Churches should increase at the expense of papal influence. The French King Louis XIV was attracted to the idea, since it allowed him to increase his influence in French religious affairs, something that was bitterly opposed by Pope Innocent XI.

French clergy often sided with their king, and began to adopt doctrines and practices that the Vatican found unacceptable. The dispute continued in France until the 1690s, but long after it finished there was much anti-Vatican resentment among French clergy. Gallicanism was a nationalist doctrine, very much in tune with the mood of Europe at the time, and other Roman Catholic monarchs followed Louis' lead in trying to reduce papal influence in their nations' affairs.

Catholic France suffered further breaches with Rome over the doctrines propounded by Cornelius Jansen, Bishop of Ypres in Flanders (now Belgium). Jansenism was based on the notion of a harsh, punishing God. Jansenists attacked the notion of human freedom and claimed that Christ did not die on the cross for the salvation of all humanity.

Many French bishops agreed, but the papacy did not. Jansenism was fiercely championed by the French philosopher Blaise Pascal, and was equally powerfully opposed by the French Jesuits; it caused a massive split in the French Roman Catholic Church.

It was in this atmosphere that French philosophers such as Voltaire, Denis Diderot and Jean-Jacques Rousseau championed the use of reason as the way to truth. Such thinking was the start of the Age of Reason in western European thought, and it contained a vigorous strand of anti-religious feeling, since the tradition inherent in the Church's practices was quite the opposite of the rationalism that the philosophers so vigorously supported. In an atmosphere of growing French nationalism, they also felt that the Catholic clergy's obedience to papal authority in Rome threatened the integrity of the French nation. Yet despite these strains, France remained a strongly Catholic country throughout the seventeenth century.

The 1600s – the growth of European colonialism

By the seventeenth century, European sailors were becoming ever more confident and successful in their discoveries of distant shores, and governments were becoming more determined to exploit newly discovered lands by planting and financing colonies. We know of the successful explorers who returned to Europe, having mapped new lands, met 'savages' and filled the holds of their ships with saleable spices and treasure, but many sailors and would-be colonists must have died unrecorded. Ships of the time were small and fragile. The Mayflower, which took the Pilgrim Fathers across the notoriously stormy North Atlantic was just 27 metres (90 feet) in length, and one of the ships that set off with the Mayflower had to abandon the voyage since it leaked so badly. Navigation was a very haphazard affair, and many explorers must have been lost without trace as ships were overwhelmed in storms, thrown on to hostile shores or wrecked on uncharted reefs.

Undaunted by these risks, and lured by the riches to be had from 'the Indies', sailors from England, the Netherlands, France and Spain continued in the exploration that was started in the sixteenth century. Portugal, the once great seafaring nation, faded from this race for colonies and trade, since its initial success in finding and colonising new lands had left it over-stretched and vulnerable. Spain invaded Portugal and seized its overseas colonies.

Spain, France and England competed for the huge Americas, with the Spanish winning influence in Central and South America, and the English and French competing for control of North America. Frenchman Samuel de Champlain landed in what is now Canada, and mapped the coast from Lake Breton Island to Massachusetts in America. In 1608 he founded Quebec as a fur-trading post. The French also made great expeditions in North America. In 1672 a fur trader accompanied by Fr Jacques Marquette, a Catholic priest, explored the Mississippi by canoe, and in 1682 a further French expedition followed the Mississippi to the Gulf of Mexico and claimed the whole area for France, naming it Louisiana in honour of King Louis of France.

However, France was much occupied with wars at home. England was less embattled and was also a great maritime nation, and its freedom from conflict allowed it to expend resources on the exploration and colonisation of America. The first English colonists landed at Jamestown, Virginia, in 1607, and by 1670 English settlements accounted for twelve of the thirteen founding colonies in North America. The English also claimed eastern Canada, following its discovery in 1610 by Henry Hudson.

The Atlantic crossing and the riches of the Americas were not enough for the discovery and trade hungry Europeans. The Pacific Ocean and the *Terra Australis Incognita*, the 'Unknown Southern Continent', beckoned. French, English, Dutch and Spanish sailors made the lengthy, dangerous voyage into the Pacific. It involved traversing the North and South Atlantic oceans before rounding Cape Horn, the southern tip of South America, that even today's well-equipped mariners treat with fear and respect.

They succeeded. In 1521 Ferdinand Magellan discovered for Spain the Philippine islands where he was killed by a native. Miguel Lopez de Legaspi followed suit in 1565 and firmly implanted Spanish domination and Catholicism. In the early part of the century, the Dutch had control of the massive archipelago of islands now known as Indonesia. Between 1606 and 1636 Dutchman Willem Jansz explored the Australian coast, and in 1642 another Dutch sailor, Abel Tasman, landed on Tasmania (which bears his name) and sighted, but did not explore, New Zealand.

Europe races for North America

The seventeenth century was a crucial century in the history of the English-speaking world. In 1607, a hundred colonists settled to a precarious life at Jamestown establishing the first English settlement in North America.

Over the following century, the French, Dutch and Swedes also sought to establish colonies to settle and exploit the North American continent. In 1624 the Dutch settled New Amsterdam, which grew into the city of New York. The Swedes also sent boatloads of colonists, establishing a New Sweden in Delaware. Yet despite the early success enjoyed by the Dutch and the Swedish colonists, the English colonists were far more tenacious, successful and resilient, and the English soon came to dominate the early American colonies.

The early American colonists were not entirely free to rule themselves, since their affairs were governed by the London companies whose capital had funded the voyages and helped finance the settlements. Despite the hard life experienced by the colonists, many people were anxious to travel to America to escape the religious intolerance that was rife in England. The Pilgrim Fathers were Puritans who had previously suffered persecution, and Maryland was colonised by the Calverts, an emigrant Catholic family. The Calverts learned from their own oppression in England, welcoming Protestant settlers and guaranteeing their religious freedom in a 1649 religious toleration act.

As the following list shows, this was the century when English settlers truly began to settle in the east coast of North America:

1607 Virginia
1620 Massachusetts
1623 New Hampshire
1624 New York
1633 Connecticut
1634 Maryland
1636 Rhode Island
1638 Delaware
1643 Pennsylvania
1653 North Carolina
1660 New Jersey
1670 South Carolina

Just as Virginia was the earliest English colony, it was also the first to establish an American representative assembly, the House of Burgesses. Although not democratic in the one-person-one-vote sense of modern democracy, it did include representatives from throughout thecolony, and received permission to make all local legislation and to control taxes. It was also a more advanced form of democracy than anything enjoyed by common people in England.

The Puritans founded colonies at Plymouth and Massachusetts Bay, initially as farmers, then progressing to establish rural industries. They also contributed to America's fledgling democracy. They framed the Mayflower Compact, an agreement among the adult males to make 'just and equal laws' for all, and held town meetings where the town's men could discuss and frame laws.

The influx of persecuted religious groups seeking freedom in America continued with the arrival of Quaker William Penn, who was made proprietor of the area now known as Pennsylvania, and later given control of the formerly Swedish area of Delaware. The king of England, Charles II, then granted the southern lands of Carolina to a series of eight new proprietors, and the new land was populated by further emigrants from England and exiled French Huguenot Protestants.

Although the American colonies were governed from London, the distances involved meant that the controlling bonds were loose and several factors conspired to cause a rapidly growing strain of independence in the American colonists. The distance from London was a factor, so was the kind of spirit inherent in the people prepared to make a long, dangerous sea voyage and risk everything starting a new life in a distant land. Also, many of the first colonists were refugees from religious persecution, for whom freedom from undue control was an article of faith.

In 1670, English colonists were founding South Carolina. Just a hundred years later, their descendants were fighting for independence from Britain.

The birth of European science

The seventeenth century gave rise to a branch of learning that would become a fundamental force in shaping the modern world – science. Science could be defined as an enquiry into the mechanics of the physical world, and even though curious minds had been asking questions and making investigations for many centuries it was only in seventeenth-century Europe that developments in technology and mathematics allowed experimental science to develop.

The intellectual soil of Europe was fertile for the development of science: the Enlightenment had made intellectual inquiry beyond the confines of religion possible, and Reformation countries had a new intellectual freedom, so that in northern and western Europe people were free to speculate, invent and theorise without risking the wrath of the pope and the Inquisition. Science is a collaborative, incremental endeavour, and the invention of the printing press meant that scientific findings could be disseminated so that researchers would be able to build on others' results. The period's most eminent scientist, Sir Isaac Newton (1642–1727), acknowledged this when he said: 'If I have seen further, it is because I have stood on the shoulders of giants.'

In Italy Galileo Galilei (1564–1642) began to develop experimental method, founding the process by which scientific experiments are conducted, and his first experiments established the uniform acceleration of falling bodies. Galileo was one of the first scientists to use the telescope (invented in 1608 by a Dutch spectacle manufacturer, Hans Lippershey) to study the night sky, and recorded observations on the Moon's craters, the Milky Way, Jupiter's moons and the progression of Venus in the night sky. His studies led him to support the views of Johannes Kepler (1561–1630) who first stated that the Earth and other planets of the solar system orbit around the Sun. These views brought Galileo into conflict with the Church, which believed that the universe rotated around a fixed Earth. He was called before the Inquisition to defend his views in 1616 and again in 1633, when he was ordered to recant under threat of torture. By this time an old and sick man, he recanted, but was said to have muttered, 'It [the Earth] still moves,' as he did so. The Inquisition ordered his detention for the rest of his life.

Italian science could scarcely flourish under those circumstances, so it is hardly surprising that much of the scientific discovery in the seventeenth century occurred in the intellectual freedom of Protestant England and the diverse, tolerant Netherlands. In 1614 logarithmic tables were published, allowing more complex mathematical calculations to be performed. The microscope was first invented by a Dutch cloth merchant, Antoni van Leeuwenhoek (1632–1723). As a cloth merchant he used lenses to examine fabric; wishing to see much smaller structures, he developed a more complex magnifying instrument which we now know as the microscope. He was the first to observe red blood cells, single-celled micro-organisms and the structure of muscles, but since he did not speak or write Latin, the rest of Europe did not find out about his work until many years after his discoveries.

Robert Hooke (1635–1703) was an English scientist whose achievements spanned almost the whole field of science: in astronomy he correctly postulated that the Earth followed an elliptical (rather than circular) orbit around the Sun, made radical improvements to microscopes and telescopes, and formulated Hooke's Law of Elasticity. He put his improved microscopes to good use, studying both microscopic animals and the structure of tissues, introducing the word 'cell' to the scientific vocabulary.

Irish-born Robert Boyle (1627–1691) did ground-breaking work in the fields we now recognise as physics and chemistry. He proved that air has weight, and formulated a theory that matter was made up of what he called 'corpuscles', discrete units that we now call atoms. He did extensive research into the nature and behaviour of gases and is credited with founding chemistry as a science.

In this first flowering of western science the discoveries came thick and fast. In 1628 Englishman William Harvey proved that the heart pumps blood around the body. In France, René Descartes' mathematical breakthroughs allowed the development of algebra and calculus, both critical developments in mathematical and scientific theory. Descartes also made the famous assertion, 'I think, therefore I am,' and from here argued strongly for the existence of God.

Back in England, however, the genius of the age was at work: Sir Isaac Newton. Newton was a mathematician and physicist, and in a long, productive life he framed the laws of gravity and the three laws of motion, added enormously to the range of mathematical theories and proofs, and discovered that white light is made up of a spectrum of colours. Newton's laws laid the foundations for subsequent discoveries in astronomy and physics, and were only partially superseded when Einstein published his theory of relativity in 1905. Newton was not entirely a hard-headed theoretical scientist, since he also spent much of his time in alchemical experimentation, searching for a way to transform base metal into gold.

The sixteenth century had closed with Europe on the brink of scientific awakening, and by the end of the century, many of the tools and methods of modern science had been discovered.

Archbishop Ussher and the age of the Earth

The seventeenth century was an age of inquiry. Experimental science and advanced mathematics began to develop, and the search for reason became the driving force in western European philosophy. In this atmosphere, James Ussher, an Archbishop in the Church of Ireland made what was at the time the best attempt to estimate the age of the earth. Ussher made a long, complex calculation, adding up the ages of characters in the Bible, and in 1654 came to the conclusion that the Earth was created by God on 23 October 4004 BC.

At the time, there was no means of suggesting an alternative view: the Genesis account in the Bible was regarded as a literal account of the creation, and the truth or otherwise of the events recounted in the Old Testament was not open to question. Both Protestant and Catholic confessions adhered to the truth of the Scriptures. Archbishop Ussher's estimate is now occasionally held up to ridicule, but it was the only means available to estimate the age of the Earth at the time.

However, Ussher's enterprising calculation caused problems for his spiritual successors. In the nineteeth century the science of geology began to develop, and many of the academics who founded the field were also Anglican clergymen. When their studies of rock strata began to suggest that the Earth was probably hundreds of thousands, if not millions, of years old, the strength of Archbishop Ussher's biblical calculation caused them immense problems, since bowing to the accumulating evidence meant admitting that Archbishop Ussher, and therefore the Bible, was incorrect in his account of creation.

This dispute set the stage for the first large religion-versus science-dispute in western Europe, when in 1859 Charles Darwin published *On the Origin of Species*, a book which suggested that organisms evolve, directly opposing the accepted Genesis account of the creation.

Seventeenth-century culture in Europe – the Baroque

In the early seventeenth century a new cultural and artistic movement developed in western Europe – the Baroque movement. Baroque thinking affected architecture, music, painting and sculpture and produced many artists whose work is still celebrated.

Three factors brought about the development of Baroque art. It was a rebellion against the formal, posed, geometric art of the Renaissance, and its scale and grandeur found favour with the secular rulers of Europe. They felt that massive, elaborately decorated buildings containing large paintings and extravagant sculptures were an appropriate reflection of their power. Baroque painting, sculpture and music first developed in Rome, which in the seventeenth century was the cultural capital of Europe. A third factor in the development of Baroque is that it was at first closely associated with the Catholic Counter-Reformation.

This does not imply that great Baroque artists were exclusively Catholic: countries where the Protestant Reformation had taken hold also produced great Baroque works. Johann Sebastian Bach is widely held as being one of the greatest composers ever – he was born in 1685 and lived and composed throughout the latter half of the Baroque period, and many of his greatest works were composed for Lutheran church services.

In painting, the Baroque cast off the posed, devotional formality of the Renaissance, and painters such as Caravaggio started to use striking contrasts of light and dark and painted scenes with people obviously engaged in normal, dynamic, chaotic day-to-day life. Once beyond the confines of Italy, Baroque influence spread through great artists including Rubens in Flanders, Rembrandt in the Netherlands and Velasquez in Spain.

When Baroque ideas developed in architecture, the rectangular, geometric simplicity of the Renaissance was replaced by a more exuberant approach to buildings. Baroque architecture developed a taste for arches, circles and columns, and included painting and sculpture as integral to the building. Examples of great Baroque architecture include St Paul's Cathedral in London, the Great Palace and gardens at Versailles and St Peter's Square that lies in front of St Peter's Basilica in the Vatican.

In sculpture, the Italian Gian Lorenzo Bernini defined a new style that was more dramatic and lifelike than the Renaissance had allowed, and much Baroque sculpture is said to be in the style of Bernini. Bernini was closely associated with the Roman Catholic Church and many of his statues adorn St Peter's and the Vatican.

The Baroque also saw amazing developments in music. The simple polyphonic harmonies of the sixteenth century were replaced by more complex harmonies, new instruments and different social circumstances. With the development of monarchs and aristocracies that owed little allegiance to the church music that was not directly inspired by religion began to develop – but the Church was still a huge influence in commissioning new music. JS Bach, Vivaldi, Monteverdi and Handel were baroque composers who made magnificent contributions to the development of sacred music. However, it was in non-religious music that the Baroque had most impact, laying the foundations of what became the classical and romantic music of Mozart and Beethoven. The music forms of the concerto, opera and the symphony were pioneered by Baroque composers, and existing forms such as sonatas were taken to new heights of virtuosity.

THE POPES
1605–1700

Leo XI (Alessandro de'Medici)

Florence; 1 April 1605 to 27 April 1605

Born from a branch of the famous de'Medici family, Alessandro was a nephew of Pope Leo X, and in later life a disciple of St Philip Neri. Appointed Archbishop of Florence (1574) he energetically applied the decrees of the Council of Trent. He was cardinal legate to France (1596–1598); the French were delighted when he was elected. He died within a month.

Paul V (Camillo Borghese)

Rome; 16 May 1605 to 28 January 1621

From the famed Roman Borghese family, Camillo trained in canon law and rose through the Curia as an outstanding legal expert. Cardinal Vicar of Rome at his election, he was devoted to reform and the implementation of the decrees of the Council of Trent. He fell into dispute with several city-states, e.g. Venice, over the extent of Church authority. An Interdict (1606) on Venice had to be withdrawn. This and a clash between Church and State, in France, severely dented papal prestige. He canonised or beatified a large number of saints, including Ignatius Loyola, Francis Xavier, Charles Borromeo and Philip Neri. He was a renowned nepotist, (e.g. his nephew Cardinal Scipio Borghese) and there was some scandal at how his family amassed considerable wealth. Patron of the Arts, Paul was responsible for the decoration of the Vatican gardens.

Gregory XV (Alessandro Ludovisi)

Bologna; 9 February 1621 to 8 July 1623

Educated by the Jesuits at Bologna, Alessandro Ludovisi, became archbishop there in 1612. After his election Gregory supported the Catholic powers engaged in the Thirty Years War (1618–1648). He had some success in the return of Bohemia to the Catholic Faith. He founded the Sacred Congregation for the Propagation of the Faith and completed the canonisations of Teresa of Avila, Philip Neri, Francis Xavier and Ignatius Loyola. He was supported throughout by his nephew, Cardinal Ludovico Ludovisi. His reign is noted for the papal decrees that regularised conclaves, i.e. a secret written ballot conducted behind closed doors. These rules have, in substance, endured to the present.

Urban VIII (Maffeo Barberini)

Florence; 6 August 1623 to 29 July 1644

Born of a prominent Florentine merchant family, Maffeo Barberini was educated there and then rose rapidly in the service of the popes. After he was elected Urban relied more on himself and his family than the Curia and, in his support of the arts, spent lavishly, giving patronage to Gian Lorenzo Bernini and other architects and artists. He consecrated the completed St Peter's. He energetically supported missionary work and condemned the slave trade in South America. Urban supported France and the policies of Cardinal Richelieu against Germany, antagonising German Catholics. Shamelessly Urban promoted the wealth and progress of his family; a brother and two nephews became cardinals. His rapacious nephews involved him in a war with the Duke of Parma (1642–1644); this brought humiliation for Urban and the hatred of the Roman populace who danced in the streets at his death.

Innocent X (Giovanni Battista Pamphili)

Rome; 15 September 1644 to 7 January 1655

A former judge of the papal marriage court, the Rota, Giovanni Battista Pamphili served as Patriarch of Antioch and papal nuncio to Spain before his election. Innocent reversed all of Urban VIII's policies and his

Barberini family were stripped of their wealth and property (see Urban VIII) Innocent favoured Spanish interests, thus damaging relations with France. When the disastrous Thirty Years War ended (1648) Innocent protested at the content of the peace treaty, which did not favour the Church; but, significant of the changed times, the European powers ignored Innocent. He condemned the heretical Jansenist movement with the bull *Cum Occasione* (1653). Innocent became dominated by his sister-in-law, Donna Olimpia Maidalchini-Pamphili, whose greed and ambition were a public scandal; her son was made a cardinal. The rapacious Olimpia abandoned him on his deathbed, and would not pay for Innocent's funeral.

Alexander VII (Fabio Chigi)

18 April 1655 to 22 September 1667

The very able and respected Cardinal Chigi, grand-nephew of Pope St Pius V, had been secretary of state under Innocent X. Deeply spiritual, Alexander was a patron of the arts and had Bernini build the great Scala Regia and the colonnade of St Peter's Piazza. Under Alexander papal power and prestige continued to decline; he was forced to accept humiliating terms in a dispute with France. He took much pleasure in the conversion of the ex-queen, Christina, of Sweden, but tired of her courtly style and lavish ways when she came to live in Rome. Alexander's coat of arms can still be seen over Bernini's colonnade in St Peter's Square.

Clement IX (Giulio Rospigliosi)

Pistoia; 20 June 1667 to 9 December 1669

Made a cardinal and appointed secretary of state (1657) by Alexander VII, Giulio Rospigliosi had previously been a philosophy lecturer at the University of Pisa. A pastoral bishop of Rome and loved by his people, Clement visited hospitals and heard his people's confessions. A poet and composer in his own right

Clement wrote libretti for sacred and comic opera.
Troubles with a domineering France continued,
although he was able to negotiate a compromise over
Jansenism. Clement was deeply distressed when no
Christian power would raise a finger to help the
Christians of Crete; besieged and then slaughtered by
the Ottoman Turks (September 1669). He appeared
never to recover and died of a stroke shortly after.

Clement X (Emilio Altieri)

Rome; 29 April 1670 to 22 July 1676

The conclave was deadlocked for four months as the
traditional adversaries, the Spanish and the French,
struggled to get the upper hand. The cardinals chose
the eighty-year-old Emilio Altieri as a compromise
solution. Infirm, Clement left the day-to-day running
of the Church to his nephew, Cardinal Paluzzi. The
main concern was to maintain peace in Europe while a
scheming Louis XIV of France set about the conquest
of Holland and the stripping of French abbeys and
bishoprics of their revenues, to fund his wars. Clement
was, at least, heartened by the Polish defeat of the
Ottoman Turks.

Innocent XI, Bl. (Benedetto Odescalchi)

Como; 21 September 1676 to 12 August 1689

An Italian from Como, Benedetto Odescalchi held a
variety of ecclesiastical posts, e.g. Bishop of Novara
and papal legate, and then retired as a cardinal because
of poor health. Deeply spiritual, he was amazed – and
at first refused – when elected unanimously to succeed
Clement X. He insisted on reform measures, social
changes in Rome itself and an austerity over papal
finances. He firmly resisted Louis XIV of France's
claims to control the Church in France (known as
Gallicanism), especially opposing the Gallican Articles
(1682). Further disruptions, including Louis' revocation
of the Edict of Nantes, deepened the rift between France
and the Papacy. Innocent's great ambition was to free

Europe of the threat of the Turks and he contributed large sums of money to this end. The Holy League of Nations was successful; Hungary was liberated in 1686 and Belgrade in 1688. His passing was genuinely mourned by the people of Rome.

Alexander VIII (Pietro Ottoboni)

Venice; 6 October 1689 to 1 February 1691

From a wealthy Venetian family, Pietro Ottoboni received an excellent education and rose swiftly in the Church; he became a cardinal in 1652 and Bishop of Brescia in 1654. Elected when seventy-nine years of age, despite his years Alexander showed great vigour in his pontificate. A reconciliation was effected with King Louis XIV of France and the return of Avignon and Venaissin, seized earlier by France; Alexander however confirmed the condemnation of the Gallican Articles of 1682 (see Innocent XI). Firm and clear in theological matters, he condemned Quietism and Jansenism. Generous by nature Alexander reduced taxes in the Papal States, enriched the Vatican Library and sent aid to Venice in their war with the Ottoman Turks. A gangrenous leg caused a lingering death.

Innocent XII (Antonio Pignatelli)

Spinazzola, Italy; 15 July 1691 to 27 September 1700

After a long conclave of five months and the threat of Roman riots, the electors chose a compromise candidate, Cardinal Antonio Pignatelli, who took the name Innocent, out of admiration for Innocent XI. He immediately pursued similar policies to his role model. He launched a thorough reform of the Curia. He put a stop to the practice of nepotism with the decree *Romanum Decet Pontificem* (1692) which forbade popes from giving land, property or offices in the Church to relatives. He condemned Jansenism and Quietism. He came to an agreement with King Louis XIV of France over the Gallican Articles and the extent of papal authority in France.

1700–1800
A century of revolutions

Timeline 1700–1800

1701 London: the Society for the Propagation of the Gospel in Foreign Parts is founded.

1716 Teaching Christianity is banned in China.

1726 America experiences a wave of evangelical fervour – 'the Great Awakening'.

1734 The Koran, the sacred book of Islam, is translated into English.

1738 John Wesley, founder of Methodism, experiences an evangelical conversion. A papal bull condemns the growing practice of freemasonry.

1759 The British capture Quebec in Canada, and guarantee Catholic freedom to worship.

1773 Pope Clement XIV suppresses the Jesuits at the request of French and Spanish kings.

1789 The French Revolution begins. Church property is seized and sold.

1792 The Baptist Church is founded in London.

1793 The French Revolution descends into 'the terror'. Thousands are guillotined, including many clergy as Catholicism is banned.

1798 The French invade Rome, Pope Pius VI flees into exile.

Introduction – A century of revolutions

The eighteenth century saw four revolutions: Agricultural, Industrial, American and French.

The first two took place in Britain, and paved the way for the growth of western capitalism, world industrialisation and the development of a largely urban western culture. Both represented far-reaching changes in what had been an agricultural, rural society, and were remarkable in that neither were intentional: in the case of both the Agricultural and Industrial Revolutions the changes occurred as a result of several complementary factors combining to accelerate the pace of change.

In industry, steam power, the development of machines and the availability of investment capital combined to kick-start manufacturing in Britain. In agriculture, advances in crop rotation, the advent of farm machinery and improvements in livestock quality had the same effect, combining to cause a massive leap in farm productivity.

In contrast, the American Revolution was against the British: the American colonists revolted against taxes imposed from London, rallying to the slogan 'no taxation without representation'. Their colonial masters both misread the mood of the Americans and overestimated the British ability to put down the revolt. Civil unrest grew into war, and in an eight-year conflict the British were driven out of America.

The French and British already had a long history of enmity, and in 1778 the French entered the American War of Independence on the side of the Americans, a move that significantly improved America's chances of victory. This was at the time an astute strategic alliance by the French kings – surely an American victory would weaken the old enemy, Britain. Alas, the French monarchs miscalculated the mood of their own people, and just six years after the Franco-American alliance threw the British out of America, the French (having been shown it was possible to revolt and succeed) rose in their own rebellion against their king, clergy and nobility.

The century continued the European tradition of warfare. In the 1730s France went to war with Austria over the question of who should succeed to the Polish throne, and in 1739 Austria turned on Turkey. Turkey occupied a strategically important point in western geography, and the Turks and Russians battled for control of the Turkish coast. Britain and France were also sporadically at war both across the English Channel and across the Atlantic, where they were struggling for control of Canada. The French were decisively beaten at the Battle of Quebec in 1759, but it was not until 1763 that the Treaty of Paris ended the war for control of Canada in Britain's favour.

The Treaty of Paris also ceded control of New Mexico and Louisiana to Spain, adding to its already considerable influence in Central and South America. However, the Spanish were having their own colonial problems: in 1747 Peru revolted against Spanish rule, and the Spanish colonial authorities were continually worried at the influence wielded by Jesuit missionaries – an order with a special loyalty to the pope.

The Jesuits' missionary activities were a political problem for the Spanish conquerors – in the previous century and 1700 they had lobbied the pope over the welfare of South American Indians. The Spanish authorities saw the Indians as potential slaves, whereas the Jesuits saw them as converts and in some places managed to secure exemption from slavery. Their efforts to protect the indigenous peoples, the strength of their spiritual authority and their explicit loyalty to the pope rankled with the Spanish. The Jesuits were so successful in their efforts to protect the Indians that during this century the Spaniards evicted the order from Paraguay and America; the Indians rioted in response. This affection from the South American Indians did little to help the Jesuits, since in 1773 Pope Clement XIV bowed to pressure from the kings of France and Spain and issued a bull abolishing the Society of Jesus.

Outside the Catholic world, the eighteenth century saw the development and growth of new Protestant religious factions. Unitarianism had first developed in Europe in the sixteenth century, and in the eighteenth century Unitarian beliefs (doubting the existence of the Holy Trinity or the truth of the divinity of Jesus) began to take hold in Baptist and Presbyterian congregations, with the first exclusively Unitarian church opening in London in 1773. In 1729 the brothers John and Charles Wesley started a prayer and Bible study group at Oxford University. The Wesley brothers founded the evangelical Anglican movement that became known as Methodism. The movement stayed within the established Church until in 1795 the differences became so acute that Methodists formally split from the Anglican Church.

The eighteenth century marked a time of revival in the English-speaking Protestant Churches. In the American colonies this uprising of religious spirituality was called the Great Awakening. Most of the American provinces were settled by Protestant emigrants from Britain, the Netherlands and Germany, and while the American colonists kept their faith alive, their clergy were concerned that their congregations were falling into religious apathy. This probably has something to do with the energy required in being part of a pioneering population. However, in 1734 the American theologian and philosopher Jonathan Edwards began a series of sermons in Northampton, Massachusetts. Evidently a charismatic preacher, he sparked off a religious revival that swept through the American colonies, to the point that churches could no longer hold the numbers of people who were turning up to hear revivalist clergy preach.

While European trade and missionary activities in the Americas and Africa met with success, attempts to make inroads into China failed. The Chinese had initially warmed to the Jesuits, but in the pope's opinion these intellectual priests went too far in coming to terms with Chinese Confucianism: in 1704 a papal legate arrived in the East to enforce Papal orthodoxy on Jesuits in their dealings with the Indians and Chinese, and in 1742 the pope condemned outright the Jesuits' efforts in China. In 1793 Britain sent a delegation to the Chinese to open trade delegations. The British were surprised to find that the Chinese were not interested in overtures from the 'Barbarians from the West'.

Africa began to figure in Europe's colonial ambitions. During the early part of the century, the British colonies in the southernmost of the American settlements developed a large-scale agricultural industry. In the absence of farm machinery, the work of harvesting cotton and tobacco was very labour intensive, and to supply these farms the African slave trade developed.

Slave ships would leave the British ports of Bristol and Liverpool laden with trade goods. In Saharan Africa, slavers would raid villages and capture whole families. These Africans would be exchanged for the goods from Britain, the ships would be crammed with slaves kept in the most cramped conditions imaginable, and the packed ships would then leave the east coast of Africa for a passage across the stormy Atlantic ocean. The surviving slaves were sold to American plantation owners. The slave ships were then loaded with export goods from the American markets, and they recrossed the Atlantic to British ports for the process to continue.

The European exploration of the world continued: Danish navigator Vitus Bering sailed far to the north and discovered the passage between Siberia and Alaska now called the Bering Strait. In Britain, a

Yorkshire tradesman's son called James Cook saw the sea and determined that his future lay over the horizon; he became one of the greatest explorers of all time. Dutch explorers had seen Australia and New Zealand in the seventeenth century, but it was not until the 1760s and 1770s that Captain James Cook explored and mapped Australia, New Zealand and the Pacific islands of Tahiti and Hawaii. In 1796, British colonists started to explore the west African interior, discovering the River Niger.

Intellectually, scientific discovery continued and the growth of reason began to dominate western European thought, with the secular philosophy of the century becoming known as Enlightenment thinking. The philosophers of the time were Voltaire, Leibniz, Hume, Kant and Rousseau. In France Diderot began to produce an encyclopædia of scientific and artistic thought. The secular and religious immediately began to clash: the encyclopædia contained subversive theories such as the idea that animals evolve over time. The prestigious French University at the Sorbonne voted to suppress such ideas, and the pope declared that anyone owning such an heretical text was automatically excommunicated.

The end of the century brought trouble for the papacy. The French revolutionary soldier Napoleon Bonaparte seized control of the French Revolution, and in 1796 he moved into the Papal States, forcing Pope Pius VI into negotiations. The French Revolution had nationalised Church property and forced the clergy to swear oaths of allegiance to the Republic. The early nineteenth century promised to be an uncomfortable time for the papacy.

The agricultural revolution

Just as Britain in the eighteenth century can rightly claim to be the home of the Industrial Revolution, it was also the birthplace of modern agriculture.

Prior to the Agricultural Revolution farming had been a small-scale, subsistence industry with significant limiting factors. Much of the work was done by hand, since farming machinery was not yet available. Crops were grown by a rotation system which required fields to be left fallow (uncultivated) for part of the year to recover their nutrient content. As a result, it was difficult to grow sufficient fodder for livestock, which meant that animals had to be slaughtered each autumn, and the meat products either eaten, preserved, sold or bartered.

The Agricultural Revolution started at approximately the same time as the Industrial Revolution, and like the Industrial Revolution several factors combined to start the revolution moving. Three changes in farming practice came about, and the ethos of industrialisation arrived on farms. People began to move from the countryside to towns and cities, and their small farming plots were combined into larger fields that could be more efficiently cultivated.

Jethro Tull (1674–1741) was an English gentleman farmer who in 1701 made the first true piece of mechanised farm machinery, a seed drill. Before the invention of Tull's drill, seed would be sown by hand scattering, which left the seeds on the surface of the soil for birds to eat, and those seeds which did survive to germinate did so patchily, reducing the yield and leaving large areas open for weeds to encroach. Tull's seed drill allowed a farmer to tow the machine behind a horse, with the drill opening a trench in the soil, dropping the seed at the correct distance apart and closing the soil over the seed.

Tull's machine allowed farmers to sow seed far faster and with a higher success rate, and it started the mechanisation of farming. This immediately reduced the farmer's reliance on farm labourers, starting a change in the agrarian pattern of British life.

Farm machinery was only one part of the revolution. Two Norfolk farmers, Charles Townsend and Thomas Coke, began independently experimenting with crop planting methods. In the early part of the century Townsend discovered that instead of leaving land fallow, planting legumes actually improved the quality of the soil, and allowed an additional crop (Townsend planted turnips) to be grown. This earned him the nickname 'Turnip Townsend', but this new humble vegetable crop dramatically increased soil productivity and allowed farmers to feed turnips to their livestock throughout the winter – livestock could be fattened up and could be killed when it suited the farmer rather than when poor grazing dictated.

Townsend pioneered the system, and found a vigorous advocate when Thomas Coke, the Earl of Leicester, introduced Townsend's and other agricultural improvements to his estates at Holkham Hall. The improvements in crop rotation became known as the Norfolk System, and allowed farm productivity to increase.

Robert Bakewell (1725–1795) started the third important contributory factor to the Agricultural Revolution through his work improving the quality of livestock. He selectively bred sheep and cattle to maximise their ability to put on muscle, and developed methods of improving the grass yield of his farms. He also gave the British sheep-meat as part of their diet. Previously the animals did not grow sufficiently to allow them to be slaughtered for meat, but with Bakewell's selective breeding and improved grass yield for animal fodder, a new, productive source of meat protein – lamb and mutton – became widely available to the growing British population.

The Industrial Revolution

As with all revolutions, many factors combined to produce the upheaval in investment and production that has became known as the Industrial Revolution.

In the seventeenth century there was a very limited form of industry, where merchants would provide raw materials to families of workers in their homes, then collect and sell the products. These cottage industries were unreliable and had poor rates of productivity, but by the early eighteeth century new inventions and a generation of merchants with money to invest began the process of changing the British economy and ultimately the world.

In 1738 the first spinning machine began to show textile manufacturers a new way of making thread. Formerly, yarn was laboriously spun on a foot-operated spinning wheel, but by 1744 the first mills in Britain were using spinning machines (including the spinning jenny and spinning mule) to mass-produce thread – it was the start of industrialisation. Machines in factories needed people to work them, and the British population began to abandon its rural life and move to the growing towns and cities to work in factories. By 1780 there were 120 textile mills in Britain.

The machines needed power to drive them – more power than could be supplied by the old methods of a water wheel or horse-power – and the second factor that allowed the growth of manufacturing was the development of the steam engine in 1698. Although crude and inefficient by today's standards, the steam engine was refined first by Thomas Newcomen and then in 1760 by James Watt. Following Watt's development, the steam engine could be reliably used for pumping water out of mine workings or driving the power-hungry spinning and weaving looms in mills. Britain's geology helped the early industrialists, since Britain had large deposits of coal, the fuel needed to run the

The growth of urban Europe

Prior to the eighteenth century, Europe had been a rural society where the population had made a sparse living in subsistence agriculture or in cottage industries.

However, by 1750 a move to towns and cities was gathering pace. The early stages of an industrial society created a demand for a workforce, and as workers migrated to the cities, the cities began to expand. By 1750 both London and Paris had populations exceeding half a million.

Cities were the home of an emerging urban middle class, whose wealth derived not from landowning but from engaging in trading goods and commodities. Rich landowners also saw urban life as attractive and invested in city house and cities soon developed into centres of entertainment, learning and culture.

They also became havens for vice, disease and poverty, as William Hogarth's engravings of London such as Gin Lane show. The underclasses lived crammed together in cramped, dark, narrow streets. There was little sanitation, diet was poor and disease was endemic. When Paris erupted into rebellion in 1789, it is hardly surprising that the British government was concerned that the 'disease' of revolution might spread the short distance across the Channel.

The rapid development of learning and culture in London did not extend to the popular toleration of Catholics. In 1780 the London Parliament proposed the repeal of anti-Catholic laws, and a volatile mob was whipped into a rioting frenzy by a fanatical protestant MP, Lord George Gordon of Wiltshire. The crowd rioted throughout central London over the course of a week, looting, burning buildings and forcing jails to free prisoners. Eventually the army was used to suppress the rioters, but at the end of the week 500 people had been killed.

The late eighteenth century marked the end of Europe as a rural society and the beginning of a move to towns and cities that continued into the twentieth century.

steam engines which came to power the ever-increasing number of factory machines.

In addition to coal, the British landscape contained large deposits of iron-bearing rocks, and a further factor added momentum to the rapidly developing Industrial Revolution – the iron industry. Previously, iron-making had been another near-cottage industry which had used charcoal to smelt the iron ore. (Smelting is the process of heating the iron ore to burn off the non-metallic impurities, leaving molten iron which can then be moulded or worked into the desired shape.) Charcoal is made from hardwood trees, and trees were a commodity much in demand for building houses and ships, so charcoal became prohibitively expensive.

Then in 1709 one Abraham Darby used coke (coal baked in an airless furnace) to smelt iron. Britain had plenty of coal which could be turned into coke, and with this large-scale iron production became possible, especially when the development of the puddle furnace in 1783 allowed higher-quality iron to be produced.

At this point, Britain's status as a colonial nation contributed to the success of the Industrial Revolution. First, the new businesses were developing a huge appetite for raw materials. Britain's many overseas colonies were ideal sources of these much needed precursors.

Second, goods need a market, and the colonies also provided a market for the finished products.

Third, this kind of development needs capital investment. In the seventeenth century British merchants had made large fortunes out of selling into war-torn mainland Europe, from exploiting the colonies and from the slave trade. The productivity gains shown by factories promised inviting profits, so the industrial pioneers benefited from private investment by rich merchants. The Industrial Revolution was also the start of modern capitalism.

Socially, the Industrial Revolution had mixed results. People left their precarious, arduous jobs working on the land or in cottage industries and moved to the towns and cities that began to grow around the factories and mills. It was a major population shift, since in the previous century only 10 percent of the European population lived in cities. Now the towns grew, and the mill and factory owners began to face competition, so they sought to keep manufacturing costs down. Factory workers worked 12–14-hour days for six days a week. The machines were unsafe, trade unions were illegal and factory owners cared little for their workers' safety. Deaths and injuries were commonplace inside the factories, while overcrowding, poverty and disease were endemic in the slum housing that sprang up around them.

A major limiting factor was transport, but once again Britain's geology and landscape went some way to solving the problem. Rivers cross much of Britain, and entrepreneurs began to invest in canals – man-made waterways that linked existing rivers and gave the inland factories access to ports for obtaining raw materials in bulk and exporting finished products. In 1777 the Grand Trunk Canal linked the ports of Liverpool and Bristol in the west to Hull on the east coast.

The British government knew that in the Industrial Revolution the country had a competitive advantage over its European trading rivals, and attempted to forbid the emigration of craftsmen. Inevitably they failed, and in 1750 an Englishman established a modern spinning factory in France. America was growing, and in 1789 a Derbyshire textile worker settled in America and soon opened the first American spinning mill. In 1799 William Cockerill, a Lancastrian carpenter emigrated to Belgium taking with him the knowledge of how to build spinning machines. The technology developed rapidly, and Belgium became the second European country to develop mechanised industry. Within twenty years there were Belgian factories producing iron parts for bridges, cannon barrels and parts for steam engines.

The American War of Independence

In the eighteenth century the British colonies in America were gaining sophistication and developing an identity quite separate from the British. In 1704 the first American newspaper was published in Boston, by 1720 a theatre had opened in Williamsburg, Virginia, and the first American orchestra was founded in 1750. In the first half of the century the American economy grew rapidly, so that by the mid 1700s the better-off American colonists were enjoying a standard of living equal to that in prosperous parts of Europe.

While ostensibly under the control of the king and their proprietors in Britain, the American colonies were developing strong local democratic government, and temperamentally the American people were developing a national identity that was different from that of their mostly British ancestry. The British did not want their prosperous thirteen colonies in America to gain too much independence, and the thriving American economy was too tempting a target for taxation.

In mid-century Britain was still at war with France, and sporadically at war with other European nations. Maintaining an army and navy is expensive, and in the 1760s and 1770s the British government passed a series of laws aimed at increasing British control over the American colonies and raising extensive taxes for the British exchequer.

The Americans began to agitate against what they saw as these 'Intolerable Measures', and acts of civil disobedience (such as the 1773 Boston Tea Party, where about a hundred men disguised as Indians hurled the cargo of three tea ships overboard rather than pay taxes on it) soon escalated into open conflict. On 19 April 1775, British soldiers and American patriots clashed at Lexington, Massachusetts, and at nearby Concord.

America was ill-equipped to fight a war. It had a vestigial army – mostly local militias – and little in the way of a command structure or a navy to protect its coastlines, but in late 1775 George Washington was named commander in chief of the Continental Army, and from then on American Patriots fought Loyalists (soldiers and colonists loyal to British Crown) for the right to govern America. If America was ill-equipped to fight a war at home, Britain was poorly positioned to fight a war abroad. The war was 3,000 miles away from home, which made for long delays in receiving commands, military supplies and reinforcements. The Patriots were fighting for their liberty and were on home territory with the support of a majority of the population.

The British forces, with their superior organisation, won early victories at Bunker Hill and in occupying New York, but there were reverses, with the British being beaten at the Battle of Moore's Hill Bridge and being forced to evacuate Boston.

The Americans formed the Continental Congress, a governing body made up of representatives from each of the American provinces, and in 1776 the Congress adopted the Declaration of Independence. At the time, the armies were not fighting for control of the entire American continent – the British colonies in America were exclusively on the American east coast, stretching from modern-day Maine approximately 2,200 kilometres to Georgia in the south, and running inland for approximately 600 kilometres.

Through 1777 and 1778 the British and Americans struggled for advantage over this large battlefield. The British were able to use their well-drilled navy to move forces along the American coast, but in many battles the inspired leadership of George Washington and the determination of the patriots inflicted significant defeats on the British 'Redcoats'. The British initially concentrated on taking control of the northern states, but in 1777 and 1778 a series of defeats saw them switch their efforts to the southern states of Virginia, the Carolinas and Georgia. A significant engagement was the Battle of Saratoga, when the Americans soundly defeated the British forces. It was a result that persuaded the French that the Americans could win the war, and in 1778 America entered into a military alliance with the French. The French had long been Britain's enemy, and in declaring war on Britain they put Britain's already stretched military under yet more pressure.

The French supplied the Americans with desperately needed money and armaments, and the French navy was able to disrupt the British navy's dominance of the American coast. The British campaign in the southern states started well with a victory at Savannah in 1778 and capturing Charleston in 1780, but the British were over-committed. They were at war with France, there was trouble in the East and West Indies, and in 1779 Spain declared war on Britain, followed by the Netherlands in 1790. Britain was now at war with its immediate neighbours at home, and fighting an increasingly determined and better-equipped army in America.

In the Southern states, the Americans won a significant victory at King's Mountain in 1780, after which the British General Cornwallis allowed his army to be trapped in Yorktown, in Virginia. Here General Cornwallis's 8,000-strong army were confronted by a combined American and French army of some 18,000. Cornwallis surrendered on 19 October 1781. While sporadic fighting dragged on, this battle marked the beginning of the end of the American War of Independence. In Britain, the defeat led to ministerial resignations, and the new ministers feared that continuing the war in America would cost Britain other parts of its Empire, so in April 1782 peace negotiations were opened in Paris.

The peace treaty was concluded in November and approved by both sides in September 1783. The Treaty of Paris then settled independence on the new United States of America, with the new nation stretching from Canada in the north to Georgia in the south, from the Atlantic coast in the east to the Mississippi in the west. The last British soldiers were evacuated from New York in November 1783.

Wolfgang Amadeus Mozart

The eighteenth century was blessed with three of the finest composers ever: Johann Sebastian Bach (1685–1750), Wolfgang Amadeus Mozart (1756–1791) and Ludwig van Beethoven (1770–1821). It was also a period of huge musical change: Bach's music was that of early eighteenth-century Baroque, Mozart's compositions were those of classical-influenced culture of the late 1700s, and Beethoven's more emotionally volatile compositions marked the opening of the Romantic period of musical composition.

Mozart was a musical genius. At three years old he was playing keyboard pieces from memory, at five he composed a technically competent keyboard concerto, and at seven he was reported to have played a complex piece on the violin without extensive instruction. His first symphonies were composed at nine years old and his first opera at twelve.

The Mozart family lived in Catholic Austria, and until 1781 Mozart was in the employ of Hieronymus Joseph von Paula, Prince Archbishop of Salzburg.

Mozart was an instinctive musician. Melody, harmony and orchestration seemed to flow from his imagination and straight on to the staves of his music manuscripts. He was also a fiercely independent, stubborn character who was aware of his own genius. However, his association with the Catholic Church gave rise to some of the most outstanding sacred music composed in Europe.

Sacred music of the Baroque had been beautiful and uplifting, but works such as *Exultate Jubilate* (K165) and the Coronation Mass in C (K317) arguably bring a whole new level of joyousness to devotional music.

Mozart's time in the employ of the Archbishop of Salzburg resulted in the Coronation Mass, the *Vesprae de Dominica*, the Mass in C (K337) and the *Vesprae Solennes de Confessore* (K339). Towards the end of his life, he composed the brief, ethereally beautiful *Ave Verum* (K618), and at the time of his death in December 1791 he was close to completing a dark-toned Requiem (K626).

The French Revolution

In 1778 the French entered a military alliance with America. Their aim was to help bring about an American victory in the War of Independence, and to weaken the British military machine that allowed Britain to fight the French and maintain its colonial expansion.

For the Bourbon kings of France, the immediate intentions worked – the British pulled out of France. However, the French economy suffered grievously as a result of its involvement in the war. In France most of the land was owned by either the nobility or the clergy and this, allied with a near bankrupt economy from their expensive engagement in the American War, led to great rural poverty, which contrasted badly with the ostentatious consumption of the throne of King Louis. Worse yet, French citizens had just seen an example of a successful revolution, and in 1789 the French king was forced to call a meeting of the national assembly (the Estates General) in an attempt to placate an increasingly restless population.

The king's attempts failed, and the French rose in rebellion, forming a national assembly. They nationalised the Church's enormous holdings and split France into *départements*, each of which would be ruled by an elected assembly. France divided into Republican and Royalist factions. The early leaders of the Revolution (Georges Danton, Jean Marat and Maximillian Robespierre) were called Jacobins, since they met and conspired in a Jacobin convent in Paris. Their demands were for freedom and justice for the people, and to gain this end in 1792 they raised an army of peasants and invaded Paris.

In the same year, a Frenchman had invented a machine for the rapid and painless beheading of criminals, and that year Monsieur Guillotin's invention was put to work in Paris, executing any nobility and clergy rash enough to oppose the Revolution. Louis XVI also went to the guillotine on 21 April 1793. Religion was in the Revolutionaries' sights, too: in November 1793 a group of Jacobins burst into Notre Dame Cathedral and enthroned a dancer (said to be 'of dubious morals') as the 'Goddess of Reason'.

The execution of the king brought about the Reign of Terror, when thousands of people suspected of anti-revolutionary feelings were summarily executed. Madame Roland, a French Jacobin poet who supported the original aims of the Revolution, observed a day's executions in Paris and later wrote: 'Oh liberty! What crimes are committed in your name.'

France's neighbours viewed this Republican uprising with great concern – if it were to succeed in France, what chance did their own monarchies stand? In an effort to suppress the Republican revolution, many of France's neighbours declared war on France, and between 1793 and 1815 France was at war with England, Austria, the Netherlands, Prussia and Spain.

Maximillian Robespierre, instigator of the Reign of Terror, himself went to the guillotine, and the Reign of Terror ceased. However, revolutionary France was ungovernable, until in 1795 a short Corsican soldier called Napoleon Bonaparte began to take control of the revolutionary French army and Paris. Europe, and especially the pope, would hear much of Napoleon Bonaparte over the following two decades.

THE POPES
1700–1799

Clement XI (Giovanni Francesco Albani)
Rome; 23 November 1700 to 19 March 1721

Highly respected for his education, intellectual capacity
and piety, Giovanni Albani had held many papal posts,
and served the two previous popes, before his popular
election. The two main crises of his reign were the
War of the Spanish Succession (1701–1714) and the
continuing heresy of Jansenism. The latter Clement
condemned with the bull *Unigenitus Dei Filius* (1713).
The clash between the Habsburgs and the Bourbons
over the Spanish throne was more difficult. Clement
tried to remain neutral, to mediate, but his authority
was ignored by all sides and Italy was a battleground.
Papal fiefs, of Sardinia and Sicily, were parcelled out
to others by the Treaty of Utrecht (1713); papal protest
brought the expulsion of thousands of priests and nuns,
a situation only rectified in 1718. Clement decided
against the Jesuit missionaries attempts at inculturation
in China; condemning what was called 'the Chinese
Rites'.

Innocent XIII (Michelangelo dei Conti)
Rome; 8 May 1721 to 7 March 1724

In the stormy conclave following Clement XI's death,
French and Imperial supporters were at loggerheads;
Cardinal dei Conti was chosen as the compromise
candidate. Michelangelo dei Conti was the son of the
Duke of Poli; after his studies he entered papal service
and rose to cardinal, serving as papal nuncio in
Switzerland and Portugal. Innocent attempted to restore
relations with the major powers, but the papacy had
become so politically weak that he was compelled to
hand Sicily and Naples over to Emperor Charles VI
and raise the French king, Louis XV's, corrupt minister

Guillaume Dubois to the cardinalate. After a further papal condemnation of Jansenism (see Clement XI) Innocent succumbed to his recurring bad health.

Benedict XIII (Pietro Francesco Orsini)

Puglia, Italy; 29 May 1724 to 21 February 1730

From the famous Orsini family that had produced several popes throughout history, Pietro entered the Dominican Order at sixteen. Desiring to live the simple life of a friar, when raised to be cardinal and later, very reluctantly, pope, he continued to wear his habit and live a frugal lifestyle. He set out to be a truly spiritual and pastoral Bishop of Rome, visiting the sick and poor. He curbed the fashionable excesses of the cardinals, forbidding them to wear wigs. However, Benedict gave little attention to wider issues, misguidedly leaving these to the care of the unscrupulous Cardinal Niccolo Coscia, who with his cronies sold favours and offices to enrich themselves. This looting of the papal treasury only ended with Benedict's death.

Clement XII (Lorenzo Corsini)

Florence; 12 July 1730 to 6 February 1740

Born of the noble Corsini family of Florence, Lorenzo earned his doctorate in law and eventually became archbishop and papal nuncio to the court of Vienna. As a cardinal (1706) he became a powerful influence in the reigns of the two preceding popes. Failing health and age (he was seventy-nine when elected) suggested a short reign, but Clement proved to be a vigorous pope. Although blind for the last eight years and often confined to bed, he set about rectifying the problems Benedict left. Cardinal Coscia (see Benedict XIII) was arrested and imprisoned; the papal finances attended to and corruption rooted out. Politically the papacy continued to lose influence; Clement was unable to stop Spanish troops terrorising the people in the Papal States and European leaders ignored him. Clement spent much of his family's money on new buildings in

Rome; he was responsible for the famous Trevi
Fountain. He condemned Freemasonry in 1738.
Clement's courageous papacy, in the face of so many
disabilities, ended on 6 February 1740.

Benedict XIV (Prospero Lambertini)

Bologna; 17 August 1740 to 3 May 1758

After a succession of papal appointments in Rome,
Prospero Lambertini became adviser to Benedict XIII.
A long conclave of six months was resolved by the
election of Lambertini as a compromise candidate; but
he proved a very able pope. His intelligence, wit and
moderation won the admiration and respect not only
of all Christians but of scientists, scholars and philosophers. Benedict's real interest was in scientific learning
and in the Papal States. He founded a number of
academies in Rome, and in the Papal States encouraged
agricultural reform, free trade and reduced taxation.
Benedict was aware that the papacy had now lost much
of its temporal power and was conciliatory in his
relations with secular powers, making concessions to
Spain, Portugal and Naples. As a scholar in his own
right, Benedict wrote many seminal books, the most
important being on the canonisation of saints. He was
munificent in his gifts to the university libraries of
Bologna and Rome. His passing was sincerely mourned
by all.

Clement XIII (Carlo della Torre Rezzonico)

Venice; 6 July 1758 to 2 February 1769

From a wealthy Venetian family Carlo della Torre
Rezzonico was educated by the Jesuits. After his
doctorate from Padua, he entered papal service and
eventually was raised to the cardinalate by Clement
XII (1737). The French vetoed the conclave's first
choice, Carlo being their second. Strongly pro-Jesuit,
Clement was immediately confronted by controversy
over the Society which had won the enmity of the
European powers for their independence and loyalty

to the Holy See. First Portugal made false claims against them and expelled the Society; France followed, then Spain (6,000 were arrested and shipped to Italy in April 1767). Naples, Parma and Corsica followed suit. Clement constantly protested and defended the Jesuits, but this worsened relationships with the European powers. Confronted by a demand from the European powers that he dissolve the Society, Clement refused, and, days later, dropped dead of a heart attack.

Clement XIV (Lorenzo Ganganelli)

Rimini, Italy; 28 May 1769 to 4 September 1774

Lorenzo Ganganelli was the son of a village doctor. He entered the Franciscans and won a reputation for his learning. He declined the office of Master General of his Order but in 1759 accepted, when offered, the cardinal's hat. A supporter of the Jesuits, he inherited the crisis regarding their future, left by Clement XIII. The Catholic monarchs of Europe were ranged against the papacy demanding that the Jesuits be dissolved. Clement delayed for three years and then gave with the brief, *Dominus ac Redemptor* (1773) officially dissolving the Society. Clement made clear that this action was to bring peace between the Church and the European powers. Jesuit missions and Catholic education received a shattering blow. The papacy was now weak in the face of secular rulers and the Enlightenment offered new challenges. Clement's last months were invaded by acute depression, fear of assassination and guilt for his treatment of the Jesuits. Rumours spread that he had been poisoned; an autopsy proved them fictitious.

Pius VI (Giovanni Angelo Braschi)

Cesena; 15 February 1775 to 29 August 1799

Educated by the Jesuits, Giovanni Braschi became first secretary to Cardinal Ruffo, legate of Ferrara, then eventually papal secretary, and cardinal (1773) being recognised as one of the most capable clerics in papal

service. In the first peaceful years of his long reign Pius
VI won the approval of the Romans as patron of the
arts and for the draining of the Pontine Marshes. His
authority was seriously challenged by Febronianism and
Josephism (named after the Emperor Joseph II) which
amounted to state control over national Churches. The
next challenge came from the French Revolution
(1789); Pius tried to maintain stable relations with the
revolutionary government, but failed. The young
Napoleon Bonaparte seized the Papal States (1796) and
a negotiated peace left French troops at the gates of
Rome. In February 1798, they entered Rome; Pius
was deposed as head of the Papal States and a Roman
Republic was declared. With dignity Pius refused to
bow to the Revolutionaries, but, frail and ill, was forced
into exile as a virtual prisoner. At his death, in Valence,
many believed that it was the end of the papacy.

1800–1900
Marxism, empires and
missionary Christianity

Timeline 1800–1900

1801 Napoleon, the French Emperor, allows the re-establishment of Catholicism in France.

1807 Christian Members of Parliament force the abolition of slavery in Britain.

1808 The Vatican appoints a first American Roman Catholic bishop in Baltimore.

1810 The Spanish Colonies in South America begin a series of revolts for independence.

1814 An Anglican Bishop is established in Calcutta, India.

1819 Catholic Bishops gather in Baltimore.

1826 Religious orders in South America experience widespread suppression.

1829 Roman Catholics in Britain are emancipated from discriminatory laws.

1830 An anti-Catholic movement begins in the USA.

1836 Both the Catholic and the Anglican Church appoint bishops in Australia.

1839 Pope Gregory XVI condemns slavery.

1845 John Henry Newman converts to Catholicism. Brigham Young establishes Salt Lake City as the centre of the Mormon Church.

1848 Revolution in Rome. The Pope flees.

1850 A Roman Catholic hierarchy is established in England and Wales.

1854 Pius IX issues a Papal bull stating that the Virgin Mary is an Immaculate Conception.

1858 Bernadette experiences visions of the Virgin Mary at Lourdes, France.

1864 Pope Pius IX publishes the *Syllabus of Errors*, a critique of modern life.

1865 The first black Bishop is ordained in Nigeria.

1869 The first Vatican Council establishes papal infallibility.

1873-76 Bismarck's *Kulturkampf* and the persecution of German Catholics.

1875 The world Alliance of Reformed and Methodist Churches is formed.

1886 Roman Catholic hierarchy is established in India.

1891 Pope Leo XIII's encyclical *Rerum Novarum* establishes Catholic social teaching.

1896 The Vatican declares all Anglican ordinations invalid.

Introduction – Development of the modern world

During the nineteenth century the shape and nature of much of the modern world was established. At the start of the century, Europe was wracked by the Napoleonic wars, the North American continent was divided between the newly independent Americans, the Spanish and the French, and Central and South America were still under Spanish rule.

By 1899 the outline of modern Europe had developed, with Italy and Germany emerging as sovereign nation-states. The United States had either bought or fought its way to ownership of North America, and the Spaniards had been driven out of Central and South America as one country after another gained independence.

Britain kept its imperial ambitions, and in this century it was said that the sun did not set on the British Empire. The British gained control of most of India and large tracts of Africa, and British colonists were settling Australia and New Zealand. The British rule of Canada was settled and the Union Flag flew over many Pacific islands.

In the Orient, both the Chinese and the Japanese attempted to stay isolated from the attentions of the British and European trading nations. China had a large opium industry, and there was great demand for this drug in the west. The British twice declared war on China ostensibly for control of the opium trade, but the underlying reason was access to Chinese ports for trading purposes.

Africa, too, became a target for Europe's colonial ambitions. Africa was a country of immense mineral wealth, and until the abolition of slavery in Britain and America, was also a source of slave labour. The French, Dutch, Belgians, German and British all sought to establish colonies in Africa, and by the end of the century most of the continent was under the control of one of these powers.

However, at the start of the nineteenth century Europe was still in the grip of the Napoleonic wars. Napoleon Bonaparte had conquered much of Europe, and it seemed his ambition was limitless. To the south he had taken Spain, and by 1812–1813 Spain's colonies in South America saw their colonial masters' weakness as an opportunity to rebel against Spanish rule. Argentina, Chile, Venezuela and Mexico either rebelled or declared independence.

Napoleon was overthrown first in 1814 when he was exiled to Elba, from where he escaped and raised an army in 1815. He was decisively defeated at Waterloo in 1815.

The end of Napoleonic France saw also the end of the Holy Roman Empire, the assembly of states including Germany, eastern France, northern Italy, Austria and Bohemia. It had come into existence around 800, and had lasted until 1806 when it fell to Napoleon's armies. With the peace of 1815 the peace conference in Vienna decided not to allow its re-establishment, a decision that paved the way to Germany and Italy becoming separate, sovereign nation-states.

The politics of the American continent were developing quickly: in 1818 the USA bought Florida from Spain, and between 1819 and 1821 Colombia, Peru and Panama declared independence from Spain. This mood of American strength and growing confidence was reinforced when in 1823 the US President James Monroe declared no European powers should interfere in either North or South American affairs. In the next two years Brazil, Bolivia and Peru gained their independence from the Spanish.

While the end of the Napoleonic wars might have ended Europe-wide war, the continent was far from peaceful or settled. Greece and Turkey were at war, in 1825 the Russian Czar Nicholas II faced and crushed a revolt by the Decembrists, and in 1831 Russia and Poland became embroiled in a war.

In 1848, Europe erupted into rebellion: the French monarchy (restored in 1815) was again overthrown, and Hungary rebelled against Austrian Habsburg rule. Britain managed to avoid outright rebellion (troops were used to quell riotous assemblies of workers). Britain had its own revolutionary gift for the world, giving a home to Karl Marx, whose revolutionary Communist writings inspired Marxist and Communist revolutions throughout the world.

Italian nationalism also began to rise: northern Italy was occupied by Austrians, and the Papal States around Rome prevented any unification taking place. There could be only one capital of a united Italy, Rome, but Rome was still a papal province, the pope's rule supported by French forces. In 1870 the Germans invaded France, starting the Franco-Prussian war. Rome's French garrison withdrew to fight the Germans and the Italian king, Victor Emmanuel, rode into Rome, proclaiming it the capital of Italy. Pope Pius IX, who had previously condemned the Italian nationalists and democrats, was virtually a prisoner in the Vatican.

Despite these conflicts, Europe was a more settled place in the second half of the nineteenth century, and with a freedom from conflict science, industry and culture could thrive: industrialisation continued to spread, and with it great engineering feats became possible. Steamships made regular transatlantic crossings, cutting the time for a voyage to America to less than thirty days. The first goods-carrying steam railway had opened in England in 1825, and in America in 1826. Soon railways were starting to spread through mainland Europe and mass land transport of people and goods was possible.

Science made numerous breakthroughs and the application of science through engineering led to remarkable feats: the opening of the Suez Canal, linking the Mediterranean to the Red Sea, and the building of the 289-metre-high Eiffel Tower.

America continued its expansion. It had doubled in size in the early 1800s through its $15 million purchase of Louisiana from the French; in 1845 Texas joined the USA, and in 1846 the USA seized California and New Mexico from the Mexicans. US pioneers crossed the Rocky Mountains to settle the west coast, displacing the indigenous American Indians in a series of wars.

However, the issue of slavery divided America so bitterly that between 1861 and 1865 the anti-slavery northern states fought a bitter civil war with the pro-slavery southern states. The north prevailed, and slavery was abolished.

Socially, industrialisation had led to the emergence of a working class, and the development of Communism by Marx and Engels gave the emerging leaders of the workers (who still often worked long hours, lived in squalid conditions and were without the vote) a political philosophy: socialism began to emerge in Europe.

The century ended with man taking to the skies: in 1896 German Otto Lilienthal took to the air in the world's first glider. It also took him to his grave following a fatal crash. In 1896 Athens hosted the first Olympic Games after 1,500 years. Much of the modern world was shaped in the nineteenth century Europe and the American continent emerged much as they are today. Australia, Canada and New Zealand gained considerable independence from British dominion but large tracts of India, China and Africa were still subject to colonial control.

The Napoleonic wars

Napoleon Bonaparte had taken control of the French Revolutionary Army in 1796 and in 1799 he seized control of France and was crowned emperor. Napoleon had massive imperial ambitions for France, and in the early years of the century he invaded and occupied Spain, Portugal, Italy, Egypt and large parts of the Holy Roman Empire. The Holy Roman Empire (which was satirised by the French thinker Voltaire as 'neither holy, Roman, nor an empire') had lasted for a thousand years, until Napoleon abolished it 1806.

Napoleon also wished to conquer Britain, a long-standing bitter enemy of France, and in 1803 he gathered a massive invasion force in northern France. However, to transport his soldiers to Britain he needed naval control of the Channel, which meant defeating the powerful British Navy. Napoleon assembled a large fleet of French and Spanish ships in Spanish ports and in 1805 ordered them to sail for the Channel to support his invasion. The combined fleet sailed, but were intercepted by a British naval fleet commanded by Admiral Horatio Nelson (who hated the French 'as the Devil himself') at the Battle of Trafalgar. The combined fleet was utterly routed, and with them Napoleon's plans to invade Britain. Instead he turned his attention to the east, where Austria, Prussia and Russia attracted Napoleon's imperial eye.

Napoleon, a soldier by training, was a shrewd battlefield tactician, and at the Battle of Austerlitz in 1805 he beat the Russian and Austrian forces, compelling the defeated Austria to negotiate for peace. In 1806 the Prussians faced Napoleon's armies at the Battle of Jena and they, too, were defeated. The Russian emperor, Alexander I, entered a treaty of friendship with Napoleon in 1807, by which time Napoleon was in control of much of Europe. However, in 1808 Spanish forces began a major revolt against French occupation and Napoleon sent a large army to quell the revolt; and at the same time the British landed an army under the command of General Arthur Wellesley (later the Duke of Wellington) in Portugal.

The British campaign to drive the French out of Portugal and Spain became known as the Peninsular War, and after initial setbacks the British Army, aided by Portuguese and Spanish guerrillas, drove Napoleon's forces north towards the Pyrenees and France.

Despite the British invasion of Spain, Napoleon turned his attention to Italy, annexing the Papal States and forcing Pope Pius VII into exile in the French town of Grenoble. The pope fought back in the only way he knew how – excommunication. The British continued to make progress against Napoleon's armies, and in 1812 they drove the French out of the Spanish capital Madrid. The French armies began to retreat across the Pyrenees into France, but despite these military reverses Napoleon opened another front in his war of European conquest.

Tearing up the 1807 treaty of friendship, Napoleon's armies invaded Russia in June 1812, defeated the Russians at the Battle of Borodino and occupied Moscow. However, the French Grand Army could not stand the appalling Moscow winter and in November they retreated from Russia. Around half a million men died in Napoleon's invasion of Russia.

Still Napoleon commanded a large (but weakened) army, and in 1813 he faced a coalition of Russian, Prussian, Swedish and Austrian armies at the Battle of Leipzig. Napoleon suffered a further crushing defeat, after which 60,000 more of his Grand Army lay dead. In 1814 the British army crossed the Pyrenees and again beat the Napoleonic forces at the Battle of Toulouse.

Napoleon abdicated and was sent into short-lived exile on the Mediterranean island of Elba. In 1815 he escaped and marched into Paris, where he once again raised an army and revived his imperial ambitions. Napoleon's new army met the British army, commanded by Wellington, at the Battle of Waterloo. The British were supported by Prussian forces and carried the day in what Wellington later called 'a damned close-run thing'. Napoleon was taken prisoner, and this time he was exiled far away, to the Atlantic island of St Helena, where he died aged fifty-one.

Invention, innovation and industry

In the early nineteenth century, war slowed the pace of progress in both European and American societies, but with the stability of peace, science, engineering, capital and industry combined in a critical mass to make this a century of innovation and industrial production.

Just as steam power had driven the start of the Industrial Revolution in the eighteenth century, a new source of power began to emerge. Electricity was to be the new power for a new society. In 1821 Michael Faraday's work on electromagnetic induction opened the way to the electric motor and the electricity-producing dynamo. The principle of 'storing' electricity in batteries was first invented by the Italian physicist Alessandro Volta in 1800. The dry cell battery was developed in 1863, and in 1890 the 'Ever Ready' battery went into production in New York.

Applications for electricity rapidly followed. In the 1840s American Samuel Morse patented Morse telegraphy, where a code made

Catholic Europe in the 1800s

The nineteenth century was a period of both setbacks and renewal for the Roman Catholic Church in Europe. France, Britain and Germany developed anti-Catholic movements at some time during the century, but the Church showed its usual resilience in the face of adversity. In 1814 the Jesuits were restored following years of suppression. They returned to active missionary work with their former vigour and played a part in countering anti-Catholic sentiments in Europe. In Britain, Catholics were emancipated in 1849 and in Germany a Catholic Union was founded in Mainz in 1851.

The nineteenth century is particularly remarkable due to the influence of Pope Pius IX, whose long reign (1846–1878) included the first Vatican Council. It was at this Council that the pope's supremacy over the Church was confirmed. Where before the pope's authority had been assumed, the Council declared the pope incapable of error when teaching on matters of faith and morals. The notion of papal infallibility dates from this 1870 pronouncement.

Pius IX was succeeded by Leo XIII. Leo took European anti-Catholicism seriously, and took pains to work towards more amicable relations between the Catholic Church and the governments of Europe. In 1891 he published the papal encyclical *Rerum Novarum* (Of New Things), which was the foundation of modern Catholic social teaching. It addressed the problems caused by 'modernism' and by the rise of the industrial society. Among its pronouncements are a marked distaste for the growing Communist political movement and a call for workers to be allowed to unionise and be free of exploitation.

up of long and short tones was transmitted over electrically charged wires. Morse telegraphy marked the start of rapid communication, and by the 1860s telegraph wires linked most US cities. In 1879 Thomas Edison used electricity to make the first electric light bulb, meaning that for the first time people could have light without the attendant risk of fire.

Morse telegraphy was part of a massive communications revolution. In 1811 the German Friedrich Konig developed the first steam-powered press, a discovery that hugely increased the rate at which a printing press could work. Newspapers could now be produced rapidly and in bulk, and the first newspaper to be produced using this method was *The Times*, which first used steam-powered presses in London in 1814. While printing was now rapid, typesetting (arranging the embossed metal blocks of letters which made up the print) was still done by hand – a slow and error-prone method. In 1884 another German, Ottmar Mergenthaler invented the Linotype machine, a large keyboard-driven machine that set the blocks of type mechanically.

The Linotype was probably inspired by another nineteenth-century invention, the typewriter, which was first produced in 1870 by the American company E. Remington and Sons.

In Britain, the early nineteenth century saw the invention of machine tools, which could shape metal to fine tolerances so that steam engines could work more efficiently producing more power, and machinery could be produced to higher specifications, producing finished products to a higher standard. Two Scottish engineers invented modern 'macadamised' roads, and steamships had developed to the point that shipping companies could run regular transatlantic crossings.

However, the telegraph meant that people no longer had to travel and deliver a message verbally, or rely on the vagaries of the post. In 1858 the first telegraph cable was laid along the floor of the Atlantic Ocean, linking America and Britain.

In Britain, mathematician Charles Babbage spent much of his life designing the difference engine and the analytical engine. Both were machines intended to solve and print the results of complex mathematical calculations, with the instructions and data being fed into the machine by punched cards. Babbage's theoretical work was ahead of the manufacturing ability of the time, but his efforts were the foundations of mechanical computing, and the principles he established carried into modern electronic computing. The Americans industrialised rapidly and one of their particular specialities was firearms. In 1833 Samuel Colt invented and produced the revolver, a new type of handgun that allowed men to kill and maim one another with greater efficiency.

Pure science discoveries continued: the speed of light was discovered in 1849, in the 1850s Englishman Thomas Dalton produced a table of the atomic weights of each chemical element, and in 1866 Gregor Mendel (a German monk) used observations of pea plants to deduce the nature of heredity and introduce the science of genetics to the world.

In 1866 Swedish chemist Alfred Nobel blew up his latest factory with his latest discovery – nitro-glycerine. He survived to make a fortune, and with it founded the Nobel prize. X-rays were discovered in 1895 by the German physicist William Roentgen, and as the century closed, the French couple Marie and Pierre Curie discovered the radioactive element radium, for which they won a Nobel prize.

At the beginning of the nineteenth century, the French and British were fighting one another with swords and flintlock muskets. By the end of the century, an Italian called Marconi was transmitting Morse code over the earliest radio sets, and at the Swiss Polytechnic Institute in Zurich, a clever young man was finishing his first degree. His name was Albert Einstein.

Karl Marx and Communism

Karl Heinrich Marx was born in Trier, Prussia, in 1818. His was to be a remarkable life, and his writings gave rise to two of the most important political movements of the twentieth century – Communism and socialism.

In 1835 Marx entered the University of Bonn to study law. Prussia was a highly autocratic state whose rulers allowed citizens little participation in public life, and Marx rapidly became a political activist, joining radical academics in urging greater democracy for the masses. Despite his obvious academic ability and gaining his Doctorate in Philosophy in 1841, Marx's political activity led to his being disqualified from teaching jobs in universities.

Marx moved to Paris, where he met his friend and long-term collaborator Friedrich Engels, and there worked as a freelance journalist, editing radical political journals that spread his revolutionary thinking. Marx and Engels co-authored the Communist Manifesto, publishing it in 1848, the same year that Europe erupted into revolution.

The *Communist Manifesto* characterises history as a continuous struggle between the classes, a struggle that would ultimately end with the overthrow of the ruling classes by the working classes. The result would be classless society, where the people owned the means of production. The *Communist Manifesto* closes by stating: 'Let the ruling classes tremble at a Communistic revolution. The proletarians have nothing to lose but their chains. They have a world to win. WORKING MEN OF ALL COUNTRIES UNITE!'

When the German revolution of 1848 failed, Marx fled to London where he lived researching and writing, although not earning much money. He spent much of his time in poverty and only survived because of financial support from Engels.

In 1867 Marx published *Das Kapital*, a monumental work that took thirty years to research and write. In it Marx made clear that he felt the free enterprise system was effective and successful, but only in the short term. He stated that capitalism was fatally flawed, since periods of inflation and depression would weaken the system, and so much money would accumulate that it could not be fairly distributed. The accumulation of riches would be paralleled by an increase in widespread human unhappiness, resulting in the collapse of the capitalist system.

Marx also kept up a voluminous correspondence with his friends and fellow revolutionaries, and even though he produced elaborate political and philosophical writings, he failed to provide a route map to the goal of Communism. Possibly this was because of his stated conviction that the collapse of capitalism and triumph of Communism was inevitable.

The political movements that followed Marx's writings variously called themselves Communists, Marxists and Revolutionary Socialists, and his lack of direction meant that emerging left-wing revolutionaries spent much time and energy arguing among themselves as to how Marx intended his revolutionary ideals to be realised.

Marx was a great admirer of Charles Darwin and his theory of natural selection, and did Darwin the honour of sending him a dedicated first edition of *Das Kapital*. It appears that the admiration was not mutual. Darwin was a voracious reader, but *Das Kapital* remained on Darwin's shelf, the pages uncut, the book unread.

Marx left an enormous historical legacy, his writings starting a political philosophy that would dominate world affairs throughout much of the twentieth century. In 1891 Pope Leo XIII explicitly condemned Communism in his encyclical *Rerum Novarum* (*Of New Things*). The Soviet Revolution of 1917 instituted a period of Communist government that cost the lives of tens of millions of people, partitioned Europe and led to the hugely expensive arms race in the Cold War. Communist China had a similarly bloody history in the Cultural Revolution. America's distrust of Communist governments caused a series of twentieth century wars in Korea and Vietnam, and covert wars throughout Central and South America.

Freud and the growth of psychology

The 1800s was remarkable for the development of three great ideas. Karl Marx developed the idea of revolutionary Communism, which would affect global politics until the present day, Charles Darwin made the first coherent attempt at explaining evolution by natural selection, and some would argue that Sigmund Freud invented the idea of human self-consciousness.

Freud was born in 1856, and following his graduation from medical school at the University of Vienna in 1881 he specialised in neurology, the emerging science of the brain and nervous system. Freud began to specialise in the study of mentally ill patients, and developed the theory that much human behaviour is governed by unconscious urges. He theorised that many people spend a great deal of emotional energy keeping painful memories and emotions buried (using a series of what he called 'defence mechanisms'), and called the resulting illness 'neurosis'.

His observations of his patients led him to conclude that people grow through a series of 'psychosexual' developments (he contended that children are sexually aware before they consciously realise it) and that any interruption of this development can cause mental illness later in life.

Freud also developed a structure for the human mind, which he divided into three parts: the id, the ego and the superego. In Freud's view, the id is the source of human instincts, such as the urge to mate or be violent. The ego is the part of the mind that modifies the id's urges into socially acceptable behaviour patterns. A further modifying effect is the superego, which is the seat of the conscience and resolves questions of right and wrong. Freud identified conflict between these three components of the mind as a further source of mental illness in adult life.

Freud also applied himself to devising treatments for mentally ill patients. He called his therapeutic approach *psychoanalysis*, a treatment which centred around free association, where the patient would talk randomly about whatever occurred to him or her. Freud would analyse both the patient's outpourings and their accounts of their dreams in an effort to identify the underlying causes of their neurosis, and the defence mechanisms by which patients hid their painful memories and experiences.

Freud's influence on psychiatry and psychology were enormous.

While some of his specific conclusions may be either questionable or incorrect, he demonstrated the importance of the unconscious on thinking, reasoning and creativity. He did immense work in stimulating the study of abnormal personalities and the development of psychology, and established the importance of childhood experiences in forming subsequent adult behaviour.

Darwin's evolution revolution

In 1859 Charles Darwin published *On the Origin of Species*. The book became a best-seller, because it contained a layman's explanation of the first workable theory of evolution. Darwin was by no means the first to suggest evolution, but he was the first to propose a mechanism by which it might happen, and to provide evidence in support of his theory.

Darwin was no revolutionary, but his theory was. It changed forever the study of biology, created a rift between the established church and Victorian science, and profoundly influenced political and social thought.

Son of a prosperous Shropshire doctor, Charles Darwin also went to medical school, but found he hated the sight of blood and in the 1830s enrolled at Cambridge University. His intention was to become an Anglican clergyman in an undemanding country parish and devote his time to his real passion: the study of natural history in general, and beetles in particular.

During the early nineteenth century, science was the province of enthusiastic clergymen who believed the Genesis account of the Earth's creation: the Earth was no more than a few thousand years old, and all its present living inhabitants were created by God and were the descendants of the survivors of Noah's flood. Against this background, the young Darwin was offered a place on *HMS Beagle*, a ship tasked with surveying the coast of South America as part of a voyage around the world.

Despite appalling seasickness and problems with the manic-depressive Captain FitzRoy, Darwin was in a collectors' and naturalists' paradise. He trekked extensively in South America, and visited Australia, the Falklands and the Galapagos Islands, where he collected rocks and fossils and shot, skinned and preserved anything that moved. He sketched, recorded, observed, absorbed and reflected over a five-year period.

On his return to Britain in 1836 he had sufficient material to occupy him in writing and research for years, and he abandoned the idea of a parish in favour of a scientific career. He developed his evolutionary ideas shortly after his return from his voyage, but kept them to himself (written in private code in secret notebooks) for many years: evolution was tantamount to heresy, and Darwin depended on the Anglican establishment for patronage in his fledgling scientific career.

Darwin was forced to publish when in 1858 a fellow naturalist announced a similar theory. It was now or never for Charles Darwin, and *On the Origin of Species* was the result. In it Darwin stated that living creatures are subject to external pressures. Some individuals are by chance better adapted to survive these pressures, and as result they breed more successfully and pass on their favourable adaptations. Ill-adapted individuals (and whole species) may die out, while well-adapted individuals (and populations) continue to breed, gradually accruing changes so that in time a new species could evolve.

Darwin's theory required an Earth that was perhaps millions of years old, where chance rather than God produced living creatures, and where Noah's flood did not happen. In 1859 the Anglican Church was very much in control of society, and the struggling young profession of science was trying to establish itself. The Church saw Darwin's theory as an attack on Genesis, and by implication the truth of the Bible and the very existence of the Church.

Darwin did not intend his theory as an attack on religion: he published because he was at heart a scientist and believed his theory to be correct, but Darwin's more aggressive supporters seized on his theory and used it to attack the Church. Evolutionary theory now underpins biological research and many branches of Christianity now accept the theory of evolution; in 1996 Pope John Paul II asserted that 'new knowledge has led to the recognition of the theory of evolution as more than a hypothesis'.

Australia

In the late eighteenth century, a British subject convicted of even a relatively minor criminal offence could be executed or transported to an American penal colony. In 1783 America gained independence and Britain had to find somewhere else to dump its convicted criminals.

In the 1770s, Captain James Cook had explored the eastern coast of Australia and named it New South Wales. The British government decided to make this rugged, mostly unknown land on the far side of the world its new penal colony. In January 1788 a convoy of eleven ships landed at Botany Bay with about 550 male and 160 female convicts, accompanied by 200 British soldiers to serve as guards. Some wives and children accompanied them. They founded the first European settlement in Australia.

Convict immigration continued, as did exploration of this massive continent. The early settlers were not sure whether Australia was a series of islands or one land mass, until in 1801 the British navigator Matthew Flinders circumnavigated the entire island, and established that this was indeed Terra Australis, the mythical southern continent. By the 1820s, the name had been changed to Australia.

In 1824 two colonists, Hamilton Hume and William Hovell, trekked overland from Sydney to the place now occupied by Melbourne, sighting a major river en route. A further explorer, Charles Sturt, followed this river to the sea in 1836, and the colonists that followed established the colony of South Australia.

In 1829 Captain Charles Fremantle claimed western Australia for Britain, and that year seventy pioneers settled on the south-west coast and founded the British colony of Western Australia, establishing the settlement that became the city of Perth.

In the 1830s explorers began to penetrate the Australian desert interior. In 1851 the first gold deposits were found in New South Wales, and shortly after a second gold strike was made in Victoria. A gold rush ensued, attracting hordes of prospectors, and between 1851 and 1861 the population of Australia rose from 400,000 to 1,100,000.

Britain abolished penal transportation in 1868; in the eighty years since transportation had first started, 160,000 convicts had been sent to the penal colonies.

Britain began to grant self-government to the Australian colonies in the 1850s, and in 1859 the colony of Queensland was established. By the late nineteenth century, Australia was developing a strong sense of national identity, and began to lobby for unified, independent government.

In 1897 a national convention drafted a new national constitution, which was approved by the population in 1898 and 1899. On New Year's Day 1901 the Commonwealth of Australia became a new independent nation.

Australia's native Aborigine population were simply conquered. For many years they were a persecuted minority in their own land, suffering a similar fate to the native Indians of the American continents.

European colonisation in the nineteenth century

The nineteenth century marked a collapse in the fortunes of Spain, which had previously been a great world power with colonial control of Central and South America. Spanish power was much diminished following lengthy wars with Britain, and early in the century Spain formed an alliance with the French Emperor Napoleon Bonaparte.

In 1805 much of the Spanish navy was destroyed at the Battle of Trafalgar and in 1808 Napoleon's armies invaded and conquered Spain. In the years that followed, most of Spain's South American colonies took advantage of Spain's weakness to rebel and declare independence. The Spanish tried to maintain control but were powerless to resist, and through the 1820s and 1830s most of the Central and South American countries gained independence and won diplomatic recognition from the United States.

Spain was left with Cuba, Guam, Puerto Rico and the Philippines, all of which it lost in 1898 following the Spanish–American War.

Britain governed much of India, and such was its power in the Asian region that in 1842 the British used gunboat diplomacy to force China to open five of its ports to British trade, and following this became a powerful colonial presence in southern China. China was a source of important trading goods including silk and the valuable drug opium, and the large country's considerable resources also attracted Russian and German colonists. The French, despite their losses in the Napoleonic wars, recovered to invade Indochina, the modern-day Vietnam, Laos and Cambodia.

By the nineteenth century, the European industrial society had created an enormous demand for raw materials, and it was increasingly clear that the 'Dark Continent', as Africa was known, was a great source of mineral wealth and, in the early part of the century, slaves. An estimated 10 million Africans were kidnapped from the West African coast and sent into slavery in the USA and Britain. The European exploitation of Africa intensified, and by the 1880s Britain, Germany, France, the Netherlands, Belgium, Spain and Portugal were all involved in a race to seize the more potentially profitable tracts of Africa. As with the previous European colonisation of the Americas, Asia and Australia, the wishes and rights of the native populations were subjugated to the colonial ambitions of the Europeans.

The American anthropologist and biologist Jared Diamond attributes the European success in colonising the world to guns, germs and steel. A retrospective addition might well add the Gospels to that list, because wherever colonists went, missionaries followed.

THE POPES
1800–1903

Pius VII (Luigi Barnaba Chiaramonti)
Cesena, Italy; 14 March 1800 to 20 August 1823

A three-month-long conclave at Venice was deadlocked due to political pressures; Cardinal Chiaramonti, a progressive-thinking, pro-democracy Benedictine, was chosen. He had been Abbot of San Calisto, Rome, and then Bishop of Tivoli, becoming a cardinal in 1785. Pius VII won universal respect for his dignity under repression and courageous handling of Napoleon Bonaparte, whose actions dominated Pius' reign. A negotiated concordat (1801) with France was violated by Napoleon's domination of the Church. Pius travelled to Paris 1804) to crown Napoleon, but was snubbed and humiliated. He tried to keep the Church neutral as war swept Europe, but the emperor seized the Papal States. Pius excommunicated Napoleon, but was then arrested, banished from Rome and continually abused in captivity. At Napoleon's defeat Pius returned to Rome amid much acclaim (24 March 1814). At the Congress of Vienna he used his prestige to secure the return of the Papal States. Pius reinstated the Jesuits (1814) and gave refuge to Napoleon's family when they were outcasts everywhere else. He signed concordats with Russia and Prussia and instituted the new Congregation for the Propagation of the Faith.

Leo XII (Annibale della Genga)
Genga; 28 September 1823 to 10 February 1829

After an unremarkable career as a diplomat in papal service, Annibale della Genga, a devout, austere and rather cheerless cardinal, was elected. His supporters, Cardinal Severoli and friends, wanted a more spiritual and pastoral pope; Leo XII did not disappoint them. He was unpopular with everyone else, as he restricted most forms of diversion and entertainment in Rome, ordered the Jews back into their ghetto and disapproved of realism in art, even having nude statues removed or covered. However, his Secretary of State, Cardinal Consalvi, was more successful on the international scene, maintaining amicable relations with the European Protestant and Catholic powers. Rome and the Papal States became like a police state, with everything checked upon, with stagnating finances and widespread inefficiency. Leo's passing was not mourned by the public.

Pius VIII (Francesco Castiglione)

Cingoli, Italy; 31 March 1829 to 30 November 1830

Educated by the Jesuits, Francesco Castiglione, an expert in canon law, won his cardinal's hat for his courageous opposition to Napoleon in the reign of Pius VII. He was favoured and promoted by Pius to be Bishop of Frascati and prefect of the Congregation of the Index which inspected publications and maintained a list of forbidden books. Not surprisingly, Francesco took the name Pius on his election. In his short reign he tried to reverse his predecessor's harsh reign. He was delighted with the passing, in England, of the Roman Catholic Relief Acts (April 1829).

Gregory XVI (Bartolomeo Cappellari)

Belluno, Italy; 6 February 1831 to 1 June 1846

Bartolomeo Cappellari joined the Camaldolese Order at the age of eighteen and rose to become abbot (1805) and procurator-general of the Order. Made a cardinal (1826), and head of the Congregation for the Propagation of the Faith, he was elected for his well-known conservative views. Gregory opposed each and every modern trend (even refusing to have the railway in the Papal States); he denounced liberal ideas in his encyclical *Mirari Vos*. Ignoring the social needs of the Papal States, Gregory was faced with continual discontent and open revolt, only contained by the use of foreign troops. He condemned slavery (1839) and enthusiastically revived missionary work around the world, encouraging the use of indigenous clergy. He left behind Papal States that were severely debilitated.

Pius IX (Giovanni Maria Mastai-Ferretti)

Semigallia, Papal States; 16 June 1846 to 7 February 1878

The longest-reigning pope, so far, in history, Pius IX (more usually known as Pio Nono) had served with distinction in the papal diplomatic service and was known to be liberal in his views and an Italian patriot. At fifty-five and with an attractive personality, he was young to be pope. Pius began with a general amnesty for all political prisoners and much needed reforms in the Papal States; however, his conciliatory approach was misinterpreted by Italian nationalists who murdered Pius's first minister, Count Rossi. Pio Nono fled to Gaeta. He abandoned his liberal views, and was restored to Rome by French troops in 1850. When these were withdrawn in 1870, the city fell; Pius proclaimed himself a 'prisoner of the Vatican', refusing steadfastly to acknowledge the new Italian government. Papal temporal power was now no more. His most famous document, the *Syllabus of Errors* (1864) condemning all modern ideas and trends including democracy, caused an outcry. Pius summoned a Council of the Church (First Vatican Council) in 1869, which, condemned liberalism and declared papal infallibility. His other achievements were to proclaim the definition of the Immaculate Conception (1854), restore the hierarchy of bishops to England (1850) and the Netherlands (1853) and, unwittingly, act as a major transitional Pope from the mediæval concept of religious and temporal power to the modern understanding of a pastoral and spiritual leader for the Church and the world.

Leo XIII (Gioacchino Vincenzo Pecci)

Carpentino, Italy; 20 February 1878 to 20 July 1903

Trained at the Academy of Noble Ecclesiastics for the Vatican diplomatic service, Gioacchino Pecci was governor of Perugia before serving as papal nuncio to Belgium (1843) and then, as cardinal(1853), Pius IX made him camerlengo (the cardinal chamberlain responsible for Church government between popes). A scholar, and in bad health at his election, Leo continued with his predecessor's policies, refusing to deal with the Italian government. He reached an accommodation with the German chancellor, Otto von Bismarck and brought the *Kulturkampf* to an end. His writings on Catholic Social Doctrine, particularly the famous encyclical, *Rerum Novarum* (1891) won Leo the title "the workers' pope". He gave much encouragement to the study of St Thomas Aquinas, to missionary work and the establishment of new dioceses in the USA (twenty-eight), India and Japan. Leo encouraged scientific study and biblical research. He restored to the papacy much of the international respect lost by his predecessor. Leo remained intellectually active up to his sudden death at ninety-three.

1900 – present
A century of warfare and
the growth of the secular society

Timeline 1900–present

1907 Pius X's encyclical *Pascendi* condemns Modernism.

1910 Beginning of the Ecumenical Movement at Edinburgh Missionary Conference.

1917 Benedict XV's Peace Plan rejected by Great War combatants.

1928 Papal document *Mortalium Animo* forbids Catholics to worship with other Christians.

1931 Encyclical *Quadragesimo Anno* reaffirms Catholic Social teaching.

1933 Hitler's Enabling Act and Pope Pius XI's Concordat with Hitler.

1937 Encyclical *Mit Brennender Sorge* condemns Nazism.

1940 Roger Schultz founds the Taizé community in France.

1948 First meeting of the World Council of Churches.

1950 The definition of the Assumption of the Blessed Virgin Mary as an article of Catholic faith.

1960 Archbishop Geoffrey Fisher's historic visit to Pope John XXIII; first by an Archbishop of Canterbury since 1397.

1962 Pope John XXIII opens the Second Vatican Council.

1965 Paul VI and Patriarch Athenagoras mutually lift excommunications.
The Second Vatican Council closes and publishes eighteen documents for Renewal of the Church.

1968 The controversial encyclical *Humanae Vitae* is published.

1971 Synod of South American bishops at Medellin, endorse 'the Preferential Option for the Poor'.

1978 Polish cardinal, Karol Wotyla, elected and takes the name John Paul II.

1979 Mother Teresa awarded Nobel Peace Prize.
Pope John Paul II, at Puebla, clarifies teaching on Liberation Theology.

1980 Archbishop Oscar Romero is assassinated in El Salvador.

1980 Pope John Paul II visits England and Wales.

1982 ARCIC I presents its 'Final Report'.

1994 The *Catechism of the Catholic Church* is published.

2000 Pope John Paul inaugurates a Holy Year.

Introduction

The years 1900 to 2000 cover such social, technological, spiritual and geographical change that the century defies summing up in a single phrase.

Economically and politically, the century was defined by the struggle between the capitalist and Communist ideologies. The Communist revolutions in Russia and China were started in conflict and perpetuated under ideologically driven police states. Dissent meant imprisonment or death. However, the inefficiency of the centrally controlled Communist economy and the economic pressure of the nuclear arms race brought about the collapse of the Soviet Union and its military alliance, the Warsaw Pact. Former Communist states in eastern Europe raced to join the capitalist European Union, and the Communist states in Africa and Asia suffered economic turmoil as Soviet subsidies and expertise were withdrawn.

One of the major factors in the collapse of European Communism was the election of Karol Wotyla to the papacy in 1978. Formerly the Archbishop of Krakow in Poland, his priestly ministry had been conducted under the repressive Communist regime. His election gave heart to the embryonic Solidarity trade union movement, and perhaps assured its survival. Without such a powerful friend, the Soviet-backed Polish government might have succeeded in crushing Solidarity. As it was, Poland started the anti-Communist movement that culminated in the opening of the borders between east and west Europe in 1989. John Paul II was the first non-Italian pope to be elected since Hadrian VI in 1522. His election was probably a turning point in the history of Western Europe.

The economic powerhouse of the world in the early part of the century was America and Britain's economy was based on production at home and on the economies of the world-wide British Empire. Even following two catastrophic wars, the end of the century saw the capitalist countries of America and Europe as the leading economies in the world. One hundred and fifty years after Marx made his prediction of the inevitable collapse of capitalism and its replacement by a Communist society, capitalism looks (in the short term) in robust health, while Communism is on the wane.

One of the factors that perpetuated western capitalism and furthers the decline of Communism is consumerism, the growth of the 'I want' society, where vigorous advertising is disseminated through a ubiquitous media. This is a phenomenon that gathered pace with the spread of television in the 1960s, and it has now arrived at the point where research suggests that a person can be subjected to several thousand advertising or marketing messages a day. When people are well fed, housed, employed and entertained, the urge to revolt on behalf of a more equitable distribution of wealth fades.

But not everyone in the twentieth century was well fed or housed. Even today, there is the developed world, and the developing or 'third' world, where poverty is widespread, infant mortality high and the average age of death is far lower than in the rich economies of America, Europe and parts of Asia. In the 1980s, a savage famine struck Ethiopia following successive years when the rains failed. The tragedy came to the world's attention through the media, and in response a huge media fund-raising rock concert, Live Aid, raised millions of pounds for emergency relief. Yet fifteen years later, western politicians and bankers still extract more from third world economies in debt payments than they offer in aid. Kenyans can no longer irrigate their subsistence farming plots because supermarket suppliers use precious water to grow out of season salads for the overfed west.

The world has never been richer, but parts of it still live in the Dark Ages. In the twentieth century, one of the few voices for a more fair distribution of wealth has been the Church: Catholic social teaching, explicitly reinforced by John Paul II's encyclical *Centesimus Annus*, imposes on Catholics an obligation to the poor. CAFOD, the Catholic Fund for Overseas Development, is one of the more effective agencies in developing countries. OXFAM also drew its inspiration from a Christian-inspired concern for the poor.

During the twentieth century democracy began to take hold in many societies. The notion of democracy was extensively explored by Greek philosophers, but was best defined by Abraham Lincoln in his speech where he called for a government 'of the people, by the people, for the people'. Democracy in the form of universal suffrage – the right of all adults to vote – came to be in the early twentieth century, since before that time women were regarded as incompetent dependants who either could or should not vote. In some central and South American countries, the Roman Catholic Church was often the most powerful advocate in favour of widespread democracy. In El Salvador, Archbishop Oscar Romero was shot and murdered while he celebrated mass. He offended the country's right-wing dictatorship by speaking out in favour of democracy and against the junta's tyranny.

In the early years of the century, groups of women in Britain and the USA began a militant campaign for voting rights (suffrage) earning them the name 'suffragettes'. In Britain, the outbreak of the First World War was the breakthrough that the 'votes for women' movement needed. With young men conscripted into the armed forces in their millions, the women of Britain provided the essential workforce that kept the voracious wartime economy running.

With this women began – slowly – to break into higher education, and into hitherto male bastions of power. Women MPs were elected to Westminster, and talented, determined women became heads of state around the world. In 1960 Sirimavo Bandaranaike became prime minister of Sri Lanka and was re-elected twice. Ukrainian-born Golda Meir was prime minister of Israel from 1969 to 1974, and Indira Gandhi served as Indian prime minister from 1966–1977 and from 1980 to 1984. In 1979 Margaret Thatcher was elected prime minister of the United Kingdom.

War defined the early part of the twentieth century. The century opened with wars in South Africa, Central and South America, but by 1914 European tensions had flashed into the First World War, where science, technology and industry assisted the mechanised killing of a large proportion of Europe's young men. The Second World War and the invention – and, more importantly the use – of the atom bomb took the ability of humans to kill one another in war to a new level. Wars erupted in Korea, the Middle East and Vietnam.

Following the active war of 1939–1945, the world lived through the Cold War, when the opposing powers of the Soviet Union, and the NATO countries threatened one another with nuclear annihilation.

There were times when the world did come close to a nuclear war. In the late 1940s, American 'hawks' (war-minded military advisors) urged the American president to make a large, catastrophic nuclear attack on the Soviet Union before the Soviets could develop their own nuclear arsenal. In the Cuban missile crisis, elements of the American military were urging the use of the new, more destructive hydrogen bombs on the Soviet Union. President John F. Kennedy, a Catholic, declined the hawkish advice.

The twentieth century saw the development of more social trends. The feminist movement came to public prominence in the late 1960s. Feminism reacted against the male domination of society, and its assumption that women were in any way inferior to males. Britain was one of the leading countries in the feminist movement. However, despite thirty-five years of feminist thought and action, and a general acceptance that woman are equal to men, women are still paid lower salaries than equivalent male colleagues, and are still widely under represented in the senior levels of industry and politics. The USA has not yet elected a female president or vice president.

In the developed western European and American economies, the demands of capitalism meant a mobile labour force, and communities fragmented. Extended families, with relatives living in a mutually supporting network within walking distance of one another, broke down. One of the few bodies that consistently argued for the value of a married family unit was the Roman Catholic Church.

The twentieth century also saw the development of environmental awareness. Both poverty and prosperity have proved to have environmental costs. In poor countries, unsustainable patterns of industry, agriculture and forestry are pursued in an attempt to survive day to day. In the developed world, the Industrial Revolution and the consumer economy it developed caused a huge demand on natural resources. By the end of the twentieth century, scientists were almost unanimously convinced of the existence of global warming – a man-made rise in worldwide temperatures that threatens to destabilise the climate.

The papacy was founded approximately thirty years into the first century. The declared followers of Jesus were probably numbered in double figures. At its height, the Catholic Church had temporal and spiritual power over much of western Europe, and Central and South America. By the year 2000, the pope's earthly power covered only the 44 hectares of Vatican City, but the size of the Roman Catholic faithful was estimated at 850,000,000.

Mechanised war

The history of the two thousand years of Christianity, and therefore the history of the papacy has had several constant factors, and one of them has been warfare. Christianity began with Jewish Palestine under occupation by Roman soldiers.

Warfare has been a powerful influence in human history – it is the urge to covet they neighbours goods writ large, and until the twentieth century it was a line-of-sight affair. To kill someone, you had to be able to see them.

With the Industrial Revolution, machine tools allowed metal to be worked to ever finer tolerances, so that more accurate and complex weapons could be produced. Artillery – large calibre weapons that could kill and destroy at ranges of up to nearly two kilometres – had been in existence in the Napoleonic wars in the nineteenth century. But with the twentieth century rapidly growing populations put ever larger strains on land and resources, and technology was used to produce ever more sophisticated, long-range weapons.

In 1914, European tensions boiled over into the First World War. This conflict genuinely spanned the globe, with battles in Europe, Africa and Asia, and troops from America involved. Men still faced one another with weapons, as they had in the Roman invasion of Palestine, but these weapons could kill at the range of a kilometre, rather than hand to hand. Artillery could throw explosive shells several kilometres, and for the first time warfare took to the air.

The first powered flight was in America, when Orville and Wilbur Wright briefly took to the air in 1903. With the outbreak of war in 1914, the opposing forces (Germany and its allies versus Britain, France and Belgium) began to develop air warfare. By 1915, the Germans were using Zeppelin airships and multi-engined aircraft to drop high-explosive bombs on British cities. Fighter aircraft, lighter, fast aircraft armed with machine guns, began to fight the battle for air superiority over battlefields.

On land, warfare bogged down into a static war of attrition, with hundreds of thousands of men facing one another from trenches, often fighting in a manner that would have been familiar to men in the Napoleonic wars 110 years previously. Once again mechanisation intervened, with the British introducing tanks at the Battle of Cambrai – large armoured motorised vehicles that carried heavy weapons and could crash through trenches and barbed wire.

The First World War also introduced chemical warfare, when the Germans deliberately released poisonous gas to drift over Allied trenches, poisoning thousands of soldiers. When the Germans surrendered in 1918, the First World War was called 'the war to end all wars'. This was a reflection of the numbers of young men who died in this four-year conflict. At the Battle of Verdun, where the French and Germans fought for a psychologically important French town, an estimated 800,000 men died. Yet cataclysmic through the First World War was, it was not the end of war in the twentieth century.

The German urge for empire – *Lebensraum*, or 'room to lie', as they called it – sparked a second world-wide conflict in 1939. The

Second World War was not merely a more technologically evolved version of the First World War. Much of the armoury on each side was the same, but in the Second World War civilian non-combatants were more involved and more at risk. Both sides deliberately used bombing against civilian targets to attack their opponents' morale, and the Germans invented a new style of remote warfare. Their V1 bomb was a pilotless aircraft carrying a high-explosive warhead that could be launched from the continent and would fly across the Channel and coastal Britain before crashing into and blowing up on its target, which was usually London. The V2 was a ballistic missile, which was launched vertically and flew in a high trajectory through the upper atmosphere before landing on its chosen target.

The Germans gave the world the weapons of the Cold War – the cruise missile and the ballistic missile. Although called 'terror weapons' they were relatively ineffective owing to the small explosive payload they carried.

In Los Alamos, a newly built research establishment in New Mexico, a team of American and British scientists spent billions of dollars building the world's first atomic bombs. Scientists had theorised that splitting an atom could release large amounts of energy, and after America entered the Second World War in December 1941 it became an urgent priority to beat the Germans and Soviets to the atom bomb. The American and British team won, and on 6 August 1945 the Japanese city of Hiroshima was devastated by an atomic bomb. The explosion was caused by just 46 kilograms of uranium, and an estimated 100,000 people died. The Japanese refused to surrender, and on 9 August a second atomic bomb was dropped on Nagasaki, killing 40,000. Japan surrendered the following day.

Within a few years of the first use of atomic weapons, the German missile technology had been combined with the US and British atomic weapons technology, and the nuclear arms race had begun. At the height of the Cold War, the NATO and Warsaw Pact nuclear arsenals combined contained sufficient explosive power to wipe out human life on earth many times over.

The Holocaust

When in 1933 the Germans elected Adolf Hitler to power, the country was still smarting from its defeat in the First World War, and its economy was in a parlous state. Photographs of the time show employees collecting a firm's wages from the bank in huge hampers so worthless was German currency.

Hitler needed a scapegoat for Germany's ills, and history had provided him with a precedent: European Jews had suffered bouts of persecution since the Crusades, and Hitler fixed on Germany's large Jewish population as the source of the nation's problems.

Jews were forced to wear distinctive badges, their businesses were confiscated, they were routinely brutalised and forced into menial jobs. Jewish academics were forced out of universities and many fled to western Europe and America.

Hitler's National Socialist party developed a political system that bordered on the religious – the Nazi rallies were parodies of religious services and Hitler inspired a messianic fervour in his supporters. Their political theories had a strong racial basis: the Aryan races (a northern European ideal) were superior to all others, who were labelled *untermench* – 'underpeople'. The Jews were *untermench*, and Nazi propaganda compared them to parasites and germs.

Having demonised the Jews, Hitler and his supporters set about exterminating them in the largest attempt at mass genocide seen in modern history. Jews were rounded up throughout occupied Europe and transported to concentration camps, where they were killed in their millions.

There is some evidence that the extermination of European Jewry was the main motivating factor of the Third Reich: Reichsmarshall Josef Goebbels was overheard to say as much.

There were individual acts of courage in protecting and hiding Jewish friends and neighbours, but people throughout occupied Europe actively colluded in the Nazis' ruthless persecution of the Jews. Both British and American military hierarchies knew of the Germans' extermination camps, but none of the camps were bombed in an effort to stop the killing. The Nazis wiped out an estimated six million Jews. Gypsies, homosexuals, anti-Nazi intellectuals and clergymen also went to the labour and concentration camps.

Inevitably, there has been a debate on whether Pope Pius XII connived in the Holocaust by an overt failure to speak out against it. His predecessor signed a co-operation pact with the Italian Fascists, and if the pope failed to condemn the Holocaust, nor did the other Allied leaders who were militarily opposing the Third Reich and its genocidal policies. As Stalin once observed, the pope has no battalions. Recent efforts at establishing the Vatican's actions in the Second World

War were compromised when a team of researchers were forbidden access to the Vatican archives relating to the Holocaust.

Catholic social teaching and Europe

Catholic social teaching formally began with the papal encyclicals issued by the reforming Pope Leo XIII (1878–1903). Catholic involvement in the alleviation of poverty and suffering had a long history, but these tended to acts of kindness and piety, for instance St Francis of Assisi's work among lepers and the work of clergy and bishops in distributing alms.

Leo XIII recognised that the Church as an organisation needed to develop a means of engaging with the liberal and socialist societies developing in Europe around the 1880s, and his encyclicals from 1888 to 1892 defined the rules for Catholic involvement in politics. Catholic political involvement grew through Catholic Workers' Movements in the inter-war years into the European Christian Democrat parties of post-war Europe.

In the wake of the Second World War, the notion of a Europe-wide community dedicated to peaceful co-operation was mooted and brought into being largely through the vision of statesmen from five countries which had been on opposite sides in the war. Christian Democrats from Germany, Belgium, Luxembourg, Italy and France were instrumental in forming the European Coal and Steel Community, the forerunner of the European Economic Community and the European Union.

While the papacy may have lost power to secular government over the centuries, the social teachings of the Roman Catholic Church expressed in papal encyclicals has strongly influenced Christian Socialist thinking in the early part of the century and Christian Democrat politics since 1945.

Christian Democrat thinking is characterised by a concern for life issues, a belief that power should be exercised as close to those affected as possible, and individual responsibility and solidarity within one's own community and with those in need beyond it. The Vatican's social teaching over the past hundred years can rightly claim to have been responsible for much of the thinking that went into the formation of the modern European Union.

The rise of the technological society

During the Second World War, the need to improve armaments and break enemy codes led to the development of computers, essentially machines that could carry out repetitive calculations at speed. In the early 1940s both Germany and America developed electromechanical computers, but it was in Britain that the first computer using valves was developed: Britain was at the forefront of the wartime effort to crack German military ciphers, and the new British thermionic valve computer, called Colossus, could sift the possibilities with incredible speed. Thermionic valves were essentially sealed thin glass containers, with all their air evacuated so that their delicate electronics could work in a vacuum. In 1947, Bell Laboratories in the USA invented the first transistor, which compressed the electronics of a valve into a solid electrical chip. Solid-state electronics was born, and the transistor opened the way to robust, portable electronics, and ultimately to the development of mass consumer electronics.

In 1866 Gregor Mendel had founded the science of genetics as a result of his experiments on peas, but it was not until 1953 that two Cambridge scientists James Watson and Francis Crick, discovered the double helix structure of deoxyribose nucleic acid (DNA), the large, complex molecules that contain information on an individual's genetic make-up. This was a breakthrough in pure biological terms, since DNA controls every aspect of the physical constitution of almost every living creature. Knowledge of the structure of DNA sparked an enormous research effort into how DNA works – just how do twin spirals of chemicals store the code to build a plant, a whale or a human? The science of genetics took off, and the industry of genetic engineering was not far behind. Genetic engineering is an industry that promises much and has enormous capital resources to fund its efforts. Despite suggestions of therapeutic genetic intervention in diseases and the non-too-distant possibility of cloned 'spare part' organ stores, the huge research effort has yet to deliver an effective safe cure.

Genetic engineering is also proving to be a field where the fields of science and religion clash as they did over evolution in the 1860s. The Church, particularly the Catholic Church, regards interfering in the human genome as interfering in God's creation, and it regards any use of embryonic products (such as stem cells) for research or therapy as wrong. Mainstream science sees the issue differently.

In 1903, Orville Wright released the brakes on the Flyer, an engine-powered biplane, and seconds later he was the first man to experience powered flight. His first flight lasted just twelve seconds. The First World War illustrated the strategic importance of flight, and in the inter-war years investment in aircraft produced multi-engined aircraft capable of flying passengers over long distances. The Second World War drove the pace of aircraft development and saw the jet engine brought into use. First developed by Englishman Sir Frank Whittle, the jet engine provided more power than a propeller-driven piston engine, and allowed the development of larger aircraft capable of hauling hundreds of passengers over long distances. Travelling to America now took a few hours rather than the four days of the fastest transatlantic liners. By the 1970s, an Anglo-French consortium had built the Concorde, a passenger airliner capable of crossing the Atlantic at speeds in excess of 1,800 kilometres per hour (1,350 miles per hour).

In 1957 the USSR stunned the world in general and America in particular when it announced the launch of the first satellite into orbit. The satellite Sputnik bleeped its way around the world, and given the rivalry between the Communist Warsaw Pact and NATO, America resolved to join the search for space technology. The post-war American economy was booming; the government flung money into the attempt to build a space programme, but in 1961 it lost the second heat of the space race when the Soviet Union announced that fighter pilot Yuri Gagarin had become the first man in orbit, blasted aloft on a Vostok rocket.

This was too much for America, and the newly elected John F. Kennedy announced that America would not merely put a man in earth orbit, America would put a man on the moon. Eight years and billions of dollars later, on 24 July 1969, mission control in Houston, Texas, received the radio signal 'Houston, Tranquility base here. The Eagle has landed.' Shortly afterwards Neil Armstrong, a 38-year-old former test pilot, became the first man to step on the moon. Historians of science are still debating the importance – or irrelevance – of the hugely expensive Apollo moon programme.

A space venture with more immediate benefits was the launching of the Telstar communications satellite in 1962. Suddenly television pictures were no longer simply transmitted between land-based transmission towers: the radio waves were beamed to the orbiting Telstar, then rebroadcast back to earth. Until this point, satellite communications had existed only in science fiction. Now satellites are used for military surveillance, gathering weather data, and carrying communications for civilian, commercial and military uses. In the Second World War, even with relatively advanced maps, pilots frequently got lost. Now, with the aid of a receiver costing around £80, the global positioning satellites can inform you of your position on the earth to within 10 metres.

Of course, technology is not always 100 percent reliable, nor 100 percent beneficial to its inventors. In 1981 the Americans launched the Space Shuttle. The project cost $10 billion to develop, and came close to being scrapped when in 1986 the shuttle Challenger exploded shortly after take-off, killing seven American astronauts. The cause of the crash was the failure of a rubber sealing gasket. In 1986 the world was reminded of the disadvantages of nuclear power when a nuclear reactor exploded at Chernobyl in the Ukraine, showering the immediate vicinity with radioactive debris and sending a cloud of radioactive gas drifting over western Europe. Fifteen years later, the land around Chernobyl is still too contaminated for people to live in safety.

Science and medicine

In 1905, Albert Einstein, at the time working in a patent office, astounded fellow scientists with his theories of general and special relativity: these dealt with the nature of gravity, space and time in the universe, and the effects that moving at velocities close to the speed of light have on matter and time. An equally important and equally incomprehensible theory was that of quantum mechanics, propounded by Max Planck at the same time. Quantum theory stated that energy is released from atoms in discrete packets, rather than as a stream, and predicted the behaviour of electrons around the nucleus of an atom.

Einstein was a German Jew, and in 1933 he fled Germany for the United States. There he convinced President Roosevelt that the Germans were interested in the military applications of atomic power, persuading him to initiate research that led to the atom bomb. Having seen its devastating effects, Einstein subsequently became a vigorous opponent of nuclear weapons.

A more prosaic but altogether more beneficial discovery was made in 1928 when Alexander Fleming noticed the antibiotic properties of the mould *Penicillium notatum*. His findings were further developed at Oxford University in 1939, when the therapeutic antibiotic action of penicillin was proved and refined into a usable drug. Penicillin-based antibiotics first became available in 1941, and caused a dramatic drop in deaths caused by bacterial infections. However, over the next fifty years antibiotics became used world-wide as a medical panacea, and overuse has led to bacteria developing resistance to most widely used types of antibiotic.

Biochemistry developed in the 1900s, and as biochemists discovered how the molecular chemistry of the body worked, pharmaceutical companies began using their research to develop drug treatments for diseases. In 1967 Christiaan Barnard, a South African surgeon, performed the first heart transplant. He removed the diseased heart of a man who had 'hours to live' and replaced it with the heart taken from a woman who had suffered fatal brain damage in a traffic accident. The recipient lived just eighteen days before 'complications' affected his lungs and kidneys causing his death.

At the beginning of the twenty-first century, technology and industrialisation have split the world into the developed world and the developing world. In the developing world, people still suffer from the diseases of poverty: malnutrition and infectious disease caught through poor sanitation. In the developed world, science and medicine are now grappling with the diseases of affluence: obesity and cancer. Medicine and affluence have extended the life expectancy of people in developed countries, while poverty and epidemic diseases such AIDs have dramatically reduced the life expectancy of people in sub-Saharan Africa. In 1918, an influenza epidemic killed more people throughout the world than had died in the recently ended First World War. Epidemiologists, the scientists whose study is the spread of disease, are waiting with trepidation for the next great viral epidemic.

Technology, industrialisation and the urge to consume fossil fuel have also begun to change the composition of the atmosphere, such that in the 1980s climate scientists began to discuss a phenomenon that became known as global warming, and warned that it could have unpredictable effects on the global climate, such as melting ice caps, rises in sea level and a change in long-established weather patterns.

The impact on history of Marx' theories

Karl Marx died in 1883 without seeing his political brainchild – Communism – successfully in action. Arguably, *Das Kapital* and the *Communist Manifesto* are two of the most significant works in modern history. It is probable that as the working class expanded and literacy became more widespread, a political system calling for greater distribution of wealth at the expense of the ruling classes would develop, but Marx was the first to describe such a system and his writings set the tone for revolutionary Communism.

Imperial Russia was cradle to the first successful Communist revolution. In 1917 the Red Guards, a Communist revolutionary militia led by Lenin, Trotsky and Stalin, stormed the Winter Palace in Petrograd. Czar Nicholas II and his family were taken prisoner and executed, and Russia fell under Communist control following a two-year civil war.

In 1922, the Union of Soviet Socialist Republics was established, and with it one of the most violent, repressive dictatorships in world history, that of Josef Stalin began to rise. Between 1930 and 1940, Stalin purged his enemies (real and imagined) and millions died. He signed a non-aggression pact with Hitler, but in 1941 Hitler invaded the Soviet Union, his forces pushing to within sight of Moscow before Stalin's Red Army stopped and in 1943 pushed the Germans into retreat. By 1945 the Red Army had driven the Germans into their homeland and occupied the German capital, Berlin.

The Soviets were allies of the British and Americans in the Second World War, and their liberation of eastern Europe gave them an opportunity to secure their own Communist Empire. Stalin seized the opportunity to bring Communism to eastern Europe, and after the Second World War much of Europe fell under Soviet control. A third of Germany, Poland, Romania, Bulgaria, Czechoslovakia, Yugoslavia and Albania became Communist states in the wake of the Second World War. Berlin became a western enclave in a Communist country.

In 1949, the countries of western Europe and America formed a mutual defence pact, the North Atlantic Treaty Organisation (NATO). NATO was to be the bulwark to prevent further Soviet expansion into Europe. In 1945 America had dropped two atomic bombs on Japan, and the Soviet Union, afraid that America possessed a strategic advantage, also developed nuclear weapons. The arms race was underway. In 1955, Russia welded its Communist satellite states into a military alliance, the Warsaw Pact, and a period of armed stand-off between the Warsaw Pact and NATO began. This became known as the Cold War, where the eastern and western powers threatened one another with ever more destructive nuclear arms. The west 'won' when the Communist Soviet Union collapsed in 1991, an ironic reversal of

Marx's original intentions. The Soviet economy had been bankrupted by the arms race. The economy of the USA had a $4 trillion debt.

The collapse of the Warsaw pact was not simply because of NATO opposition. In 1978 Karol Wotyla, archbishop of the Polish diocese of Cracow was elected pope. Having taken the name John Paul II, and now residing in the Vatican rather than Soviet-dominated Poland, he was a significant factor in precipitating the collapse of the Communist alliance. In 1979, he made a papal visit to his Polish homeland. One million Poles attended his open-air mass. A year later, the Poles defied their Communist government (and their Soviet masters) and formed Solidarity – ostensibly a trade union, but also a vehicle for anti-Communist opposition. Poland, with papal support, sparked the anti-Soviet movements of the 1980s that ultimately contributed to the collapse of the Soviet Union and Warsaw Pact. Without a Polish pope, recent history could have been very different.

But before its death, the military and industrial might of the Soviet Union spread revolutionary Communism around the world. Following the Second World War Mao Zhedong led Communist forces in a civil war that defeated the Chinese Nationalists led by Chiang Kai-shek, and Communist insurgencies gained power in Vietnam (defeating the French colonial rulers and resisting American military might in the Vietnam war), in Korea and Cambodia. Marxists briefly gained power in Central and South American countries such as Chile and Nicaragua, but the fiercely anti-Communist USA did not tolerate 'Reds' on its own doorstep, and funded elaborate military coups to rid the Americas of governments with Communist sympathies.

The Soviet Union has been consigned to history, but Communist China continues, and it is likely that the world will feel the effects of Marx's writings for many years to come.

Suffragettes and the growth of feminism

Women make up 50 percent of the population of the world, but from the history of the last twenty centuries an impartial observer might have thought that women were a subservient species rather than half of the intellectually dominant population of this planet.

The exceptions of history, where powerful women happened to gain some influence localised in time and place, do not detract from the fact that women have spent most of the past two thousand years entirely subjugated by a male-dominated society. However, the advent of printing allowed the dissemination of many ideas – religious, scientific, creative and social. Inevitably, it was not long before a woman recognised the injustice of the situation, then wrote and published on the subject. Words in print have a permanence lacked by those in conversation, and a movement was founded.

In 1792, Mary Wollstonecraft published *A Vindication of the Rights of Women*. The Chartist movement of the 1840s espoused rights for women. The renowned philosopher John Stuart Mill assisted his wife Harriet in promoting the cause of women's rights, and in 1865 the first women's suffrage movement was established in Manchester, England. But despite this, in the late nineteenth century, successive reform bills proposing votes for women failed.

However, in the twentieth century, several factors conspired to begin to change this situation. In the late nineteenth and early twentieth century, women in Britain and America became educated and therefore literate and politically aware. Ironically, one of the most staunch opponents of women's rights was none other than Queen Victoria. However, in 1869, legislation was passed that allowed women taxpayers to vote in local elections and sit on county and city councils.

Around the turn of the century, the 'Votes for Women' movement became more organised, political and coherent. It met with no success, so a wing of the Suffragette movement, led by Emmeline Pankhurst, became more militant. Their protests became more radical and the women were imprisoned, where they in turn refused to eat and were brutally force-fed.

In the First World War, the men of Britain went to fight and the women replaced them in the factories, keeping both the domestic and the war economy running. Recruiting posters showed women urging their young husbands and sons to go and fight for Britain's freedom. As a result, the British House of Commons passed the Representation of the People Act in 1917, allowing British women aged over thirty to vote. In 1928, a further Act of Parliament lowered the voting age to twenty-one, the same as that for men.

Despite voting equality, sexism pervaded western culture. The prejudices of the previous 1,900 years held: women were believed to be inferior to men, especially by the men who ran the hierarchies of society.

However, in the 1960s female intellectuals began to develop feminism, the intellectual and social movement that demanded social and economic equality for women. In 1949 Simone de Beauvoir published *The Second Sex*, which stated that liberating women would also liberate men, and in 1963 American Betty Friedan published *The Feminine Mystique*, which attacked female domesticity and male dominance.

The growth of feminism coincided with the availability of reliable artificial contraception. A woman could now have a sexual relationship without the previous consequences of repeated, unpredictable pregnancies. This helped to allow women to make professional progress, but despite compelling evidence that women are in every intellectual respect the equal of men, the third millennium still sees women under-represented in the hierarchies of business and government. The phenomenon is known as the 'glass ceiling' – society accepts the equality of women, but there is a resistance to allowing women to be promoted as far as their talents allow.

The Church's response to the results of the availability of contraception is different. Contraception allows people to indulge in sex without the risk of pregnancy, which only encourages a growing trend to sex before marriage and the tendency to live together rather than marry in the Church. Fundamentally, what should be a special act is debased.

Issues of life

Sex was an issue even for early Christians. Early Christians believed that sex for procreative purposes was irrelevant, since the Second Coming was imminent and the world would end. Sexual ethics was also a matter of identity. Early Christians wished to distinguish themselves from pagan Romans, and there was one area of life where this became possible. The Romans were fond of feasting and were reputed to be sexually licentious, so an emphasis on sexual chastity became a hallmark of early Christians.

In 418 the theologian Augustine wrote *On Marriage and Concupiscence*, in which he said that male semen transmitted both life and Adam's original sin, establishing a precedent that became important in the subsequent Church debates on contraception.

In 1930, Pope Pius XI's encyclical *Casto Connubii* condemned all artificial birth control as a 'grave sin'. In the 1960s, pressure built for the Church to liberalise its teaching on contraception, but in 1968 Pope Paul VI reverted to the teaching of Pius XI in his encyclical

Humanae Vitae when he asserted that 'every conjugal act has to be open to the possibility of the transmission of life'.

The Church insists that sex is permissible only within marriage, and that within marriage birth control can be practised by the rhythm method, where a couple avoid intercourse during times when the woman is likely to conceive. The Church's teaching about contraception is absolute. In sub-Saharan Africa, where AIDS is endemic, the Church will not approve the use of condoms to try to halt the sexual transmission of the HIV virus. It states firmly that sexual continence would be a more effective preventative measure.

The 1990s brought a new threat to the concept of life with development of genetic engineering and cloning. When the monk Gregor Mendel discovered the basis of genetic inheritance in 1866, he would have been horrified to think that 130 years later genetics would become one of the main intellectual battlegrounds between the Roman Catholic Church and science.

Genetic engineering is the science of using genes for therapeutic medical purposes. Many medical conditions have a genetic cause. A defective gene (or set of genes) inherited from one or both parents. Fundamentally, either directly causes a disease or leaves a person unduly susceptible to suffering a disease. The premise inherent in genetic engineering is that 'correct' copies of a gene can be spliced into the genetic material of a sufferer, resulting in a cure.

Germ line therapy is more controversial yet: it involves altering the genetic make-up of an embryo to eliminate genetic disorders before birth. Cloning advances the technology further. At one end of the technology, it postulates the possibility of taking 'stem cells' from early embryos and directing their growth into becoming organs for transplant. The middle case is reproductive cloning: producing a genetic copy of a person using genetic manipulation. At the time of publication, an Italian doctor is promising reproductive cloning by 2003, and claims that he has hundreds people waiting for the opportunity to have cloned offspring. At the extremes of such technology, genetic engineering postulates that it will be possible to take a human body cell, disable the genes for the development of the head, and stimulate it to grow so that a headless (and therefore personality-less) copy of a body can be grown as a source of transplant organs. The advantage of this technology is that the organs derived from your headless clone would be genetically identical to your own, and would therefore not risk rejection, as often happens following a transplant sourced from another person.

The Roman Catholic Church is one of the few organisations opposing such developments, although in 2001 American President George Bush, under pressure from Christian lobbyists, placed severe restrictions on stem cell research using material derived from embryos. Science has made great, sweeping predictions for the potential of this technology. So far, however, the science has not lived up to its own predictions.

Abortion

The history of the first two thousand years of the Church has been one of survival, acquiring almost supreme power over monarchs and nations, then a gradual loss of influence as national governments gained confidence.

One area where the papacy directly opposes the policy of many governments is that of abortion. The papacy has long held a firm view on the sanctity of unborn life. Pope Gregory IX (1227–1241) stated that to treat any person 'so that he cannot generate nor she conceive, or offspring be born, let it be held as homicide'.

Pius IX (1846–1878) decreed that abortion was a sin punishable by excommunication, and the papacy's absolute opposition to abortion was stated in the encyclical *Humanae Vitae*, issued by Pope Paul VI (1963–1978) in 1968: '... above all direct abortions even for therapeutic reasons are to be excluded as lawful means of controlling the birth of children'.

In the same year, the Abortion Act came into force in Britain, where, by the year 2000, 170,000 pregnancies ended in abortion every year. In 1973 a court case in Texas, Roe v. Wade, stated that to ban a woman's access to an abortion was not compatible with the American Constitution. Abortion on demand was available in the Communist countries of eastern Europe, and in China forced abortion is a state-sponsored means of population control.

The Catholic Church nonetheless maintains its opposition to abortion, and some see the Catholic Church and some Protestant churches developing a 'Constant Ethic of Life', applying to abortion, euthanasia, genetic manipulation and capital punishment.

South American Catholicism and liberation theology

Central and South America were colonial outposts of Catholic Spain throughout the seventeenth and eighteenth centuries, and when in the nineteenth century Spain succumbed to Napoleon's armies, the colonies rapidly rebelled and declared independence.

While they threw off Spanish rule, the newly independent nations of Central and South America ostensibly retained the language and religion of their conquerors. In the late twentieth century, the Latin American Catholic clergy began to combine their religion and social experiences into a social Catholicism which became known as liberation theology.

Liberation theology was championed by left-wing priests who believed that God speaks particularly through the poor, and that biblical revelation is best seen through the eyes of the poor.

Liberation theology was inaugurated at the Latin American Bishops' Conference held in Colombia in 1968, when the bishops stated that the industrialised nations of the west gained wealth at the expense of the peoples of developing countries. Liberation theology found charismatic leaders in Archbishop Oscar Romero (who was assassinated in 1980) and Franciscan Leonardo Boff.

The politics of Central and South America meant that liberation theologians were criticised and occasionally violently suppressed by right-wing governments, and the anti-Communist sentiments inherent in Pope John Paul II's Vatican meant that many liberation theologians suffered censure as being naïve Marxists.

African and Indian independence

The twentieth century opened with large tracts of the world still under the colonial control of European governments.

Britain ruled India, the French had control of Indochina, and the African continent was ruled by colonists from Belgium, Germany, France, Italy and Britain. The 1920s and 1930s were the heyday of colonial rule, since the western European governments benefited from advanced technology in their dealings with the colonies: air travel enabled rapid communications between the colonial rulers and their agents in the colonies. The Europeans had well-equipped armies that were able to put down insurrections, and the European economies benefited enormously from the economic plunder of the colonies.

By the 1920s, India was tiring of British rule, and a charismatic leader in the form of Mohandas Gandhi (1869–1948) began to lead Indian resistance to British rule in 1914. The British were not sympathetic to Indian independence, and Gandhi's non-violent opposition to British rule during the 1930s and 1940s led to his frequent imprisonment. British wartime prime minister, Winston Churchill, dismissed him as a 'naked fakir', but obviously Indians thought differently; Gandhi was president of the Indian National Congress from 1925 to 1934. He was held in great esteem by most of his nation, which conferred on him the name 'Mahatma', Sanskrit for 'Great Soul'.

In 1942, Gandhi championed a 'Quit India' vote in the Indian Congress, and the British again imprisoned him, but times were changing. In 1945, Churchill's Conservative Party was voted out of government and in September Clem Attlee the Labour prime minister promised India independence 'as soon as possible'.

As independence approached, the tension between Indian Hindus and Muslims erupted into rioting, leading to a partition of the sub-continent into Hindu-dominated India and Muslim Pakistan. Gandhi died in 1948, assassinated by a Hindu extremist.

France occupied Indochina (the countries we now know as Laos, Vietnam and Cambodia) in the nineteenth century, keeping control until France fell to German occupation in 1940. With this Japan invaded Indochina, and kept control until the Japanese surrender in August 1945, when the French regained control of Laos and Cambodia and tried to reassert control in Vietnam. They did control some Vietnamese cities, but in the countryside a Communist nationalist movement led by Ho Chi Minh was gaining ground. The Communist insurgency, supported by China and Russia, gained strength and in 1954 took the main French stronghold at Dien Bien Phu. The beaten French withdrew from Indochina.

In Africa, European colonies began to agitate for independence, and through the 1950s and 1960s most European countries withdrew from the African continent. Colonies work during times of peace, but the Second World War had devastated large tracts of Europe and the Europeans needed to turn their efforts to internal rebuilding rather than colonial rule overseas.

Belgium liberated the Republic of Congo, the Mau-Mau revolted in Kenya, and in 1965 Rhodesia rebelled against British rule. In 1975 Portugal gave independence to Angola, and in 1977 the Central African Empire came into existence under Emperor Jean Bokassa. In 1980 white Rhodesia ceased to exist when Robert Mugabe became the prime minister of Zimbabwe, but white rule in Africa persisted with the South African apartheid regime.

The South African regime was a nakedly racist government, quite prepared to use violence against its black citizens when they agitated for their civil rights. In 1960, the South African defence forces shot and killed fifty civilians at Sharpeville, and despite international condemnation and internal civil unrest, the Boer South African government kept the country's black population in subjugation until the release of Nelson Mandela from prison in 1990. Free elections in 1994 led to Mandela becoming the first freely elected president of South Africa. Colonial rule in Africa was at an end.

Conclusion

In Palestine 1,970 years ago, a few terrified men and women gathered in a room. Their leader, Jesus Christ, had been crucified by the Romans, and they feared the same fate. By 2000 AD, adherents of the Christian faith were thought to account for between 1.5 and 2 billion people out of a world population of 6 billion.

The papacy, the religious tradition that started with Jesus telling his follower Simon Peter (a fisherman by profession) that 'you are Peter, and on this rock I will build my church', is still in existence, and the present pope claims his authority from that moment and from the heroic former fisherman who travelled from Palestine to Rome to spread the teachings of Christ.

The Church was born in a world of outright military oppression. It continues in the face of a commercial, individualist, cynical, media-driven secular world. But it continues, and this is probably the open-mouthed comment of historians throughout the two thousand years of the papacy's existence.

Through the folly, brutality, violence and vanity that grabbed the headlines of history, the humility, charity, faith and goodness of the people of the Church persisted, and flourished. The survival of a faith does not guarantee the future survival of the species, and human beings have begun to radically change the environment on which they depend. Biologists point out that species have (on average) a life span of 1–2 million years before they are driven into extinction. By that reckoning, human beings are not long for this world.

A population biologist, looking at the disciples shut in that room in Roman occupied Palestine around 33 AD would have doubted the survival of the followers of Christ. There are few things that are certain in life, but the history of the last two thousand years suggests one. As long as humans walk the earth, there will be a Bishop of Rome, called the pope, who traces his spiritual heritage to a man plucked from his fishing nets on the shores of the Sea of Galilee.

THE POPES
1903 to the present

Pius X, St (Giuseppe Melchiorre Sarto)
Riese, Italy; 4 August 1903 to 20 August 1914

After his ordination (1858), Guiseppe Sarto, who was the son of a village postman, served first as a simple parish priest and then as the rector of the seminary of Treviso. Consecrated bishop in 1884, he won a reputation for the pastoral care of his diocese. Leo XIII elevated him to cardinal (1893) and Patriarch of Venice. Reluctantly he accepted his election, but then worked with his famous secretary of state, Cardinal Merry del Val, to introduce pastoral reforms and resist all anti-Catholic measures, particularly those introduced by the governments of Portugal and France. He sternly condemned, with draconian measures (the decree, *Lamentabili* in 1907 and the encyclical *Pascendi* in 1907) a liberalising movement in the Church, which he called Modernism. Pius reorganised the Curia (1908), started a revision of canon law, reformed Church music, promoted Catholic Action and encouraged Catholic lay people to receive Holy Communion more frequently. Deeply troubled by the progress of European powers towards war, he tried desperately to stop it, but failed. He died only days after the start of World War I. He was canonised on 29 May 1954.

Benedict XV (Giacomo Della Chiesa)
Genoa; 3 September 1914 to 22 January 1922

With doctorates in civil law, theology and canon law, Giacomo Della Chiesa trained for and entered the papal diplomatic service. Pope St Pius X made him Archbishop of Bologna and, in 1914, a cardinal. Elected pope a month after the outbreak of World War I, Benedict used his diplomatic skills to remain neutral, devoting himself to relief work, especially for prisoners-of-war. In 1917 he proposed a plan for peace and to further reconciliation Benedict asked both sides to state their aims. Neither side would co-operate, both accusing him of favouring the other side (had they done so several million lives would have been spared). From 1920 Benedict devoted himself to efforts at international reconciliation, with some success. He promulgated the new code of canon law in 1917, and published twelve encyclical letters. His last years were spent in readjusting the organisation of the Church in the wake of the disastrous conflict, and in promoting missionary work, encouraging missionary bishops to ordain native indigenous clergy.

Pius XI (Achille Ratti)

Milan; 6 February 1922 to 10 February 1939

Born in 1857, by the age of twenty-five Achille Ratti had been ordained to the priesthood and attained three different doctorates, in theology, philosophy and canon law. After a short period of pastoral experience Ratti distinguished himself as a scholar and rose to be the Prefect of the Vatican Library (1914). Within seven months of being raised to the cardinalate (June 1921) Achille Ratti was elected pope. His earnest desire for peace dominated his pontificate. Using his able secretaries of state (until 1930 Cardinal Gasparri and then Cardinal Pacelli), he negotiated the Lateran Treaty (1929),with Mussolini's Italian government and, believing Communism was more to be feared than Hitler's National Socialism, a Concordat (1933) with Germany. Shocked by Nazi violations of the Concordat Pius denounced Nazism in his letter *Mit Brennender Sorge* (1937). The same year he condemned Communism in the encyclical *Divini Redemptoris*. He vigorously promoted missionary work, particularly in Asia and the East. Pius encouraged the work of the Pontifical Academy of Sciences and the Vatican Observatory; he founded the Pontifical Institute of Christian Archaeology, and installed radio in Vatican City. Pius had the distinction of being the first pope to be an enthusiastic mountaineer and the first to be heard on radio.

Pius XII (Eugenio Maria Giuseppe Giovanni Pacelli)

Rome; 2 March 1939 to 9 October 1958

The Pacelli family had served the papacy for many years; Eugenio, of fragile health, entered the Vatican diplomatic service soon after ordination. A specialist in canon law he rose rapidly to become personal assistant to Cardinal Gasparri, secretary of state whom he assisted with the codification of canon law. As papal nuncio in Bavaria – and later the German Republic – he negotiated a Concordat with that country and with Prussia. Succeeding Gasparri, Pacelli negotiated (1933) a Concordat with the Nazi government. Groomed for the papacy by Pius XI, Pacelli, with his wide experience, high intelligence, gift for languages and wide political skills, was the obvious choice. As pope he was immediately faced by a world at war. Failing to prevent war, Pius spent immense energy and resources on the relief of its victims, refugees, prisoners of war and particularly the Jews of Rome. His diplomatic training, intelligence of Hitler's intentions regarding the papacy and a natural indecisiveness led him to act cautiously, (which prompted much later criticism) rather than speak out prophetically. Pius saw Communism as the great enemy and sought to counter it with an immense outpouring of teaching and literature. Austere and intensely devout, Pius declared 1950 a Holy Year and defined the teaching of the Assumption (that the body of the Blessed Virgin Mary had been assumed into heaven). His three great encyclicals *Mystici Corporis* (1943), *Divini Afflante* (1943) and *Mediator Dei* (1947) pointed up the theological way to the Second Vatican Council. However, in his last years, attempting to be the universal teacher, Pius retired into more and more isolation becoming more conservative. He was the first pope to be familiar to the general public, through radio and television.

John XXIII (Angelo Guiseppe Roncalli)

Sotto il Monte (Bergamo), Italy; 28 October 1958 to 3 June 1963

Born at Sotto il Monte, near Bergamo, in northern Italy, of a large peasant family, Angelo studied at Bergamo and Rome before ordination (1904). He served first as secretary to the local bishop and then taught in the diocesan seminary, gaining experience of army life, when a chaplain during World War I. Drafted into the Vatican's diplomatic service he served as an archbishop, first in Bulgaria, then in Turkey and finally as papal nuncio to post-war France in 1944. Pope Pius XII, in recognition of his outstanding conciliatory pastoral work in France, appointed him as Patriarch of Venice in 1952. Due to his poor health and age (seventy-seven years) many considered that he was a 'caretaker pope', but John XXIII started changing things from the start. His principal interest was Christian Unity; he established a Secretariat for Christian Unity (1960), received the Archbishop of Canterbury in Rome, permitted Catholic observers to attend the World Council of Churches and, his most important act, summoned the Second Vatican Council (1962–1965). John believed that the modernisation of the Church was a preliminary step to reunification with her 'separated brethren'. He issued several notable encyclicals, including *Mater et Magistra* (1961) and *Pacem in Terris* (1963). John attempted, with some success, to open a dialogue with the Soviet Union and the Communist world; he played a pivotal role in the 1962 Cuban missile crisis. This won him universal respect. Greatly loved by all and highly respected by Protestants, who nicknamed him 'Good Pope John, his painful last illness was followed by many millions throughout the world. At his passing the flags on all British public buildings flew at half-mast, a tribute never before paid to a pope. John XXIII was undoubtedly the most beloved pope in history.

Paul VI (Giovanni Battista Montini

Concesio, Italy; 21 June 1963 to 6 August 1978

Son of a lawyer, Giovanni Montini endured poor health throughout his childhood and youth. After his ordination (May 1920) he was appointed to work in the Vatican Secretariat of State. While acting as assistant to Cardinal Pacelli (later Pope Pius XII) he travelled widely; after his election Pius XII (1939) had him working for refugees and victims of the World War. When offered a red hat (the cardinalate) by Pius XII, Montini declined and was appointed Archbishop of Milan (November 1954). Many believed that he had fallen out of favour with Pius XII; but John XXIII made him one of the first new cardinals on his election. Montini played a leading role in the Second Vatican Council and was highly regarded by John XXIII. On his election Paul VI immediately affirmed his intention of continuing with the Council. It concluded on 8 December 1965 and the greatest test of Paul's skills followed, as he encouraged the implementation of the Council's decrees while striving to prevent a schism between those conservatives who resisted change and liberals who took the decrees too far. He continued the reforming spirit of his predecessor, reducing court ceremonial and disbanding anachronistic bodies. He was the greatest travelling pope (before John Paul II) visiting the Holy Land, India, Australia, USA, etc. He was the first to address the United Nations Assembly. Enthusiastic for ecumenism, Paul met with the Patriarch of Constantinople, the Archbishop of Canterbury and representatives of many world faiths. He issued many documents; his two most notable encyclicals were *Populorum Progressio* (1967) and *Humanae Vitae* (1968). This unleashed a critical backlash, which demoralised Paul. He survived an assassination attempt in Manila (1970), but careworn by the weight of office and the murder of his friend, the politician Aldo Moro, he died of a heart attack shortly after his friend's funeral.

John Paul I (Albino Luciani)

Canale de'Agordo, near Belluno, Italy; 26 August 1978 to 28 September 1978

Remembered affectionately as 'the smiling pope', Albino Luciani was born (1912) of a poor family. After ordination he served as a simple curate and then taught in the local seminary. After World War II he gained a doctorate in theology and was appointed vicar general of his diocese and then, in 1958, Bishop of Vittorio Venetto. Pope Paul VI appointed him Patriarch of Venice in 1969, and Cardinal in 1973. In Venice his unassuming simplicity of life endeared him to the people. He wrote *Illustrissimi* (fictional letters to famous figures) and enjoyed spending time with the city's students. Elected on the first day of the conclave, it was clearly his pastoral skills and personality that attracted the electors. Impatient with papal ceremonial he did away with many traditional papal customs, preferring a simple investiture to coronation with the traditional tiara. He was the first pope to choose a composite name, to make clear that he wished to continue the work of his two predecessors. The world was shocked and saddened to hear of his sudden death, probably a coronary embolism, on the night of 28 September, after a reign of just thirty-four days.

John Paul II (Karol Wojtyla)

Wadowice, Poland; 16 October 1978

The first non-Italian pope for 456 years, and the first Polish pope, Karol Wojtyla was born at Wadowice, near Cracow, on 18 May 1920. A gifted scholar (he obtained two doctorates) and linguist, he excelled at sports and acting; many thought he would seek a career in the theatre. When the German armies invaded Poland (1939) he was forced to work as a labourer in a quarry. He studied secretly for the priesthood and after the war was ordained in 1946. He lectured in ethics at Lublin University (1956) and was appointed bishop (1958), and then, five years later, Archbishop of Cracow. At only forty-seven he became a cardinal and supported Cardinal Wyszynski in resisting Polish Communist repression of the Church. He took an active part in the deliberations of the Second Vatican Council. At election, 16 October 1978, he was the youngest pope since Pius IX. John Paul's stated aim, from the start, was a 'universal pastoral ministry', to which end he has been tireless in his travels and visits to all the principal countries of Africa, Asia, Oceania, the Americas and Europe, with incalculable results (five million people attended one Mass in Manila in 1995). A prodigious output of sermons, talks, addresses (e.g. over 550 in 1979) have included notable encyclicals, like *Laborem Exercens* (1981), *Centessimus Annus* (1991) (both on the dignity of work and capitalism), *Veritatis Splendor* (1993) on moral theology, and *Evangelium Vitae* (1995) on modern moral issues and fostering a 'culture of life'. Sternly authoritarian, John Paul has centralised power in the hands of the Roman Curia and limited the authority of the local hierarchies; many critics have felt that his conservatism has hindered necessary development. He has proved to be a sign of unity for some and strife for others. His unique first-hand experience of Nazism and Communism dictated his firm approach to totalitarian regimes. The almost fatal assassination attempt in St Peter's Square on 13 May 1981 was thought by many to have been a direct response by Soviet Communism to John Paul's influence upon liberating movements in Poland and throughout the Communist bloc. History will judge the extent of his role in the final collapse of the Soviet Empire.